INVITING PARENTS

into the

YOUNG CHILD'S WORLD

Kevin J. Swick
Professor, Early Childhood Education
University of South Carolina
Columbia, South Carolina

Copyright 1984
STIPES PUBLISHING COMPANY

ISBN 0-87563-254-8

Published by
STIPES PUBLISHING COMPANY
10–12 Chester Street
Champaign, Illinois 61820

135927

TABLE OF CONTENTS

Page

PREFACE   i

ONE: Learning About Today's Families   1

TWO: Toward a New Concept of Parenting   9

THREE: Understanding Special Needs Families   17

FOUR: The Many Roles Parents Perform   29

FIVE: Parents As Catalysts For Children's Learning   37

SIX: Fathering: New Roles and Relationships   43

SEVEN: Ecological Assessment and Family Functioning   55

EIGHT: Parent Education: Focus On Needs and
          Responsibilities   65

NINE: Critical Issues In Parent Education   73

TEN: The Home Learning Environment   85

ELEVEN: The Home Visit: Educating and
          Supporting Families   101

TWELVE: Parent-Teacher Involvement:
          A Developmental Process   113

THIRTEEN: Strategies for Organizing Parent
          Involvement Programs   125

FOURTEEN: Ways to Involve Parents   137

FIFTEEN: Involving Parents in Decision Making Roles   145

SIXTEEN: Assessing and Improving Programs   153

SEVENTEEN: A Support System Design for Parents
of Learning Disabled Children   167

EIGHTEEN: The Parent-Teacher Communication Process   175

NINETEEN: Communication Styles for
Parents and Teachers   187

TWENTY: Parent-Teacher Communication Techniques   193

TWENTY-ONE: Supporting Families as Learning Systems   205

TWENTY-TWO: The Work Place: Supporting Families
and Schools   213

TWENTY-THREE: The Neighborhood as a
Family Support System   223

TWENTY-FOUR: Schools as Family Support Systems   231

REFERENCES: 239

PREFACE

The isolation of adults from the development and learning of young children has been a costly venture. The need for *involved* parents and teachers has been established through various studies. Parents need to be involved in the "child's" world from the outset, continually refining and extending their participation in guiding the child toward self-development. Teachers need to be "inviters" of parents—engaging them in educational activities, supporting their efforts with children and utilizing parents as co-partners in designing effective programs. The benefits of linking home and school, parents and teachers—into productive learning and development teams—are apparent in improved functioning on the part of all members of the community. So far reaching are the influences of productive parent involvement that the recent report of the *National Commission on Excellence in Education* (1983) recommends that schools utilize parent involvement as a major strategy for increasing the child's potential for school success.

While the involvement of parents in educational programs may initially appear to be a simple process, the intricate mechanism of bringing together the dynamic and diverse members of home and school settings is a challenge to all who work with young children. It is this challenge that is examined in this book. The attempt throughout the book is to provide the reader with a perspective and a process for use in developing effective parent involvement programs. There are five major components to this process: 1) understanding parents and families, 2) educating parents, 3) involving parents, 4) communicating with parents, and 5) supporting family development.

The theme: "Understanding Parents and Families" is examined in chapters one through seven. The process of studying and learning about families is critical to forming a successful relationship with parents. Understanding parent roles, the unique contribution of parents to the child's education and the process by which families can be strengthened are some of the issues dealt with in these early chapters. Chapters eight through eleven provide information and strategies for use in educating parents regarding their involvement in home and school learning settings. The basic focus of parent education is presented as well as an overview of major issues involved in implementing parent education programs. The use of the home as a learning ecology and modes educators can use in fostering effective home learning are also identified.

The organization, implementation and assessment of parent involvement programs is dealt with in chapters twelve through seventeen. The developmental nature of parent-teacher-child relationships is used as a basis for advocating specific techniques to use in developing productive home-school settings. Special attention is given to the involvement of parents of learning disabled children. In addition, the collaborative nature of educational decisionmaking between parents and teachers is discussed.

The communication process, which is critical to effective home-school programs, is examined in chapters eighteen through twenty. Included in this section of the book is a presentation on communication styles and an examination of specific techniques parents and teachers can use in improving their communication system. The concluding chapters focus on ways to support families. The various ecologies in which families function are examined as they can be activated to be supportive places for parents and children to work, learn and develop to their full potential.

The success or failure of children and adults is linked to their functioning in productive environments. The strategies presented in this book are directed toward improving the possibilities of home and school becoming viable places for children and adults to learn and develop. Thus, certain concepts are reinforced throughout the book and while this may appear to be repetitious, it serves the purpose of focusing on the essentials of productive parent-teacher involvement programs.

KJS
January, 1984
Columbia, South Carolina

CHAPTER ONE
LEARNING ABOUT TODAY'S FAMILIES

In attempting to educate young children early childhood educators must relate instructional as well as other modes of learning to the family context. The child is part of the family system and is affected by the many events that happen to parents and siblings. Likewise, the family is part of the broader social system and is impacted by social, by economic and political forces taking place in the macrosystem. For example, a teachers behavior toward the child at the Head Start center influences the parent-child relationship at home. In a similar manner the parents experiences at work influence the child in many ways including his social orientation at home. (Swick & Taylor, 1982). Critical to understanding the child in the learning and development context of the school is a clear understanding of the child's family. Such an understanding provides us with a basis for acting—designing and implementing programs that promote positive learning programs for children and their families.

Studying Families In Your Community

While global perspectives on family dynamics in the society are valuable, it is critical to study about the local needs and situations of families. Data generated from national family studies, for example, will synthesize demographic information into a "big picture" of the family. Some recent studies dramatize the dynamic shifts in family structure, size, status and processes of living. Today's family is small in size, very diverse in structure, has fewer adults than in the past and is very mobile, clearly our families are heterogenous and thus children bring to school many value orientations and unique needs. In acquiring information regarding the families you teach there are many ways to carry out this process.

Gathering demographic data on the families in your neighborhood or local community can be very helpful. Demographic profiles can provide you with a "local picture" of the families you work with and involve in programs for young children. You may find, for example, that 80 percent of the children reside in single parent households or that a significant number of children live in homes that are unheated. A demographic profile provides us with a basis for involving the family in learning and development experiences which can aid them in becoming skilled and functional human beings.

The use of parent surveys can provide another type of information pertinent to the family and its role in educating children. For example, a survey of parental talents, skills, interests and hobbies provides us with information not only on family values but on a basis for using parents as resource people in the classroom. Other surveys can be conducted to acquire parental input on the formation of parent education and parent-teacher involvement efforts. In addition, questionnaires can be used to find out how parents and children perceive the school and/or other parts of the community. Parental perceptions of the school and community provide us with a view of their attitudinal orientation to life — which certainly impacts their learning approach and influence their children's school performance (Bronfenbremer, 1979).

Teachers of young children are taught to critically observe children and to use such information in planning the educational program. A similar process should be used in terms of observing family behaviors and considering these orientations when planning programs for young children. What are family interests: Are families spending time together in recreational and social activities? Do parents attend school activities when they can? Are families spending time together in recreational and social activities? Do parents attend school activities when they can? Are parents involved in exposing their children to responsible community living? Answers to these questions will (or should) influence our instructional approach as well as the ways in which we relate to families of children in our early childhood programs.

Direct contact with parents and children is one of the most beneficial modes of learning about total family needs. Contacts at school, in the home or through community programs help us see parents in action. Face to face meetings between parents and teachers provide one mechanism for clarifying common and unique situations of families and schools. Further, such contacts are the beginning of parent-teacher efforts to use home and school as a means of nurturing children and adults toward being better individuals. Schaefer (1983) explains that continuous, meaningful communication between parents and teachers is the best method for assuring that we as early childhood educators are aware of the total family situation as we plan and carry out our programs.

Theories in Family Study

As we study families there are useful theoretical perspectives that enable us to better understand family behavior and-in-turn-help us to plan useful learning and development experiences with them. Theories are important in any scientific theory building, one first forms a hypothesis or a best estimate about a relationship between two variables. This hypothesis is then tested through research and is either confirmed or disconfirmed as a result of the research findings. When a hypothesis has been confirmed again and again it gains the status of a proposition, a principle, or a generalization (these three terms are used interchangeably).

In the behavioral or social sciences, hypotheses can gain the status of a proposition if they are true in a majority of cases. Propositions which are related to each other may be gathered together to form a theory about human behavior. Then this theory and the prepositions that it includes can be used to predict and explain other behavior.

The best theories are based on a great deal of empirical research. In family studies, theories are only in their beginning stages since the systematic study of families was only begun in this century therefore, the beginning family theories are called theoretical frameworks to distinguish them from the more highly developed theoretical formulations in other sciences. Currently, four of these theoretical frameworks are important for students to consider in thinking about families and in attempting to clarify and to predict and explain the many customs, rules and patterns of behavior associated with families (Nass, 1978). The four frameworks which will be introduced here are: 1. The Structural-Functional Approach, 2. Exchange Theory, 3. Symbolic-Interaction Theory, and 4. The Developmental Approach.

The Structural-Functional Approach

The basic idea in this approach is that the family is a subsystem—or institution—in society. Society is a social system made up of many subsystems including families, school, governmental bodies, law-enforcing agencies, churches, and other groups. The idea here is that what works for the maintenance of the system—that is, what is functional—will survive. Whatever is dysfunctional to the maintenance of the system will disappear. The question asked by proponents of the structural-functional theory is "What function does a subsystem serve in maintaining the total system?" (Nass, 1978). It must be remembered at this point that each subsystem is itself made up of subsystems. Thus the family is also a system made up of its individual members.

In discussing the family as a subsystem of society there are three main categories of functions to be considered:

1. The functions of the family for society.
2. The functions of the family for self-maintenance.
3. The functions of the family with respect to individual family members.

The family serves many functions in society. One might generate a long list but for certain the procreation function would be included in the list. If families did not create new members for the society, then the society would cease to exist. Look at Aldous Huxley's *Brave New World* to see how a society provided for the procreation of new members when the family institution had been abolished. Besides the procreation function, in our society the family serves to transmit the cultural values of the

3

society to young children. Some of the family's traditional functions have been usurped by other societal subsystems. For example, the family used to be the primary educator of its children, but in recent years the school has taken over that function. More recently, of course, the emphasis is shifting back to the family as primary educator of children. It has been found that schools are not succeeding in replacing families in the education of young children.

The family itself is a system that is being maintained and anything which contributes to the survival and maintenance of that system is functional. The major stabilizing mechanism in the survival of the family has been considered to be the sex and age-related division of labor. According to this particular view, a small group will not function effectively or survive unless role differentiation occurs (Nass, 1978). It will be interesting to see what happens to families as more and more women are sharing in the role of bread-winner and as more and more men are sharing in household maintenance and the caretaking of children. One might predict that the family would be less stable and that the divorce rate would increase as a result of this greater ability on the part of men and women to fill the various roles.

Social and biological needs of the family members are met by the family system. The family provides companionship as well as education, protective, and economic functions for its own members. An emphasis in current thinking is that the importance of the family as an institution providing functions in our society is diminishing while the role of the family in filling the companionship needs of the family members is increasing in importance. An optimistic suggestion for the preservation of the family has been offered by Burgess and Locke (1953). They believe that the companionship function of the family will increase in importance and that this function will maintain the family system as the family changes from "institution to companionship".

A main criticism of the structural-functional approach is that it is too simplistic. For example, divorce would be considered dysfunctional in this approach since it would be considered to be disruptive for society, families and individuals. But in some cases divorce is functional since it provides for the orderly separation of potentially destructive relationships. Another criticism is that too much emphasis is placed on the maintenance of the status quo. Balance and system stability are emphasized to the exclusion of growth and change. A final strong objection to the structural-functional approach to studying families has been to their traditional role definitions of men as instrumental and women as expressive. An instrumental role designation for men has suggested that they are task oriented while the expressive role of women has emphasized their emotional role in family life. These exclusive sex-role categorizations omits consideration of a great deal of flexibility and a variety of options for individual family members (Nass, 1978).

4

Exchange Theory

An important theoretical development in the 1960's was the elevation of exchange theory to a place of importance (Broderick, 1971). Exchange theory has stimulated research and theory and is best described by Lederer and Jackson's (1969) principle of *quid pro quo*. This is the idea of "something for something" or that a person will do something for another person in order to obtain something from that person.

Many principles of exchange have been applied to courtship and mate selection and a current interesting applications has been in the analysis of family power in parent-child relationships. Exchange theory suggests that differences and hostilities among family members can be negotiated in order to achieve the benefits of family cooperation. Thus, a child is born with few resources available for exchange. Later though, the child learns that his or her parent values affections and the child uses this knowledge to bargain for goods and materials (candy, new roller skates) from the parent. Then the child may learn that the parents value such things as good grades, conservative sexual behavior, and so on. The child may use these resources in exchange for others from parents.

Symbolic-Interaction Theory

The structural-functionalist emphasizes societal systems related in an organized manner, exchange theorist consider people involved in confrontation, and the symbolic-interactionist focuses attention on individuals as they react and interact in social roles. Emphasis is placed on individuals as significant sources in the development of social behavior. Interaction is the complex process whereby one person's social behavior results from and is modified by another's actions. This approach is derived from the field of social psychology.

In this theory, behavior is to some extent predetermined by the roles that individuals play. Thus, the behavior of a father toward a child is to some extent predetermined by the role he fills. This theory views the family as a unity of interacting personalities and the focus is on communications within the family and on the family in its companionship functions rather than in its function as an institution. If the role of the family as a companionship of interacting personalities continues to increase in importance, then this theoretical orientation should be expected to likewise increase in importance.

The Developmental Approach

This theoretical approach is a composite one borrowing from the structural-functionalist's view of the family as a social system and from the interactionist's view of the family as a unity of interacting personalities. Developmentalists have added to the concepts borrowed from the other theories a time dimension or the idea that a family's behavior can in part be attributed to the developmental stage of the family.

5

The typical family life cycle can be divided into roughly eight stages progressing from newly married couples, to couples in the childbearing years, to families with preschool children, to families with school-children, then to families with teenagers, and to families whose children have begun to leave home, to "empty nest" families, and then families in retirement (Duvall, 1971). The number of years spent in each stage varies from family to family and an interesting activity is to make a chart representing a personal family life cycle and to compare this with life cycles from other families.

As in other developmental theories, families must accomplish various developmental tasks at each stage of the family life cycle. Failure to accomplish tasks at their appointed times leads to complications and problems as families move to later stages in the life cycle. (Students should take time to generate a list of developmental tasks for each stage of the life cycle.) Some of the tasks of newly married couples are to establish complementary roles, to establish economic independence and stability, to develop a satisfactory sexual relationship, and to build effective communication skills. If these tasks are not accomplished during the stage before children are born, one might accurately predict that the marriage would be less stable than marriages in which the birth of the first child is delayed for several years.

A criticism of the developmental approach to studying families is that it has most often emphasized a modern, suburban, middle-class American family rather than being considered with respect to the wide range of family styles that characterize the modern world. This framework may be limited in its scope and may not be functionally applied to a broad array of families. Another problem with the approach is that childbearing is an implied value. Developmental stages have been based on the ages of the children thereby eliminating permanently childless couples from consideration (Nass, 1978).

Implications for Facilitating Family Development

Each family theory provides educators and other helping professionals with perceptual tools they can use to gain insight into the families they hope to assist. A major advantage of understanding and appropriately utilizing these different theories is that, as a family facilitator, you can acquire a multi-dimensional perspective of the families with which you work.

Appropriate usage of each family theory would take into consideration at least the following suggestions.

1. In applying any single theory to studying families, it must be remembered that it represents only *one* possible view of the family— albeit an important view.

2. As different theoretical frameworks are applied to studying families, it should be remembered that these are theoretical constructs and as such are open to changes as new empirical data are generated by social science researchers.
3. In studying families, regardless of which framework is used, the information acquired *must remain confidential.*

Each theoretical framework for studying family life has some value in terms of identifying family needs and proving the basis for meeting those needs in a systematic way. The *structural-functional approach* provides a view of the functional nature of the family while *exchange theory* offers a view of the existing social matrix of the family. *The symbolic-interaction* perspective provides insight into role relationships among family members and the *developmental approach* is valuable in understanding the context and requirements of the family's stage of life functioning. Appropriate usage of each of these theories can provide family facilitators with a knowledge base which, in turn, can be used to encourage effective home-school relationships.

As professionals attempt to study and facilitate, the following ideas should be useful in maximizing their efforts:

1. What perspective am I using in studying the family?
2. Will this perspective provide the king of information desired?
3. How can the data gathered be used to facilitate family development?

An important consideration every helping professional should (and must) deal with relates to *how they view the families they work with.* Only as educators and other professionals develop and understand their framework for studying families can they better facilitate family development toward a growth-oriented role in society. For example, Bronfenbrenner views ecological influences affecting families as an important step in helping families function at their best.

CHAPTER TWO
TOWARD A NEW CONCEPT OF PARENTING

The family today is not as it was in 1940, nor should we expect it to remain static as the culture changes. Many economic, technological, political, social, and psychological forces have influenced the way families function. When these forces are taken in combination, their influence on family life has been dramatic. An understanding of how families have changed is essential to developing any effective home-school relationship. Each force (or influence) will be considered as it has affected changes in the way families live.

Forces Affecting Family Life

Economic Forces

Economic forces influencing the way families live include the shift from a simple, rural economy to a post World War II industrial-nuclear economy. The roles of parents and children have become quite different than simply producers and consumers. As more goods and services have become available, more time outside the home must be devoted to acquiring these material goods. Thus more time is spent by family members in "working" outisde the home to earn money to pay for goods and services and less time is spent in working at home with other family members to produce goods and services. Although many families have been negatively affected by economic pressures, other families have positively responded to a rather complex and potentially harmful social situation. In these cases, families are involved in trying to determine real needs as opposed to culturally determined needs (Solnit, 1976). For example a television set is not a human necessity but a culturally defined need.

As the cost of living continues to increase at an alarming rate, parents are becoming more skilled in determining needs and organizing resources to meet those needs. Educators (and other helping professionals) must understand the economic aspects of family living and, in their own way, assist families in making economic arrangements a positive force in family living (Keniston, 1978).

Technological Forces

Technological forces which have influenced the way families function are illustrated by the following comparative descriptions of household utensils and tools in 1883 and 1983:

1883: wash basin, oil lamp, coal stove, well water, wood cooking stove, ice box, plow and horse, straw broom, clothes drying line, and home-made foods.

1983: automatic dishwasher, television, radio, vacuum sweeper, washer and dryer, electric lights, centralized heating and cooling systems, freezer, refrigerator, tractor, automobile, stereo system, and home computers.

This simple comparison of home use items in 1883 and 1983 indicates the dramatic changes in life styles that have taken place due to technological developments in the society. As technological refinements occur, the kinds of jobs, services, recreational activities, and family styles also change.

Some of the changes that have taken place as a result of technological developments includes a decrease in family interaction, an increase in the number of families in which both parents work outside of the home, a change in what families do when they are together, and an increase in the number of small families (Kanter, 1978). Technology has, in effect, freed family members from tasks which once consumed most of their daily life. Thus parents and children have changed their daily schedules and currently select activities previously unavailable to them. These changes have been difficult for many families to cope with. Educators and other helping professionals can be aware of these changes and assist parents and children in developing family management techniques to better cope with the technological culture in which they live.

Political Forces

Political forces influencing the family are characterized by the ever-growing bureaucracy of human services. The number of family-related government programs testifies to the societal concern for improving the human condition. Unfortunately, the ineffectiveness of many programs to facilitate family living has led many people to become cynical about institutional services. In addition, as many service groups assumed responsibilities which had been family functions, there arose a tendency for parents to assume less responsibility for their children.

At least three distinct political trends that have influenced the family are: a thrust to protect the child from abuse and neglect, a focus on assuring families of minimal economic and social security, and a move to provide families with special services when the situation so dictates. The *intent* of federal and state legislation related to these trends was to *facilitate* family life. However, the issues involved are so complex that implementation of the programs have not always accomplished the original objectives.

10

As families have been placed under much stress (due in part to rapid economic and technological changes) the incidence of child abuse and/or neglect has markedly increased (Schmitt, 1975). This problem alone is indicative of the complexity of family life and of the difficulty in determining appropriate social responses to problems by community members. Political action has led to the development of a *National Institute on Child Abuse* and the formation of community agencies to protect children and parents from abuse and neglect. These programs have made many people aware of proper child care techniques, the need for protecting children, and the need for helping families under stress. A very positive aspect of many child abuse programs is their preventive and/or rehabilitation orientation.

Complementing the development of child protection programs has been the emergence of social programs designed to meet minimal basic needs of all members of the human family. An emerging concept in all human service professionals is that without healthy and functioning parents and teachers our children's future is bleak. Fortunately this concept is beginning to have impact on political changes taking place within federally and state funded programs designed to assist families and schools. A major weakness in past legislation is that too much has been done *to* the family and too little *with* the family.

Another political trend has been the move to create programs designed to meet the special needs of families. Parents of physically or mentally handicapped children or learning disabled children, and families who find themselves under unusual pressures are beginning to find that help is available via various state, local, and federally sponsored programs. This trend is indicative of a broadening view of parenting as a process to which all members of the community must contribute.

As the costs of these family services continues to increase, the need for reducing money spent on management in order to increase dollars for actual services is urgent (Cardenas, 1978). As political action groups formulate plans for future years, a primary goal must be to maximize the service aspects of each family facilitation program and to begin funding programs at the local level.

Social Forces

Social forces influencing family life include the decreasing size of families, the greater life-style expectations of people, and the origination of a nuclear family as a result of increasing mobility and an emphasis on individual living as opposed to the once predominant rural community concept of life (Talbot, 1976). In addition, a variety of family forms are continuing to emerge such as the single parent family and families created by group marriages and communal families (Talbot, 1976).

11

A brief examination of how these factors alone interact to include family living is noteworthy. For example, the increased mobility of people means that, in general, many families will live in at least two or three different communities during their lifetimes. The chances for continuous relationships with friends, relatives, and grandparents is lessened. Likewise, the increased lifestyle expectations of people usually mean that both parents must work to pay for conveniences and this, in turn, affects the quantity and sometimes the quality of family relationships.

The emergence of a more individualized style of life has created a situation where, in many cases, personal desires take priority over family needs and desires (Levinger, 1977). A result has been a decrease in size of families and a concurrent decline in the number of years people spend in direct parenting roles. These social changes in the way families function are not necessarily negative changes. Rather, family living has changed and new perceptions of family life are required in order to facilitate the development of parents and children in positive ways.

Psychological Forces

Psychological influences on family life are a result of the effects of changes in our society as elaborated in the previous sections of this chapter. In the past, individuals usually perceived themselves as members of a tightly organized family group in which grandparents, parents, children, relatives, and neighbors cooperated and facilitated each other in meeting the demands of everyday life. As our society has become more mobile, urban, and individualized in life orientation, it is rare to even hear of an extended family in the middle-class white population. These changes have influenced the way individuals within the family perceive themselves and others.

The identity issue within the family unit itself is just one psychological result of the social and cultural changes in our society. Women no longer perceive themselves as housewives. Rather, the typical mother may perform career roles and other social roles and perceive herself quite differently than in the past. Children also perceive themselves differently than in the past when they were important economic arms of the family. As members of the family begin to perceive themselves in more individualized modes, the psychological nature of family life changes. A major role can be played by educators (and others) in facilitating parents and children in their quest to develop a psychologically stable and meaningful home arrangement. As the substance of family life has changed due to the many influences examined in this chapter, *so our concept of parenting must change.*

Developing A Meaningful Parenting Team

The concept of parenting as it must emerge in the future should resolve around a team approach to child care which does not replace or inhibit the functioning of the main players (father, mother, children) but rather expands the option of human development through the involvement of others from the extended family, neighborhood and the community. As Armin Grams puts it:

> The future may see more frequent decisions to provide children with optimal parenting, utilizing a combination of parenting persons. Included may be the child's father and mother, as well as a variety of parent surrogates. Some may be siblings or other relatives, and some may be individuals who choose to work as parent substitutes on an individual basis in the child's home or with groups of children in a child care center (Grams, 1973, p. 8).

As is suggested in the above statement, the parenting process, as it emerges in the 1970's and beyond, must be based upon a flexible yet responsible approach to meeting the child care needs of the next generation. And it must be made clear that "the kind of parenting a child receives is the responsibility of the entire community, and our objective must be to make all who wish to commit themselves to the task optimally effective." (Grams, 1973, p. 8).

The concept of parenting team suggests that there may be a variety of team structures, each designed to meet the specific needs of individual children. Because of the very nature of our society, children and parents exist within a variety of settings. There are children from two-parent families, one-parent families, parent-surrogate families, and from non-familial social settings. We have parents who work outside the home, work within the home, who are divorced, who provide the sole support for their children, and those who receive support from many people in their extended families and communities. Although the kinds of parenting and family situations described above have existed in the past, such situations are presently occurring more often and in more complex settings. Thus more people are required to facilitate family development in positive ways (Swick, 1978).

Key factors in bringing about an expanded parenting team are the attitudes that people bring to their involvement with young children. The attitudes of parents, child care workers, educators, and citizens must change if the concept of a parenting team is to be a reality. The idea that mothers are the sole child-care agents within a family must be replaced by a more uniform and balanced perspective including the contributions of fathers, siblings, grandparents, and community-wide child-care workers.

The significance of promoting positive, confluent, and mutually respecting attitudes among teachers, children, and parents has been established

13

by various studies in the fields of education, sociology, and psychology (Swick, 1973). Community attitudes toward child care, parenting, and toward children are significant factors contributing to the kinds and quality of human development programs that exist in the community.

The adhesive which binds together the parenting team will be the attitudes and behaviors exhibited by various team members toward each other and toward the children they are nurturing. The behavioral origins of school success and the resulting successful society are found in the home (Swick, 1973). And the home, in the meaningful sense of that term, is composed of all caring members of the human community.

Developing a Human Community That Values Children

Every community in our society is faced with value choices of such dimensions that men and women of the past never imagined they would exist. As communities value and invest more finances in the material environment than in the human environment, the ecological imbalance of the quality of life (especially for our children) moves in the favor of technology rather than humanity. Should we have another car, boat, highway, or shopping mall in lieu of quality adult-child relationships? Has what we do *for* our children become more enhancing to the adult ego than what *we do with our children as a parenting team.*

Every parent, teacher, child-care worker, citizen, and child of every community should be reminded of the current status of children today!

- The U.S. ranks 42nd among nations of the world in relation to infant mortality rates.*
- Millions of American children today remain hungry and malnourished.
- In 1973 one out of every seven children was in a single parent family.

Further, community leaders should take stock of the following situations in which *our* children exist.

- Physical abuse alone occurs in 70,000 children per year and results in the deaths of some 700 (Schmitt, 1975).
- In 1970, of the 48 million children between the ages of six and seventeen, 7 million were reported to be living in poverty as were 3 million children out of 23 million under the age of six.**

---

*See Keniston, *Childhood Education,* 1975, pp. 4–12 for a complete view of the status of children in our society as of 1975.

**Gottlieb, D., Ed., *Children's Liberation.* Englewood Cliffs, New Jersey: Prentice-Hall, Inc., 1973, pp. 8–10.

— Although more professionals are now being trained and there has been an increase in service-related agencies, possibly no more than half of the children in need of aid (economic, social, educational, psychological) are receiving help from child welfare agencies.**
— Only an estimated 5 percent of children who need psychiatric care are receiving it.**

There are people and social groups that are trying to correct the child abuse and neglect situations depicted above. The key to narrowing the gap between ideal child-care situations and the real inadequacies of current child care programs and practices is a parenting team that is competent and caring in every way. With the proper development of a parenting team that is both competent and caring, the future of our children can be healthy and fulfilling. The parenting team that is characterized by continuity, flexibility, and by consistent, mutual facilitation can bring about human environments in which competent children are the norm rather than the exception (Holloman, 1976).

What can children be like when capable parenting teams exist and are at work in the society? They can be secure, trusting, healthy, well-nourished, growing, learning, and exploring human beings (Cooper, 1976). This ideal view of human development can become a reality if our approaches to infant and early childhood education are broadened to include support services such as "housing, jobs, adult education, adequate access to social services, sanitary conditions, and the whole sweep of social arrangements." (Gordon, 1976).

What our children can be, vividly reflects what the adult population wants them to be. The preamble to the 1970 report of the White House Conference on Children suggests what we want for our children:

— Let us ask what we want for our children. Then let us ask not less for all children.
— We want for our children a full opportunity for learning in an environment in which they can reach and grow and take pride in themselves.
— We want for our children a home of love and understanding and encouragement.
— We want for our children the right to be healthy, to be free of sickness. But if sickness comes, to have the best care humanly possible.
— We want for our children the right to have the respect of others.
— We want to have respect and dignity as a right because they are, not because of who their parents are.***

***Partial quote of the preamble to the report of the White House Conference on Children, 1970, p. 5.

15

Let us begin to help children reach their full potential by forming a unified parenting team of mothers, fathers, siblings, child-care workers, educators, citizens, and other children. With a truly unified parenting team the human family can move toward a more actualized and meaningful existence. As Urie Bronfenbrenner's recent research (1979) indicates, the ecological system in which families function can be either a positive or negative force in our efforts to make human beings humane.

CHAPTER THREE
UNDERSTANDING SPECIAL NEEDS FAMILIES

While a case can be made that all families are special in some way, few people would disagree that "special needs families" such as child abuse families need intense and unusual attention. It is during the early childhood years that a majority of these needs emerge as problems for families and this provides a good opportunity for preventing, treating or resolving the unique situation faced. Thus it is essential that child care workers, teachers and all who work with young children be familiar with the characteristics of special needs families, understand the types of special needs different families may face, and be skilled in utilizing different techniques and resources in helping families deal constructively with these situations.

General Characteristics of Special Needs Families

There are some general features that continuously appear within special needs family situations regardless of the uniqueness of their different predicaments. Parents of handicapped children, for example, *experience an intense sense of isolation* from the usual life routine. It appears that they use so much energy in coping with the child's problem and their new life context that feeelings of resentment and insecurity temporarily isolate them from their former friends and acquaintances. Depending upon the severity of the situation and the personal competence of the individuals involved this sense of aloneness may last a short or long period of time. It is essential that all who work with parents in such situations establish some basis for helping them re-establish self confidence and social linkages with the outside world so they can foster constructive family living and be functional community participants. Parents confronting severe problems of any sort experience this phenomena and need special attention in coming to deal with over a period of time (Klein, 1982).

In addition to the development of social isolation, special needs families such as families where a member has died *may well go through a period where emotional responses to reality are distorted* and/or used to restore a reality that no longer exists. The denial of a terminal illness by a family member is a natural shock reaction to an immediate situation where one has no control over it. With support and social linkages to the real world of daily living most individuals overcome these feelings of denial and distorted life perceptions. For example, by having contacts with supportive relatives, teachers, neighbors and other helping professionals special needs families can piece together a new and workable set of circumstances (Birtchnell, 1969).

A part of any unique and disruptive event in the lives of families is *the temporary breakdown of normal communications.* Emotional overload, physical exhaustion, and disruption of normal social interactions — in isolation or in combinations — tend to interfere with our communicative abilities. Cognitive functioning is impaired (for example when one is exhausted) and communications are less than rational and sometimes totally inept. Under duress our listening abilities lose their sharpness and may deteriorate to where we process very little of what others are trying to say to us. In child abuse cases, for example, the abusing parent tends to filter incoming messages toward a defensive self justification orientation. Through parent support groups, family counseling and generally supportive people the process of functional communications can be restored (Kagan, 1979).

Families under severe pressure due to various problems usually experience *more than normal stress levels.* Some stress is, of course, necessary for functioning. Indeed most families today must cope with above average stress. However, in cases where a family is under unusual stress their coping mechanisms may break down — causing even more severe family situations. The following is a pictorial representation of different stress levels.

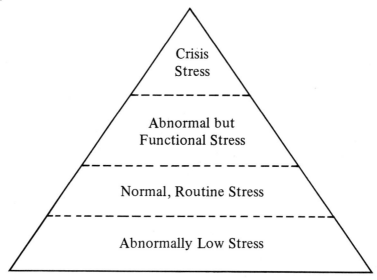

As the pyramid suggests when little or no stress exists (like a vacation) and when crisis stress appears (as it does with many special need families) very little room exists to psychologically function. Thus the need for human support systems increases with the increments of stress special needs families experience. Consider the following *Family Stress Barometer* as one way of calculating the needed level of support for families.

18

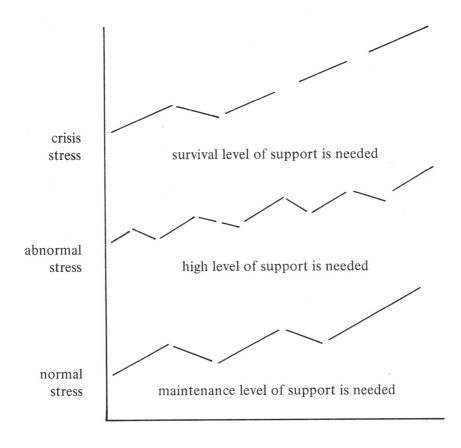

crisis
stress

survival level of support is needed

abnormal
stress

high level of support is needed

normal
stress

maintenance level of support is needed

As the *Family Stress Barometer* indicates when family needs increase to a level where they can no longer function we have a crisis. This may occur when one member of the family (due to some handicapping condition) draws so much of the others energy that normal living is impossible. It is in such cases that schools and other human support systems must come to the family's aid. In many cases this "crisis support" may be needed for only a brief period of time during which the family learns to handle the situation at least somewhat independently. However, all families need external supports and special needs families will usually need supports of a special kind even after they have passed through the adaptation stage. Being aware of the abnormal stress special needs families face is essential to facilitating their abilities to handle some very critical situations (Bronfenbrenner, 1979).

Clearly families with special problems exist within a web of forces that are connected and impinge on the family's well being. Financial problems, for example, are related to stress increments in the family and a sense of isolation delimits the family's ability to use available human resources. The interdisciplinary nature of early childhood education provides a basis for intervening in positive ways to help special needs families sort out the negative factors affecting them and develop mechanisms for renewing the status of the family.

Parents With Special Needs Situations

It is impossible to portray every situation that influences parents and children in negative ways. Examples of unique parenting situations, however, can increase our sensitivity to various family neeeds. An understanding of the problems single parents confront on a daily basis can provide us with fresh perspectives on both the designing of instructional programs and the formation of family support programs. Realizing that poverty families often feel less valued can and should alter our ways of working with them and their children — hopefully in a direction of restoring the integrity and competence levels of every family member? Consider the following as examples of unique parenting situations which require alterations in our usual approaches to educating young children.

A *death in the family* creates major disonance in family relations both internally and externally. The sudden loss of a significant human being is traumatic to all family members. Parents and children experience a sort of dislocation in their social relationships as well as psychological anguish and cognitive disequilibrium. While each person faces the loss of another person uniquely, it usually takes up to a year or more for reorganization of life styles to occur. In working with children and parents a highly supportive orientation to meeting their special need in classroom and out of classroom settings. For example, spending more time with a child whose father died is one way of helping him through this difficult time (Kagan, 1979).

A *critical illness in the family* creates unique demands on all family members. What were at one time routine tasks become burdens on the limited time and energy of each person in the family. Simple tasks such as shopping, cleaning, working, meeting adult and child needs and community participation efforts may be disrupted when one family member is bed ridden. The stress from this situation may influence a child's school behavior negatively unless the teacher is aware of the family predicament and acts accordingly in adjusting the learning setting to the new needs of the child. In dealing with this type of family situation we can support the family by linking them up with available support services. For example, every United Way programs sponsor home-assistance programs when a family in trouble is assisted through a helper in the home. Such efforts reduce stress and enable everyone to function more effectively (Hartup, 1979).

There are many *handicapping conditions* in the lives of parents and children. These will range from minor hearing loss to severe mental retardation. Depending upon the condition and the severity of the impediment, teachers of young children will want to realize such events and calculate

20

methods of dealing with them. In families where a child is severely handicapped, for example, the need for services may be urgent and long term. Early childhood educators have advocated, whenever possible, mainstreaming handicapped children into a quality program. Designing or redesigning early childhood learning environments toward meeting special needs such as ramps for orthopedically handicapped children is one mode of assisting families in functioning effectively. Fostering continuous communication with parents regarding their role in the educational and development lives of handicapped children is yet another way of facilitation. Learning about the myriad of handicapping conditions (physical, mental, social or psychological) that affect families and how they influence family dynamics is an essential part of our skill kit (Umansky, 1982).

Families experiencing the various stages of a divorce must deal with some rather unique problems. Internal family relationships are often shattered — at least temporarily and external family relationships become difficult to carry on until some new equilibrium is formed. Children, for example, may show new and/or unusual forms of behavior in the forms of attention span problems, excessive dreaming, aggressive — attention-getting behavior, sulleness, or other socio-emotionally related behavior syndromes. This is understandable as the early and middle stages of divorce (disillusionment, erosion, detachmant, physical separation and mourning) are highly emotional leaving little room for parents and children to sort through their internal and external lives in a cognitive manner. Family arguments and parent-child conflicts may increase during this time and in some cases may "spill over" into the school via erratic behaviors of the child and possibly by the parents. By helping the family establish a well-functioning support system through referral to counseling groups, listening to parental concerns and providing the child with extra help — especially of a nurturing orientation — we can ease the family's burden and help them build a basis for re-organizing their lives in a constructive manner (Hetherington, 1979).

The emotional stress existent in *child abuse families* is only symptomatic of deeper and more severe pathologies within the persons and the social system of the family. The following are characteristics of child abuse/neglect families

- Existence of pathological tendencics among those in the parenting role.
- Existence of extreme stress due to many factors such as marital conflicts, alcoholism and economic problems;
- Inadequate support system which promotes a feeling of powerlessness in all family members.
- Existence of a disorganized family system (Helfer & Kempe, Fort Ore, 1976).

21

135927

In attempting to prevent or remediate child abuse and neglect early childhood educators must see themselves as helping professionals. Helping professionals must view themselves as a family support team. Whatever role we play, our concern must certainly be focused on promoting human quality. The use of "visiting nurses" to help parents of newborn infants (especially high risk cases) can go a long way toward improving family life. Parent education and parenthood education programs, whether sponsored by schools or other agencies, can assure us of a better future. As helping professionals focus on the family as a humane place to be, the prospects of reducing child abuse will increase (Swick, 1980).

Single parents in the words of Bronfenbrenner (1979) must learn to be "superhuman" in handling a job originally designed for two or more people. The tasks of child rearing, job/career responsibilities, homemaking, community tasks and maintaining some semblance of personal identity all combine to create the need for special support systems. The recognition that single parents face unique situations will provide us with a basis for aiding them and their children in organizing a workable life pattern. Providing single parents with supports such as flexible conference times, extended school care projects for their children, summer school/ recreational and enrichment programs, and necessary counseling resources are roles we can perform in support of their efforts. Hetherington (1979), for example found that single parents who had a highly support team of people in their "world" performed the parenting role better than their peers who lacked such a support system.

Additional special needs situations occur in family settings such as unemployment, financial problems, mental health problems and problems related to extra-familial interactions. For example, an increasing number of mid-life parents are finding their lives complicated by the necessity of caring for their elderly parents. Two terms appear to be related to all of these special needs situations — *stress and lack of resources.* For example, unemployment reduces family income drastically — thus decreasing resources for maintaining family functioning and increasing stress levels among every family member. A positive psychological view of life is the most effective way of dealing with these problems. As educators we can attempt to help special needs families by linking them to needed resources and facilitating their positive interactions in the family and with community groups such as churches and schools.

Patterns of Reaction In Special Needs Families

While each person and family react uniquely to "special needs situations", there are some stages most individuals experience as they deal with these life jolting predicaments. What follows is a description of these stages as they often occur. While these "stages" provide a framework for understanding exceptional family situations they do not reveal the uniquely

22

human response of individuals to their personal encounter with these life events.

Anticipation: An approaching problem is often anticipated by one or more family members. For example, couples about to separate or divorce report they have "sensed" the ensuing conflict over a period of time. Less verbal interaction, increase in major disagreements and/or a general malaise within the marital relationship have usually been happening for some time prior to the breakup. Most human events unfold over a time continuum and thus provide people with clues to an approaching disruption in their lives.

Shock-Disbelief: Whenever our equilibrium is disrupted in a major way shock and disbelief (unwillingness to accept reality) overcome our human psyche. The degree of shock will, of course, depend upon the perceived dissonance of the individuals reality base and the actual events taking place. For example, an individual who has had time to anticipate a divorce for a long period of time will experience a different type of shock than the person suddenly facing the loss of a husband due to an automobile accident. Regardless, shock is a state of life that parents and children experience during life crises situations. Disregard for reality, psychological malaise, social isolation, extensive moodiness, cognitive malfunctioning and physical illness (often of a psychosomatic nature) are symptoms people exhibit while in shock.

Shock and disbelief are natural ways of the mind for insulating us from harsh and real world events until we can re-tool ourselves. A nurturing, supportive environment is very helpful in easing a person back to reality. The sooner our mental fabric senses an acceptable reality the healing process can begin in earnest. For example, as parents of handicapped children begin to see that a workable life pattern is a possibility they initiate rational steps toward handling the predicament. This does not happen all at once but rather occurs in bits and pieces of daily routines. Healing and resolution are cyclical processes which take time but which do bring new possibilities for people when they have supportive people around them.

Anger: The acceptance of a sometimes very difficult reality brings anger to the surface in the lives of special needs families. A feeling of "why me" or "why us" is quite common among families experiencing distressful life events. This anger may be expressed through parental arguments and misbehavior by children at school or in the neighborhood. Obviously angry people are poor at communicating with others in a rational manner. However, a supportive teacher, helpful pediatrician or a "good neighbor" can be helpful by listening (allowing the person to vent their feelings) and then suggesting ways for that person to channel their frustration into problem solving behaviors. We need to remember that anger is a necessary step in forming the basis for action. If a person is upset enough to reach a state of anger they must care about finding ways to handle the situation.

Adjustment: As the feelings of anger are directed toward constructive resolution the special needs family begins an adjustment process that leads toward living with their special situation. The young mother of a handicapped child stated it well when she said: "once I realized that being angry at the world only made me and my family miserable did I see that I had to step forward into the world once again — no matter how difficult — and try to find ways of living." Adjusting to new demands, dealing with unique problems, and learning about new modes of living are very demanding processes. As special needs families begin to seek out needed resources and communicate with each other about planning activities they are taking initial steps toward resolving crisis level functioning.

Decision Making: As special needs families explore possible modes of dealing with their situation they begin to formulate ideas on how to work out their life pattern. This decision making process will last for some period of time. Experimenting with new daily routines, seeking advice from trusted others, retreating to old habits, trying new ideas and failing, and realizing these are all steps toward a more functional life are parts of the decision making puzzle. Helping professionals can be extremely useful to special needs families during this time by offering ideas, responding to parent and child inquiries about their problem and in general becoming a part of their world. Sitting down and talking with a single parent who is trying to work out a new home schedule is just one example of how we can positively influence the lives of parents and children.

Resolutions: While there is never a permanent resolution to any life situation, special needs families gradually arrive at a "workable life pattern." This return to equilibrium is essential for the survival of every family member. Arriving at an acceptable daily routine, agreement or new and acceptable family roles, and the formation of functional linkage with the school and community are symptomatic of an emerging resolution of a "new life" for special needs families. The degree to which the family can find acceptance of its plan in the outside world will influence the workability of that plan.

Refinement - Continual Adaptations: Although special needs families arrive at a "way" of handling their situation, a continuous process of refinement will be used to adapt to changes as they occur. Developmental changes within the family, extra-familial events and a variety of personal-social changes in family members all influence family adjustment behaviors.

While all special needs families go through some or all of these states the experience for each family (indeed each person) is unique. This uniqueness of the human response to any life experience is critical to our role as helping professionals if we are to be effective in "helping" and not hindering special needs families.

24

Helping Special Needs Families

Teachers of young children have a special opportunity to help families confronting problem situations or even experiencing a crisis. Understanding special needs families (through establishing a knowledge base) is a first step in this process. Becoming familiar with the particular family in need is another step. Once a basis exists for helping exceptional families the ideas presented in this chapter should prove useful in organizing an approach to assisting them in a functional manner.

The interdisciplinary nature of early childhood education provides us with many modes of serving special needs families. The utilization of the many professionals who work with young children and families (educators, medical professionals, social workers, ministers, family counselors, etc.) is essential if we are to support families in the most effective way possible. By "teaming" these various family support groups can utilize each others skills and talents in not only remediating special family problems but also in preventing a large number of problems from ever happening (Swick and Duff, 1978).

In order for effective teaming among early childhood professionals to take place individual professionals must make the effort to know what others are doing. For example, teachers need to make themselves aware of services and resources available through other professional groups in the community and make use of these in their contacts with parents. Through participation in conferences we can bring together people from the different fields of study that impact the lives of parents and children. Local, inter-agency family support groups can also be used to forge an interdisciplinary approach to early childhood education.

One example of this "teaming" effort exists in the focus on proper maternal and infant health care. Individuals from many professions work together to encourage proper maternal/infant health habits. Nutritionists working with parents before the birth of the child on diet, rest and exercise lay a foundation for preventing many birth defects and other birth-related problems. Pediatricians who counsel and provide parents with regular health care guidance for the child as well as health educators who serve in constantly reminding the public of the need for quality maternal-child health education and services are additional examples of an interdisciplinary approach to service special needs families.

A major service to families and community members is the provision of information and services related to preventing (as much as possible) handicapping conditions from happening to children. Early childhood educators along with their many allies in the helping professions are making major strides in this prevention effort. The utilization of parent education programs, media information packages, community awareness projects and other educational modes have provided avenues for creating a new awareness of the need for parental involvement with the child at every stage of development. For example, the prevention of birth defects by educating people about their major causes (such as drug abuse during pregnancy) has proven successful – at least to some degree. The current campaign in many states to require safe baby seats in automobiles should lead to minimizing another cause of special damage to young children. Genetic counseling is yet another example of how human service professionals have provided parents (or potential parents) with information relative to preventing birth defects.

Critical to the effective functioning of special needs families is their having access to "support services" that enable them to deal with the situation. In cases where the problem can be corrected remediation services should be provided as early as possible in the child's life or when the courses occurs to the family such services need to focus on the total family. By profiding a malnourished infant with proper foods (and the parents with nutrition education and resources to acquire food and vitamins) a series of problems can be corrected before they become major crises. The availability of counseling services for parents of mentally retarded children can – if conducted properly – provide the parents with a resource group to use in making decisions relative to what is best for the child and the other family members. Infant stimulation programs for handicapped and normal children have proven effective in helping individuals maximize their human potential. The work of Kempe (1978) has shown that in-depth rehabilitation programs for child abuse families can alter family interaction patterns toward more normal levels of functioning.

Early childhood educators, are of course, familiar with the many success stories of educational programs such as Head Start, Home Start, Follow Through and various other intervention and/or remediation projects. The most successful of these programs were comprehensive in design and had an emphasis on supporting families.

The mainstreaming of handicapped children (where appropriate) and the provision of special educational services for special needs children are further evidence of the way we can support families through direct services to their children. A key ingredient in developing these programs is the involvement of parents in appropriate and supportive roles in the education of their children. The increased self respect parents develop in such involvement efforts further their self development and improves the total functioning of the family.

An emerging support role helping professionals are performing relates to helping special needs families assess their situation and develop priority means of improving it. While some family situations may be so pathological that self-assessment is not feasible, many families are able to benefit from such a process. This process focuses on helping family members to assess where their "life support system" has deteriorated and involves them in organizing mechanisms for rebuilding it – albeit different than it was and certain to occur only over a period of time. According to Overton (1982) this rebuilding of support systems should aim to help the individuals involved establish a network of relationships that builds confidence and reduces stress factors in their daily lives. This ecological self assessment by the family should focus on the following questions:

1. What support systems are no longer available?
2. Specifically, what did these systems offer you that you on longer receive?
3. Specifically, what would you like from future support systems?
4. List support systems that are current available to you!
5. Now, prioritize the three most available to you and develop some strategies for utilizing them in revamping your family situation! (Overton, 1982)

The matching of special needs families with needed resources can be best accomplished with their involvement in the problem solving process. Bronfenbrenner (1979) notes, for example, that as people regain cognitive control over their destiny (at least as much control as possible) their affective balance and physical health generally improve and a sense of well being is restored.

CHAPTER FOUR
THE MANY ROLES PARENTS PERFORM

In order to fully understand the American family it is essential to grasp the challenges today's parents deal with on a day to day basis. In the recent past parental roles were basically homogenous and these roles were complemented by other socializing institutions in the community. Today's parent must perform a multitude of roles and do so within a dynamic culture which often provides few support systems to carry out these roles. Many of our social issues relate to parental ability or inability to carry out their tasks. With increased expectations and family responsibilities many parents find themselves overwhelmed in their attempt to parent. School failures, delinquency and even adult criminal behavior have been linked to pathological beginnings in ineffective home environments. Possibly, by better understanding parental roles, we can organize early learning environments that support and—indeed—involve parents and children in their attempt to become effective human beings.

The Parent As Developing Person

The most critical role a parent performs is that of being a developing person. Their personal development is essential to the performance of all other parenting tasks. For example, the research on child abuse indicates that parents who abuse their child are personally insecure and socially incompetent. The static parent is a poor model for the child who is seeking a guide in an attempt to learn about human functioning (Kempe 1978). In contrast to failure prone parents, Burton White (1979) states that effective parents are secure and competent human beings. It is impossible to separate the developing person from the developing parent.

There are indicators of the developing parent as a person. Effective parents have a sense of self and how this self functions in the family and in many other contexts. Their self awareness leads towards continuous improvements through their contacts with adults and children in many different environments. An understanding of strengths and weaknesses and the development of strategies to improve and refine the self is apparent in the effective person.

As a part of this "sense of self" effective parents use the past to learn from and to build the present and future into meaningful events — in effect they have a sense of purpose. Their sense of trust, autonomy and generativity combine to provide them with a set of psychological tools to apply in parenting and in personal situations. Stinnett (1979), for example, says that fully functioning families use resources within and from outside the family to strengthen their network of relationships. Such an ability is certainly rooted in the parental leadership provided for the family. Developing parents can thus draw upon their personal identity in dealing with family crises.

An understanding of the adult stages of development can help us see parents in a different way. For example, many young persons (20–35) are still attempting to establish a basic set of "work world" competencies. Their success or failure in this endeavor heavily influences parental behavior toward children and affects their transactions with home support agencies such as the school. Parents in mid-life often confront their self-identity in a new light such as job changes, marital conflict or the responsibility for caring for their own parents or assisting a teenage parent (daughter or son). By being sensitive to these personal — developmental influences on parents we can design and adapt early learning programs to match the parent-child context and thus facilitate the learning and development of the total family. (See Erik Erikson, 1982 for a complete life cycle portrait).

Parents behave within a cultural framework they have developed over a life time. Values, interests and attitudes are shaped through our experiences from childhood throughout the life span. Thus parental values, for example, will vary according to their experiences. While some parents will encourage exploratory behavior in their children, others may see this as a threat to a way of life they cherish. It is critical to examine parental values and accommodate them in our planning of programs for young children. By including family mores in curricula experiences we can have a positive influence on introducing parents and children to new ideas in a trusting and mutually respectful environment. Fantini (1980) purports that the relating of early childhood education settings to the multicultural backgrounds of families is a key to successful home-school programs.

Successful educators of young children have recognized that parents are the key people in bringing about lasting changes in the lives of children. They have also recognized that parents function within personal and developmental frameworks and have planned learning programs to relate to both parent and child needs and interests.

The Parent As A Community Participant

Erik Erikson's concept of the "generative adult" extends our discussion of parenting roles to the broader community setting. Many family problems are directly linked to parental impotence in terms of relating to the community in a productive manner. This impotence reduces parental self image and may influence their family relationships negatively. Conversely, a productive parent (one who is gainfully employed or positively engaged in citizen roles in the community) usually feels secure and has a sense of self-worth that permeates their family involvement in positive ways. For most parents their community participation is a continuous process of learning, doing and then refining their behavior. A key part in this discussion is that contributing parents usually develop a network of friends and supporters who in turn make their lives more functional which in turn has a positive impact on the total family.

Given the multiple community participation roles parents perform it is possible for conflict to develop in their attempt to carry out these roles and yet maintain adequate family involvement. For example, it has been estimated that today's parents spend less time with their children than in past generations — largely due to parental job requirements and resultant recreational opportunities that often accompany such jobs (Bronfen-brenner, 1979). Other research indicates that many "latch key" children return home from school to find no one there — which is especially critical during the formative years of the child's life (Duff and Stroman, 1982). Stress factors created through out-of-home work and social con-tracts can influence marital relationships and/or parent-child relationships in negative ways. Some schools and community agencies are attempting to assist parents in coping with these issues by developing extended school-day programs and through offering family management seminars where parents can step back — examine their daily lives — and plan a more orderly program of living.

Just as parents suffer from too much involvement they can experience the dismay of being unemployed, underemployed or devalued in a role they saw as a contributing one to the society. The "degenerative" parent — one who is economically and/or socially isolated — is often unable to meet family maintenance requirements. A cycle of human incompetence can begin and eventually result in various family mental health problems. Young children are influenced by parental situations and suffer (possibly more than adults) from the effects of an unemployed parent. A role we can perform is to advocate for more education and training programs for adults and the development of job/career counseling programs to assist parents in dealing with these problems in functional modes.

In addition to job or career roles parents are involved in many com-munity support activities. Parents serve on school boards, city councils, church boards, health support groups, youth recreational planning com-missions, volunteer fire and police departments and many other vital community service groups. These activities, if kept in balance, add to the parents skill kit and provide young children with opportunities to see adults in productive roles. In less formal but certainly important roles, parents perform many assistance tasks in their neighborhoods. For example, a parent may help a senior citizen do their weekly shopping. These kinds of tasks can accumulate to many hours of "good neighbor" work. Parents who perform these human service jobs in complementary fashion to their family tasks are certainly providing children with a positive experience in values education in action.

A developmental perspective of parenting is essential for parents and their support team (teachers, employers, etc.) in order to balance the multiple expectations we have of parenting with the realities of everyday life. For example, parents of infants and toddlers will – in all probability – exert more effort in child care tasks than in community support roles. As children develop more autonomy, parents will engage in more community service roles. Family support agencies can help parents in utilizing a developmentally based approach to parenting by designing early childhood programs that take the developmental needs of the family into consideration.

Parent Roles Within The Family

A family photograph presents a holistic and rather simplistic view of family relationships. Yet the personalities behind each person in the family are fairly complex and handling these relationships – as parents know – is a full time job in itself. Consider, for example, that in parent-child-relationship we are dealing with more than two people; we are dealing with them and "significant others" they deal with. This certainly highlights the need for human relations education for parents and children. It further substantiates the very demanding but potentially rewarding job of parenting. Parent-parent, parent-child and parent-child-parent relationships present some important roles for parents to perform and those of us in the family support professions to understand.

Parent-parent relationships are the basis for developing other intra-familial relationships (Bronfenbrenner, 1979; Stinnett, 1979). Thus an obvious but often overlooked role for parents is to establish and continuously refine their involvement with their spouse. In the initial stage of dating and later during the early years of marriage couples experiment with and eventually organize a set of compatible relationships that become the basis for later involvement with children. When these relation building experiences are lacking or evolve in an incompatible manner the fabric of the marriage is usually weak. For example, couples who learn to handle external stressors in a constructive way during their pre-children years are likely to use these skills in handling family problems throughout their marriage. Positive parent-parent interactions influence children toward the development of prosocial behaviors.

Parent-child relationships emerge from the initial bonding of mother and infant at birth to become more abstract and sometimes complex as both the child and parent develop and learn. Even at birth this relationship is a mutual and reciprocal interaction process. As Bell and Harper (1977) indicate the parent-child relationship is continuously forming, refining and re-shaping itself. Parent and child influence each other as

32

well as being influenced by the myriad of cultural factors in their environment. Yet, it is also clear that parents establish the basis for other productive or destructive socialization of future generations. Indeed the developmental nature of social relationships is influenced by the initial yet ongoing dyadic relationship between mother and infant. Consider Stern's (1977) perspective on this "relationship forming" process.

> If we could capture the essence of the nature of characteristic interactive patterns of any individual infant-caregiver pair, it might be possible, even feasible, to predict and chart the likely course of future interpersonal relatedness. Yet this task eludes us. Both parents and researchers maintain that some temperamental features of infants, such as activity level, remain consistent during development. Furthermore, at a different level, most parents experience that the interpersonal "feel" of what it is like to be with the person who is their child maintains some indescribeable yet pervasively recognizeable unbroken strain from infance on, even though the manifestation of this "feel" may change considerably during different developmental epochs (pp. 109, 110).

Considerable energy is put forth by parents in relating to their children as the data on the socialization process indicates (Erickson, 1982). Four basic roles emerge as critical processes in making the parent-child relationship meaningful both within family environs and beyond into various human constellations. These roles are: (1) nurturing, (2) guiding, (3) problem solving and (4) modeling.

Research related to effective development in young children reveals that parents who form a close relationship with their children are in a better position to provide the various kinds of experiences necessary for them to function capably in society. The meeting of basic human needs (love, security, food, etc.) and the development of a competent child are *nurturing skills* parents perform. Nurturing infants and young children toward developing continuity of self is the "stuff" of developing generational continuity (Gordon, 1976). This nurturance role does not end at two years of age. As middle childhood approaches, parents continue helping children broaden their scope of acceptance and understanding of life conditions by involving them in various community and school tasks related to learning about the connectedness of life (Swick & Duff, 1982).

The guidance role is critical because children learn productive behavior only when someone shows them through setting limits and/or offering alternatives to existing behavior patterns. The significance of the guidance role can be seen when children are severely neglected. Such children seem to wander in search of direction, withdraw into themselves and/or become highly aggressive and antagonistic toward rules and structures which are a part of functional living. Parental guidance, within intra-family relationships, sets the stage for children to eventually become self-managers and effective social beings in the family and in extra-familial environments.

Not only are parents called upon to use *problem solving* skills in the work place but of vital importance to the child is the parents skill in applying instrumental behaviors in resolving family issues and concerns. The management of family schedules, resolving human conflicts and maintaining the economic and social stability of the internal family network requires much time, skill and human committment on the part of parents. Learning to use intra-familial resources as the "core" of family strength which can then be used to foster family contacts with community resource groups. Ira Gordon (1976) was certainly correct when he observed that it was through family living experiences that children learn skills for later use in solving human problems in the community.

A synthesis of all the roles parents perform can be found in the examples they set for children. Whether performing nurturance, instrumental or guidance roles, *parents model a way of life* for children. The way they behave toward other family members and people in the community sets the stage for what children internalize as modes of living within a social system. Various research reports in early childhood education confirm that early parental modeling is among the most powerful of all teaching tools the child will ever experience (Fraiberg, 1977).

In carrying out various intra-family roles, parents (if they are to be effective) must develop an internal support system. This necessitates some role changes by mothers and fathers of young children. Fathers, as Lamb (1979) points out can perform nurturing roles as well as mothers and the sharing of roles is, of course, most effective in building supportive relationships that will last. Teaming among adult family members can be the start of what can become a total sharing of family tasks by children and parents. Intra-family pathologies emerge when parasitic and destructive relationships are allowed to occur. Lack of teaming, family networking and ineffective communication systems can only lead to insecurity and possibly family dissolution.

Supporting Parents In Their Efforts

The internal functioning of families is only as effective as available community resource teams make it. We must find ways to support families as primary caregivers and the parents as the child's earliest and most influential teachers. In the words of Ira Gordon (1976, p. 126): "Connections need to be forged across all agencies as services to support rather than to supplant the family. Agency dichotomies and barriers must tumble. We need to build harmony between family, school, health, social services, housing, transportation, and work."

Some guidelines that early childhood educators can use in designing supportive family oriented programs are discussed here to stimulate a re-thinking of our role in making the important job of parenting more possible. As Bronfenbrenner (1979) and Gordon (1976) substantiate "time" is critical to healthy family development. All family members need time to relate to each other in meaningful ways. Yet this commodity seems very difficult for parents to acquire. Making citizens (especially community leaders) aware of this need and encouraging them to develop flexible work hours, adequate maternity/paternity leave policies, and planning school and community projects with this "time need" in mind. In the formative stages of parent-parent and parent-child relations this factor of time is crucial to establishing a positive basis for extended human relationships to develop.

The strengthening of the "family team" is dependent upon our (society) redefining the role of the father and then providing fathers with opportunities to engage in the family living process (Swick & Mann-ing, 1983). Through "parenting experiences" young boys can learn about nurturing and guiding as roles they too can perform both as young people and later as parents or citizens (Swick & Duff, 1982). The involvement of fathers in the birthing process and in infant care and educational experiences with their preschool child can form a positive father-mother-child connection that has been sadly lacking in our society. The use of fathers as homeroom leaders, tutors and school volunteers is a recent but encouraging sign that educators of young children are beginning to capital-ize on total parental resources in their centers and schools (Manning & Swick, 1982).

Intergenerational human resources provide a natural support system for families and schools. Consider, for example, that our children are involved with adults (or for that matter even children of different ages, etc.) less than any previous generation in history. The use of high school tutors, senior citizen volunteers and foster grandparent programs are only initial steps in bringing about more connectedness within children and parents. Schools that have used intergeneration and multi-age teaching strategies report that academic and social skills are learned and used more effective-ly than in isolated settings. By introducing parents and children to human resources in their community we can improve their chances for successful development and involved them in situations where they can contribute to others (Stinnett, 1979).

Additional support networks exist in the form of neighborhood co-operatives, preschool educational programs, church sponsored parent centers and through the more formal structures of various social service agencies in the community. As James Hymes (1972) indicates the entire thrust of early childhood education is to bring together all community resources to facilitate parents and children toward becoming effective social members of the community.

CHAPTER FIVE
PARENTS AS CATYLISTS
FOR CHILDREN'S LEARNING

Children learn the essential skills for living within a web of human re-lationships. Their potential to become significant contributors to society is dependent upon the kinds of experiences they have with their parents, teachers, siblings, peers, and other people they transact with during their life span. Learning to acquire and use information, for example, is learned simultaneously in the home, school, and in the community. Building upon the idea that learning and development occur in ecologically con-nected settings, Bronfenbrenner (1979) exclaims that children function best when the home and school are involved in mutually supportive endeavors. Recent research supports Bronfenbrenner's point of view. Studies examining the performance of children in school settings indicate that young children who have had positive preschool settings as well as supportive and involved parents do better on academic and social skills than children who lack such positive environments (Lazar, 1976).

Emerging from the research and study on how children learn best is a not so surprising discovery — children learn best wehn significant adults are continuously involved in helping them interpret and find constructive ways to act upon their world (White, 1979). For example, the first skill the infant must acquire is to trust his parent. This takes shape naturally if a caring, capable parent exists, but in many "failure to thrive" infants no such competent adult exists to guide them toward the acquisition of this skill (Fraiberg, 1977). The role of "significant and competent adults" is by far the most influential factor in the young child's attempt to become a fully functioning person. The generative adult, as Erickson (1982) points out, is able to care for the people and things he or she has been responsible for creating. Erickson uses the following example to focus on the significance of capable adults in nurturing the younger members of civilization.

As he lay there with his eyes closed, his wife whispered to him, naming every member of the family who was there to wish him shalom. "And who," he suddenly asked, sitting up abruptly, "who is minding the store?" This expresses the spirit of adulthood which the Hindus called "the maintenance of the world" (Erickson, 1982, p. 66).

Parents: A Child's First and Most Powerful Teacher

Parents are the first people to interact continuously with the newborn infant. In these early contacts with infants, parents "teach" children about how people live. Parental behavior, in effect, teaches the child about life. The nonverbal behaviors of parents (for example, when and how they hold the infant) communicate to the child more clearly than words. Research indicates that young children seem to place more credence in examples set by parents than in their words. Thus, the learning of essential skills begins in infancy and is carried out through parent-infant contacts (Swick & Duff, 1979).

The type of atmosphere conducive to productive learning in children is recognized by effective parents as containing simple, safe surroundings which allow children to explore, solve problems, ask questions and receive answers, observe, and interact with others. Such an environment allows children to act out, imitate, meet new situations, and retreat to familiar ones — all with the support and encouragement of a caring, supporting adult team (Lane, 1975).

In addition, the type of atmosphere which tends to promote effective learning is one which provides children with opportunities to observe parents and/or other significant individuals in the process of living together and working through the full range of problems and situations that confront families today. As children experience associations with other individuals who are willing to help them understand the happenings around them, numerous opportunities for productive learning unique to each family situation present themselves.

Basics of Parenting

The cumulative set of parenting behaviors infants and young children experience represents a curriculum that influences them throughout life. When parents talk, sing songs, gently touch or feed the baby, they are conveying the messare: you are important! In addition they are facilitating the infant's physical and social development. As parents respond to the needs of the infant, they are giving the assurance of a secure and trusting environment (Swick, 1983).

During these formative years parents have opportunities to help young children to begin the development of their basic human capacities. Children, for example, learn to talk and develop language faility only when they have people to *converse with, to think with,* and *to follow as models.* By talking with and listening to children, parents set the stage for language acquisition at the same time they establish a social and emotional bond with them (Gordon, 1975).

Parents teach children to trust or distrust, love or hate, feel secure or insecure, to value or not value life itself (all of which are essential skills). As children grow, parents continue to be their facilitators and leaders.

By setting limits for positive behavior, with reasonable expectations which allow for human errors, and by being consistent in home management, parents set an example. Through their interactions with children — praising, showing, involving, and rewarding — and in responding to children's inquiries, parents can lead them toward an understanding of the nature of learning.

Further, when parents take children on walks or to parks and encourage their curiosity, they enhance the natural proclivity of children to learn. Spending quiet times together, visiting friends, and making things a part of natural family activities are all very positive parenting behaviors that combine to expand the learning capacities parents and teachers value.

Parents Perform Many Catalyst Roles

Parents perform many roles in their attempt to stimulate the child toward growing and learning in productive ways. Not the least parents are the child's "safety network" by taking care of basic human needs such as food, clothing and shelter. Without this maintenance of the home setting by competent parents very little learning and development could occur in the child. Thus, while it is often taken for granted, the work parents do to support the child and themselves is critical for the total family to function.

In order for parents to carry out their many roles they must give attention to their "personal skill kit," or they will be unable to provide the child with any long-term support. Swick and Duff explicate the significance of parents as persons in the following manner.

> Parents must have a personal life which allows them to explore, enrich and develop their interests in constructive ways. Parents who appropriately balance their work lives with hobbies, social interests, and other activities not only develop their individual selves but are in a better position to provide their children with models of positively functioning human beings (Swick & Duff, 1978).

As fully functioning human beings parents are equipped to perform what Burton White calls the "educational, support, and planning roles" that are critical to fostering in the child a zeal for learning.

The "educational role" of parents is exemplified in their management of first the home setting and later the school-community contexts as meaningful places for children to develop in intellectually and socially skillful modes. Consider, for example, that during early childhood parents involve children in many cognitive-perceptual development activities such as puzzle games, picture stories, and everyday parent-child dialogue regarding objects and events in the home setting. Later, during the elementary and middle school years parents expand the child's educational world through travel and strengthen the child's school performance by being involved in various school functions — especially those that enhance the parent-child-teacher triadic relationship.

The "support role" of parents — while often carried out in an indirect fashion — has a very direct and dramatic impact on the child's learning potential. In noting the characteristics of effective parents, White cited parental ability as "environmental support planners" of the child's world as the critical role they perform (White, 1980). During the early childhood years parents use their energies to establish a safe, healthful, and intellectually interesting environment. They "take care" of the child in terms of proper nutrition, medical care, and critically large doses of love and care. While parents continue such supportive activity during the school years, they also extend their involvement to introducing the child to books, ideas, people, and the "fabric" of the culture in which the child will live and hopefully contribute.

Successful parents *plan and anticipate* events that have or may affect children's learning and development. In studies of "high risk" parents (parents likely to abuse or neglect their children) Kempe found they failed to plan for the baby's arrival and generally were unable to anticipate even the most basic needs of the developing child (Kempe, 1978). In contrast to this finding, Stinnett found effective parents imbued a sense of purposeful planning in the entire family. Some of the ways they accomplished this was to utilize regular family meetings, evening meals, and family get-togethers as times to join as well as individual events and activities. And as Stinnett points out, *the "art of anticipation" is at the basis of learning essential skills* such as problem solving, reading, socialization and other human coping mechanisms (Stinnett, 1979).

Family Impact on Child as Learner

When parents are effective in their various roles, children benefit (and so does the school and the society). Various studies have been conducted to determine factors that influence a child's performance in school. Ira Gordon, for example, in his "Florida Studies" found that by improving parental language skills and their "teaching" skills children's performance in the primary grades was positively influenced. These children were better readers and in general did better than their peers whose parents were not involved in Gordon's parent education programs. A side effect of the program was that parental self-concept improved, and these parents spent more time with their children — especially in terms of educationally related activities (Gordon, 1977).

Further studies conducted by White (1979), Watson (1983), Lazar (1976) and Swick (1979) have established the following as "benchmarks" of the impact effective parents can have on young learners.

1. They are usually ready to benefit from formal school experiences.

2. They are less apt to be placed in special education courses or to be held back a grade in school.
3. Generally speaking, these children are consistently "high performers" throughout the school years.
4. Such children (and their parents) are curious, creative problem solvers and exhibit a high level of self-reliance in school and community situations.
5. They tend to score high on IQ tests and on other measurements of school success.

Families in which successful children develop are not perfect but do have characteristics that typify a success cycle of living. For example, a recent study in the field of family life education indicates that effective families are characterized by a sense of purpose, teaming among family members, continuous and intentional communication, a coherent spiritual belief system, regular family get-togethers (usually at meal times), a sensitivity to each other's lives, high value of education, positive social interactions in the community, and an emphasis on solving conflicts through the problem-solving process. Families of this orientation, says Stinnett, produce successful children and adults (Stinnett, 1980).

Educated Parents Equal Productive Children

Educated parents tend to use a combination of behaviors that encourage children to learn to solve problems, to communicate effectively, and to seek adult assistance when needed. Some behaviors used by effective parents are:

1. Listening to their children with their eyes as well as their ears. Eye contact is a way of showing the adult is listening.
2. Offering answers to children's questions that cause children to think creatively and develop alternative solutions.
3. Reflecting an active interest in numerous topics and activities. Parental enthusiasm about learning and doing serves as a model of continuous learning for the children.
4. Reading avidly. Effective parents enjoy and feel comfortable reading. They read regularly to their children and for personal growth. Such adult behaviors set an example for children of the use of cognitive as well as other essential skills for daily needs.
5. Pointing out aspects of their surroundings that children are likely to overlook. They take time to discuss and describe happenings that children may understand.
6. Offering praise and encouragement for their children's growth efforts. They are sensitive to the needs for honest praise and simple encouragement. Such adult behaviors assist children to develop the ability to accept honest appraisals of their efforts (Talbert, 1976).

Increasingly, parents are coming to recognize the importance of their own active involvement with their children and are, in numerous cases, beginning to assume greater responsibility for understanding and assisting their children in appropriate ways throughout the various growth processes. To reach and teach a child is a process that requires growth, energy, and an ideal vision of tomorrow. As parents are the child's first teachers, they certainly hold the power in their hands to provide children with a humane vision of what life can be!

CHAPTER SIX
FATHERING: NEW ROLES AND RELATIONSHIPS

The role of the father is changing from the economic provider role to a more comprehensive and involved caretaker. The image of the father as a builder of log cabins and protector from nature is anachronistic to our modern society (Maxwell, 1976). However, in our culture the father has been considered the primary source of financial support for the family and often relinquishes child rearing activities to the mother (Sawin & Parke, 1979). Fatherhood, once described as a social invention, has been given a clear message regarding its status and value: man's place is not in the home with the children (Resnick, 1978).

Recent trends toward father recognition are reflected by magazine articles on father roles, advice columns for fathers, and by family oriented hospital practices (Sawin & Parke, 1979). Definitions of birth and family life are broadening with the growing recognition of the importance of fatherhood, changing cultural definitions of masculinity, and opinions of father involvement in pregnancy, birth and infant care-taking (Fein, 1976).

Other factors contributing to the current interest in paternal roles are a concern with father-child interactions, the growing realization that little was known about fathering (Gearing, 1978), and fathers perceiving themselves as partners in both childrearing and domestic responsibilities (Lamb & Bronson, 1980). In addition, a few fathers have experimented with role reversal with their wives and found new insight into the father-child and husband-wife relationships (Cammarata & Leighter, 1978).

Additional events influencing the changed direction of father role include: break down in American family life, increase in divorce and separation, increase in the number of single-parent families, and the decrease in the marriage rate (Katz, 1979). Also, Lewis (1979) reports that both women's and men's liberation movements have changed opinions toward fathers. The role transition is summarized by Lamb (1979, p. 941):

> Although the impetus for change has come largely from women and the major changes have been in female roles, some redifinition of paternal roles appears to be inevitable and desirable.

Fathers, while certainly experiencing many new challenges, are showing a new desire to become integral family members. For example, their family relationships are providing them with more affectionate roles than past times. Fathers, no longer discouraged from displaying physical affection toward their children, are showing support, involvement, and responsibility toward the care of infants and children (Redina, 1976). Thus new roles and relationships are emerging in the lives of fathers. An exploration of these roles from involvement in the birthing process to father involvement in family development will enable us to better meet their needs.

The Birthing Process

Fathers who recently have become "visible and involved coaches" before and during the birthing process are learning they enjoy being a part of the human development team. Fathers can and do perform many valuable and critical roles in this process. For example, the "third party effect" fathers have on the mother — newborn dyad is very positive when carried out in an effective manner. Father support during labor and delivery has been observed to enhance the mother's self perception and to provide an aura of security critical at this point of her life. Further, such support releases the mother from external pressures so she can focus on first having a successful birth and then establishing an intimate and positive relationship with the newborn (Bronfenbrenner, 1979).

When men assist women in carrying out birthing techniques and become involved with the infant (such as holding the baby, changing diapers and other tasks), they also accomplish two other human functions: (1) establish themselves as fathers in the authentic sense of that term and (2) form bonds with the infant that can only occur at the moment of birth — at least according to recent studies (Klaus & Robertson, 1982).

The Infant Years

Researchers studying human development and learning are convinced that infancy is a critical stage of the individual's life. The father is a key person in making sure the infant has access to the necessary opportunities for a successful beginning in life. There are at least three "involvement roles" men can perform to maximize the development of the infant and indeed the total family during this period of life. It should be noted that father involvement in these roles is critical during the initial formation of the family (that is with the birth of the first child). The roles are: (1) supportiveness, (2) nurturance and (3) educational facilitator.

Urie Bronfenbrenner (1979) cites various studies that indicate the need for a triadic approach (3 party system) to sustaining and creating positive conditions for humans to develop. Mother-infant interactions, without supportive people in their "world" can and often do deteriorate into cycles of deficit producing behavior. The litany of tragedies that occur among isolated dyadic teams (mother-infant) need not be repeated; it is documented ad nausem (Green, 1982). What does deserve attention is

44

what happens when fathers (or father surrogates) perform *the role of support system for mothers and infants.* When the mother-infant dyad becomes extended to the mother-infant triad team everyone benefits. And when this is extended via neighborhood, community and societal support systems, the entire social fabric of the culture is strengthened (Swick, 1982). Consider the following as examples of supportive behaviors fathers can perform during the infant period.

— Adapting work schedule (where possible) to assist wife in handling family management tasks.

— Being positive and reinforcing of your wife's efforts in child care.

— Be flexible, allow for changes in what used to be routine and facilitate things by helping establish a new routine (this is especially critical for first-time parents).

— Be a good listener! During the early months of the newborn's life, your wife needs an active communicator who assists in making the home a comfortable place to live.

— If your infant is in a day care center, be supportive of the teachers and take part in the activities at the center.

Infants are learning and developing at a pace they will never again experience. *Fathers can play an active role in making this period of development a beneficial time for infants.* By creating an orderly but stimulating environment, fathers can promote a sense of security needed for learning to occur. Infants, as they develop, are mobile, curious, and seek knowledge of the world around them. Often times, mothers are so involved in the direct socialization and needs-meeting of infants that fathers and relatives perform the vital role of filling the environment with substantive materials such as mobiles, malleable (safe) objects and meaningful human contacts such as informal play and holding infants closely. In a more direct fashion, fathers can take part in this educational adventure by talking with the infant, responding to infant utterances both verbally and via gestures, and through direct play interactions with the infant (where fathers and infants engage in meaningful but informal language, motor and other learning activities).

Many infants must spend their days in centers outside the home. Fathers can play a major role in assuring these centers are safe, pleasant, and educationally meaningful places for infants. For example, fathers will want to check for infant-caretaker ratio, the composite physical facility, philosophy of the center staff, and the "curriculum" used among many other items of consideration. (See Burton L. White, *A Parent's Guide To The First Three Years* for a comprehensive perspective on this topic). Being an active supporter of center activities is yet another role fathers can perform in their efforts to make infancy a positive time for their children.

During the early development of the child, the socialization process is linked to the security and psychological atmosphere existent in the entire family. Fathers, as recent research indicates, play a significant role in nurturing everyone in the environment toward productive living (Resnick, 1978). Of course in order to be nurturing persons, fathers must feel secure and positive about their role and see its significance in making family and society productive places. As Manning and Swick (1982) point out, the world of work and the extended family system (relatives and neighbors in particular) must free fathers from their isolated roles so they can become more caring individuals. The following are activities fathers perform when they feel accepted within the fathering role context (Schlesinger, 1978).

— spending creative, open-ended play time with infants

— making meals, cleaning, and performing tasks that visibly place value on the family's new place in the world

— being affectionate toward mother and infant by spending time in physical and social contact with them

— increasing availability time during this phase of family development so the tasks and jobs of parenthood can be shared and thus integrated into a life style that will last throughout the family's life.

The Preschool Years

Fathers will continue to perform many roles (instrumental, nurturing, educational and modeling) throughout the family's life span (Swick and Duff, 1982). The preschool years provide fathers and children a time to refine their relationship and extend it to new settings. Continued nurturance of the child toward his positioning for experiencing autonomous activity, educating the child in his consciousness of surrounding events through concrete experiences, and modeling caring modes of behavior for the child are some significant involvement possibilities for fathers.

The preschooler seeks validation as a person within his/her social context. Fathers, by encouraging the child's autonomous acts such as commenting on particular accomplishments or reinforcing positive social behaviors of the child, can foster the development of positive and secure self constructs in the child. Father-child interactions can take place in many settings and can be adapted to their personal interests and qualities. The important thing is that a direct, continuous and meaningful relationship exists between the father and child. Some guidelines for fathers of preschoolers are listed for consideration and use as appropriate.

46

— Set aside "time for being with your child on a regular basis". Sporadic involvement does not have the long range effect that consistent and enduring relationship building has.

— Respond, whenever possible, to your child's questions and statements. Remember, you are an important person to him and your response or lack of it is critical to his developing view of life. As you take time to listen to your child, he will begin to listen and communicate in similar ways.

— Utilize every opportunity to be directly involved in your child's play. Your involvement in water play, building block games, putting puzzles together, hide-n-seek gaming, etc. provides you an opportunity to stimulate the child toward new thinking and validates your child's interest in learning.

— Observe your child's total development and learning. Your daily observations help you to see changes and any problems that occur — thus enabling you to help your child. Your observations also are valuable for the pediatrician and teacher in being supportive of the child's development.

— In selecting a preschool center, consider the environment in which your child will spend most of his/her working hours. Is the environment safe, interesting, pleasing to the eye, stimulating and most importantly a warm — caring place where you would *like* to be? Are the adults who run the program personal, interested in and knowledgeable about the children, and desirous of having parents involved as partners in the education of young children?

— Be involved in your child's preschool education. Make visits to the center, serve as a resource person, support the teaching staff, and encourage other parents to do likewise. Adult involvement in school programs expands and enriches the learning setting and validates teachers and children as important members of the community.

Fathers are, in many cases, the family's window to the world. Your example in establishing a caring, teaming relationship with your total family sets the "model" for your preschooler to follow.

Kindergarten-Primary Years

The attitude parents hold toward education influences the way children approach the formal school situation (Watson, Brown, and Swick, 1983). While women have traditionally been the child's guide in being introduced to school, fathers need this experience, too! When both parents participate in home — school transitions, the ultimate outcome is usually of mutual benefit to all family members (Swick and Duff, 1978). An additional observation is that when fathers are involved in the initial school experiences of their children, they tend to continue this practice throughout the school years.

While reality dictates that fathers and mothers will never be able to attend all school functions, their "teaming" and planning for as much involvement as possible will influence the child's success potential in terms of academic and social performance (Swick and Taylor, 1982).

Critical to the transition from home (and informal preschool involvement) to school for the child is the involvement of fathers in making this change a productive one. Fathers can take the lead in contacting the school prior to the child's entrance into kindergarten. Visit the classroon with your child and introduce him/her to the teacher and the school environment. Talk with your child about the exciting things he will learn in school and the many new friends he will make there. If possible, go to school with your child the first time and make it a pleasant experience. Many schools have "transition programs" for children and parents to experience the beginning of school in a positive manner. Take advantage of these opportunities and if none exist, take the lead in initiating them in your community.

Throughout the early years of school, fathers are looked to for guidance by young children. Sex role development, development of social skills, learning to care for self and others and becoming involved in school and community events are skills and roles heavily influenced (positively or negatively) by father involvement. Children seeing fathers involved in various roles in the home, at work and related to school functions are likely to develop androgynous sex role constructs and thus synthesize their selves into a harmonious social relationship with other individuals (Hobson, Skeen and Robinson, 1980). Learning how to share, solve problems, and to become self reliant are skills they need for caring, facilitative adult involvement. While children in the early grades have many contacts with mothers and female role models, their exposure to men are too few and in very structured settings. Father attendance at parent-teacher conferences, participation in classroom functions and active encouragement of the child's educational aspirations are essential to the total development of young children. The following are some basic guidelines for fathers of young children.

- Be supportive of your child's efforts at school. Remember, each child is unique — do not compare siblings or your child to a neighbor's child. Your full support of the child as a unique person will enable him/her to develop in a complete manner as a person.

- Your child looks to you as a guide. Be the best guide you can be. Respond to his inquiries and help him over the problem spots. Your belief in him is critical to his self concept development.

— Communicate with your child and his teacher on a regular basis. Ask your child about his day at school and encourage his mastery of school-related skills. Your communication with the teacher not only indicates your interest to the teacher but more importantly impresses upon the child that you care about his educational performance.

— Participate in school functions and be visible in your child's classroom whenever possible. You have many talents to share with young children. Your service as a resource person, tutor, and teacher-aide are roles that will impact your child and all the children in that classroom.

Elementary And Middle Years

The literature documenting active and successful father involvement and caretaking responsibilities (Manning & Swick, 1982) provides evidence that the fathering role can extend beyong the home and early childhood years. Fathers can play a significant role during the development of elementary and middle years children, both in the home and in the school. Fathers can be quite competent and responsive (Parke & Sawin, 1976) and are eager to assume an active role in the rearing and development of children (Lamb, 1979).

The research provides considerable evidence to document the importance of the *father's influence on the sex role identification* of both boys and girls (Bradley, 1980). Provided the father is warm, accepting, and involved with the children, the influence on sex role identification will occur regardless of the father's masculinity.

The evidence allows the conclusion that fathers can and should provide appropriate sex role identification in both school and community. The rising divorce rate and increased number of one-parent homes (Katz, 1979) lend support to proposing that fathers are needed to model appropriate sex role behavior. Both boys and girls living in one-parent homes will benefit form this opportunity to relate to a father figure. The father's previous interest and participation in PTA and school advisory councils provide evidence of successful experiences in educational situations. The following provide ideas for fathers involved with children in sex role development.

— Work with parent and community involvement programs. The presence of a warm, accepting, and involved father serving as a class assistant or class father will allow children to see the role of masculinity in a new light.

— Be supportive and accepting of your child's questions and concerns over changing sex roles. Remember, although considerable change has occurred in your lifetime, changes are becoming more dramatic and rapid.

Two related aspects are important and worth mentioning. Father involvement, not limited to the classroom, may include other school and community activities after regular school hours and during the weekends. Also, involved fathers must portray appropriate and reasonable sex roles and avoid implications of the "macho" image often suggested by the media.

Warm, accepting, and involved fathers play an important role in the socialization of both boys and girls. In addition to modeling and teaching sex roles (Lamb, 1979), additional research by Hoffman (1961) further suggests that "a warm companionship with the father is clearly related to peer-group adjustment" and "a positive father relationship is associated with a high degree of self-confidence with respect to abilities."

The research suggesting that positive father interactions with children can enhance social development also infers that father presence in school and community activities can promote social development in children other than his own. Substantial amounts of research dealing with socializaiton support the proposal that the presence of positive male figures will lead to increased self confidence and improved relationships with others (Bradley, 1980; Hoffman, 1961; Lamb, 1979). Consider the following ways a father can enhance social development.

— Serving as a teacher's aide, special project volunteer, or a community group sponsor, your interactions with both your children and others will provide appropriate examples of social development.

— Serve as a positive mediator in disputes without taking sides. Explain and give examples of positive behaviors such as discussing calmly, seeing both sides, compromising, and reaching mutually agreed decisions.

Broderick (1977) concluded that caring and involved fathers with frequent and positive father-children contacts have children with higher moral and school achievement. Similar findings by Blanchard and Biller (1971) provides additional evidence that high father contact fostered academic achievement.

Father involvement with children in school and community services can take many forms, all positive and beneficial for both boys and girls. The research indicates that benefits can be accrued mainly by father availability and participation showing an interest, a sense of caring, and sometimes just a person to encourage a child troubled with a school, home, or other personal problem. The father can assist children in academic development in many ways.

— Commit yourself to share your areas of expertise or interest with students as lesson plans and units are developed. Follow-through with interesting experiences designed for the level of development of the children.

— Using your untapped resources, energies, and skills, volunteer to work with teachers and administrators to begin a special interest club or organization.

— Provide first-hand assistance to small groups or students needing individual attention.

These projects, however, must be without sexist implications and with both girls and boys participating, should be conducted assuming non-academic activities provide experiences fostering academic interest and achievement, and the realization that sex role identification and social development are being influenced.

According to Payne and Mussen (1956) and Lamb (1979), a major influence of the father is to model and transmit values, mores, and encourage societal rules and expectations. Lynn (1974) succinctly summarizes the position:

"Fathers — working in the community, knowledgeable of its rules and principles, aware of the price of their violation and eager that his children take their responsible place as citizens — might be expected to urge his children to internalize the culture's basic rules and values." p. 194.

Essentially, the father's role in the child's moral development will depend on the relationship between the father and the child. Lamb (1975) concluded that boys identifying with their fathers tended to make more moral judgements than those that did not.

Perhaps a note of caution is needed before continuing: The father involved in school and community activities should not and probably would not want the responsibility of teaching values and mores sacred to parents and religious institutions. This does not mean, however, that the children cannot at least be made aware of some basic societal expectations. The following are some suggestions for assisting in moral development.

— Exercise caution! Acting as an exemplary model, attempt to transmit an awareness of societal expectations to children.

— Transmit the idea that some decisions must include a consideration of other people and often are reached only through difficult and thoughtful consideration.

— Provide problem-solving situations allowing each child to reach a conclusion based on her or his beliefs as taught by parents and religious institutions.

The role of the father acting as a friend — someone in time of need, loneliness, curiosity, or confusion — may be the most beneficial for both boys and girls. Too often children may not seek assistance or advice from the teacher on delicate matters because they feel the teacher "may report them to their parents" or consider their problems unworthy of consideration. A volunteer father may make the difference. Tasch (1952) in a study of the role of fathering found:

> "Companionship was highly valued by the fathers studied and emphasized in their many reportedly jointly shared activities with their children, their satisfactions, and reiterated in their concepts." p. 358.

Evidently, the fathers in this study had come to grips with allocating time between employment and time spent with children. Tasch continues:

> "Doing things with the children in the time they have available appears to be more important than the consideration of how much time they spend with their children." p. 358.

Lamb (1975) in a discussion of father absence considered the fathering role of "playmate" and "socializer" more difficult to mediate than the "provider" role. Payne and Mussen (1956), describing the father capable of fulfilling a companion role, includes warmness, rewarding, gratifying, understanding, and the ability and willingness to establish a sound psychological relationship. A father understanding the importance of companionship to all children can work wonders in home, school, and commjnity activities.

— Develop the habit of talking with your children on a regular basis. Let them know you want to listen to their concerns. You may not always agree, but let them know you will listen to their opinions in an objective manner.

— First and foremost, be a friend with a kind and accepting statement to both your children and the children in the community. Be a person the community children can talk with of concern and need.

— Follow-up with a children in school and community concerning their concerns and problems.

— Be sure to speak to the lonely, quiet child at school. Do not be too aggressive; just say a few words each day.

52

Fathers capable of fulfilling a volunteer assistant or companion role have a challenge in today's schools and communities. Educators need to look beyond tradition and include fathers as partners in academic matters, advisory roles, extra-curricular activities, and in any area where need, expertise, and willingness allow.

The literature on fathering has provided evidence that fathers, acting in nurturing and caretaking roles, have both the necessary desire and competence to succeed with children. Also, research studies substantiate the importance of the role of the father in sex role identity, social development and adjustment, academic achievement, and moral development. Educators and community leaders must recognize that fathers serving on a voluntary basis can be as influential in the classroom and community as research has shown them to be in the home.

CHAPTER SEVEN
ECOLOGICAL ASSESSMENT AND
FAMILY FUNCTIONING

The formation of successful parent involvement programs is based on having families that function in healthy modes. Too often school personnel assume that many parents lack sufficient interest in the educational process. Researchers such as Bronfenbrenner (1979), White (1980), and Schaefer (1983) purport that it is not a lack of interest that prevents parental involvement as much as deficiencies in family functioning which impede parents and children from fully functioning in the home-school partnership. Educational leaders, therefore, need to consider the "ecology of family functioning" as they design parent-teacher programs. This chapter contains material pertinent to fully functioning families, some assessment issues that can be used in acquiring a picture of families as they function, and some ideas on how school personnel can incorporate family assessment into their planning mechanism.

Family Functioning and Ecological Assessment

Relationships among family members have traditionally been studied in microcosmic modes. Dyadic (father-son interactions) relationships and individual behavior patterns have been predominant concerns of people studying families. Only recently has the family been viewed in broader, more systematic and ecological perspectives. This broader perspective enables us to see family functioning as a composite of many human relationships within the family and external but linked to the family's ultimate destiny. For example, in this perspective various individual and dyadic relationships are extended to triadic relationships and then viewed within systems perspectives. This larger view of families has provided us with a better understanding of how some families perform effectively and others seem to suffer from isolation and negligence (Starr, R.H., 1979).

In viewing family functioning as a "network of dynamic and complex relationships" we can study the ecology of the family and generate more realistic and useable modes of involving parents and children in the educational process. Ecological assessment of families attempts to gather information regarding how members of the family relate to each other and to their extra-familial life contexts. *An important part of this eco-logical view of families is how family members perceive themselves as they relate to various situations.* In other words, what do people perceive as important and relevant to their identity and functioning in both family and societal settings. Figure 1 presents a picture of how the family can be viewed in an active-functional sense (Swick & Taylor, 1982).

It is in these settings of family, neighborhood, school, and work that parents and children carry on the business of learning, developing, and attempting to function as members of the human community. By viewing families in an ecological-developmental perspective, researchers have generated some ideas on how effective families function.

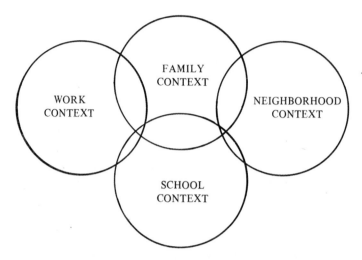

Figure 1. Inter-relationships of parent-child perceptions of family, school, neighborhood and work contexts as related to child's school performance.

Characteristics of "Healthy" Families

Recent studies of families contain information of extreme importance to those individuals planning parent involvement programs. We are beginning to acquire a picture of how effective families work. This information is important for at least two reasons: (1) it enables us to see how families can function positively and thus contain the skills critical to being an involved parent; and (2) it provides us with some parent behaviors we can attempt to nurture throughout our contacts with parents and citizens.

CHARACTERISTICS OF HEALTHY FAMILIES

- They have a sense of purpose and some goals as a team of human beings should in any social unit.

- They express a great deal of appreciation for each other. They build each other up psychologically by focusing on the positive contributions of family members.

- They spend a good deal of time together. This is not a "false" togetherness, but genuine enjoyment of each other.

- They have very good communication patterns. For example, they listen to each other and respond to each other in substantive ways.

- They are deeply committed to each others' happiness and welfare. They show this committment by structuring their life styles to accomodate family needs.

- They have a high degree of religious orientation. This religious orientation is more than mere church going, it is a commitment to a spiritual life style.

- They deal with crises and problems in a positive way. This is not to say that they enjoyed crises but that they had developed family bonds essential for coping with life predicaments.*

These characteristics of healthy families seem to combine to create a successful "press of events" that further influences successful development of family members. At the center of the "ecology of functioning families" is effective parenting. Ecological assessments of effective families point to successful parenting as the key ingredient in making this process work. Capable parents are characterized as having developed a life style that is based upon active participation in home, school, and community events (Swick, 1983).

Schaefer and Edgerton (1983) have identified parent behaviors that correspond with the development of successful children as well as promote supportive family relationships. Their research indicates that parents who have high verbal intelligence, are task oriented, have developed a strong sense of curiosity, encourage considerateness in family interactions, and are socially involved in the world beyond the home are most likely to have successful children and feel positive about their own lives. Passive, dependent, hostile, introvertish, and rigid parents have a negative influence on the family ecology.

Additional work in this field by Swick, Brown, and Watson (1983) indicates parental effectiveness influences the child's academic success in a positive way. Effective parents (which sets the stage for having healthy families) develop within supportive environments that reinforce productive human behavior and encourage positive parent-child interactions.

---

*For a more detailed explanation of characteristics of healthy families see Nick Stinnett, et. al., *Building Family Strengths*, Lincoln, Nebraska: University of Nebraska Press, 1979, pp. 23-30.

The ecological perspective toward developing healthy families and positive settings for children is supported by the following recommendations from a recent study on parental impact on children.

1. Parents must have an ecological support network from which they can draw in carrying out their roles.

2. Parents must perceive their role as "educator" and their children's role as learner as important and vital to the functioning of the family.

3. Parents must act on their perceptions that learning is essential for healthy family living.

4. Parents and teachers must form an active partnership beginning at birth so the appropriate home-school match can be achieved.

5. Neighbors, relatives, and citizens must join the home-school network in fostering an ordered, sensible, and supportive climate in which children can translate their education into positive community events (Swick, Brown, & Watson, 1983).

Unhealthy families appear to lack the needed support systems and direction for organizing their human energies into meaningful functions. These families are often characterized as powerless, chaotic, passive, and very dependent on external forces regarding their life choices (Stern, 1977). As we will discuss in the next section of this chapter the "ecology of the family" influences the way family members function both as individuals and as social group members.

Ecology of the Family

A major goal of all social institutions is (or should be) to nurture the learning and development of human beings. The family is the institution that historically has carried the burden of initiating and then maintaining the learning and development of its' members. There are four levels of functioning which influence the effectiveness of the family in accomplishing this objective of learning and development: primary level, secondary level, third party support level, and fourth party social linkage level. These levels of functioning combine to make up what might be called the "ecology of the family" (Bronfenbrenner, 1979, pp. 844–850). In viewing the family as it operates within these social systems we can acquire some useful information to apply toward the development of effective parent involvement programs.

The primary level of family functioning is the family system. It is within the family that children and parents learn how to function and develop as competent human beings. When it works effectively, the family provides the child with a place to gain skills, acquire a positive self image, and a setting where parents can actualize their abilities in a close, supportive environment.

The secondary level of functioning is any social system that provides the child and parent with opportunities and resources to engage in activities they have learned in the primary environment. For example, the child learns the rudiments of his language in the primary environment (the family) but applies his language in many different ways in secondary environments (such as the school and the neighborhood). Obviously the primary and secondary levels of family functioning are interdependent and thus meaningless when operating in isolation from each other. *This connectedness of the primary and secondary levels of family functioning is a major premise at the core of the parent involvement paradigm.*

The third party support level is comprised of those forces that encourage or impede the interactions of family members. It is the functional level that can maximize the development and learning of parents and children. For example, Bronfenbrenner (1979) found day care services to be of support value to parents in that they enabled parents to carry out their work without undue fear of how the children were being taken care of in their absence. Additional studies have supported this concept that supportive work, school, and neighborhood environments increase parent and child effectiveness in the family system (Swick, 1983; Schaefer, 1983). In the absence of supportive resources families tend to become overwhelmed and function in deficit ways.

The fourth level of family functioning occurs as family members have opportunities to practice, refine, and apply their skills in various community settings. The community plays a critical role in helping the family become fully functional. Youth work projects, school-based talent programs, recreational and civic opportunities as well as church sponsored programs are places where children and parents can "link up" with life in a constructive manner. One of the characteristics of effective families is their ability to engage in meaningful community behavior (Stinnett, 1979).

The dynamics of family life are such that the four levels of functioning are continuously interacting with each other and influencing the total makeup of the family. In this sense, the "ecology of the family" and the "community ecology" interact to shape each others' destiny. In organizing our thinking regarding educational programs we must move beyond a "content paradigm" to a more comprehensive view of the "ecological nature" of learning and development.

For example, we need to assess what is happening in the family, to the family, and how these interactions influence the development and learning of family members. Information acquired from this type of assessment can help us plan and implement parent involvement programs that are effective in supporting children and parents in their attempts to become contributing community members.

There are many views on family assessment and a variety of modes to use in acquiring a picture of how families work. Unfortunately, too many assessment approaches are based on a "deficit paradigm" that is of little value in promoting the development of healthy families. The goal of assessment is (or should be) to promote family development by better understanding the dynamics of families and then creating resources to support family members in their endeavors. This type of assessment can best take place in the actual life of families as they interact with themselves and the world in which they function. Further, effective family assessment should include the perceptions of family members of their family and how it functions and is influenced by social institutions it interacts with.

An ecological/perceptual assessment approach to family study involves gathering the views of family members on how it functions and relating these perceptions to what is empirically valid (Swick & Taylor, 1982). We must keep in mind that it is how we perceive things that influences a large part of our behavior. Thus, our assessment can be designed to correspond with the four levels of family functioning described in the previous section of this chapter.

Parent-child perceptions of what happens within the family. When we ask the question: How do family members see each other and their interactions within the family we acquire a broad picture of how their "life curriculum" works. Consider the following as statements that provide insights regarding how families function at the primary level.

– My family is generally happy at home.
– I think of my family as a group of capable people.
– We help each other in our family.
– My family has a good sense of humor.
– We do things together as a family whenever we can.
– I like being a part of my family.
– We discuss our school and work lives at home.

Responses to these statements, when synthesized into a family perception profile, provide a view of how the family sees itself as functioning. The purpose of this type of assessment is to acquire an idea of how the family functions (based on its' perceptions) and to plan home-school activities that will be facilitative of the family. For example, if family members perceive themselves as helpless, ineffective, unhappy, and isolated from each other, a major parent involvement objective would be to develop family oriented educational programs. Families that see their human interactions in the primary unit as facilitative and productive endeavors are ready for more intense involvement in the extra-familial settings such as the school.

Parent-child perceptions of what happens outside the family. In assessing family functioning in community settings it is important to again focus on how various family members see themselves in extra-familial settings. A series of statements can be used for family members to respond to in acquiring a picture of this part of the familyecology. We can begin by asking children to respond to statements such as the following.

- I like school.
- I am doing a good job in school.
- In my neighborhood I am usually involved in playing or working with others.
- I have an after-school job and am successful at it.
- I am involved in church and/or civic opportunities in a successful way.

Responses to these statements will vary according to the child's development and her experiences in school and community settings. A note of caution: avoid focusing on isolated responses; look at how the child perceives his situation in a wholistic manner.

Insights can be gained regarding parental involvement in secondary social units by having them respond to statements such as the following.

- I like where I work.
- I am successful in my work.
- I am involved in my child's school.
- I know my child's teacher.
- I am involved in church and civic activities.
- I am viewed as a helpful and involved neighbor.

Parent responses to these statements, taken in combination, provide a picture of how they see themselves as functioning in community situations. Parents who see themselves as successful in work and community roles will have a different view of parent-teacher relations than parents who see themselves as having major difficulties in linking up to the community (Schaefer & Edgerton, 1983).

Parent-child perceptions of their support systems. Critical to the development of successful families is the existence of a viable support system which parents and children can use in becoming fully functioning human beings. In gathering information on how families perceive their "support systems" statements such as the following will prove useful.

- My child's school is a helpful place.
- The school program is helping my child.
- My child's teacher is a very helpful person.
- I interact with my neighbors on a regular basis.
- My neighbors would or have helped me when the need exists.

- I try to make my neighborhood a better place to live.
- The people I work with care about my personal life.
- My work place is an enjoyable place to be.
- My parents enjoy their work.
- The people my parents work with care about us.
- I play a lot with the children in my neighborhood.
- In our neighborhood we help each other.
- My teacher likes me.
- Our school principal is a helpful person.

Responses to these statements may be indicative of how individual family members see their surroundings as well as indicative of the interaction of perceptions within the family. For purposes of establishing meaningful home-school programs it is important to understand the perceptions of families regarding their ecology as supportive or nonsupportive. For example, if the school is perceived as a nonsupportive place then a priority of parent involvement planners must be to alter this view of the school through substantive actions.

Parent-child perceptions of community potential. In the development of families the potential for actualizing family talents in the community is essential for fostering continuity of success in the family and the community. Parent responses to statements such as the following can give some insights as to how they see the community.

- As a parent I see many avenues for our family to develop and contribute to the community.

- There are places for young people to find meaningful employment in our community.

- Cultural and recreational opportunities are available in our community.

- Our community has a bright economic and social future.

Parent-child responses to these statements (and others like them) will indicate their views of the community as a functional place to live. For example, do parents see the community as a place where the family can engage in meaningful educational, social, and work experiences? Empirical data on community characteristics can be used to correlate with family perceptions. Community settings in which few opportunities exist for families to participate in functional activities are detrimental to fostering positive learning environments at home and in school.

The assessment of family functioning at the various levels of social performance must be viewed from an interactionist perspective. For example, the way parents and children function in their primary environment (the home) is influenced by their interaction with happenings at all other levels of the society. It has been found that parental behavior

62

toward children is influenced by the peopleparents work with, the child's status at school, and the viability of support systems in which parents and children function. Further evidence supporting the interactionist perspective exists in our study of child abuse. Child abusers usually have had negative interactions within all four levels of societal structure. They have, in a real sense, experienced a systematic denigration of self concept and consequently have few psycho-social skills for being an effective parent (Sasserath, 1983). Healthy parents appear to have developed an organizational pattern for having positive and productive interactions within various social systems (Schaefer & Edgerton, 1983).

While not all the variables that promote healthy families are known, a great deal of useful information can be acquired by viewing the operations of families in an ecological perspective. In conducting this kind of assessment educators of young children will find the following questions useful provided they have conducted some of the previously described activities.

1. How do parents perceive themselves as functioning in various social systems?

2. Have parents developed a successful pattern of interacting in various ecological contexts (family, neighborhood, school, work place, and community)?

3. How do parents perceive the various components of their family support system (such as their family relations, relatives, neighbors, and work partners)?

4. Have parents developed a viable pattern for linking up with the community in applying their skills and talents in a positive manner?

5. How do children perceive themselves as functioning in various social systems? For example, do the children see themselves as successful in school?

6. Have children developed a successful pattern of interacting in various ecological contexts (family, neighborhood, school, work place, and community)?

7. How do children perceive the various components of their family support system (such as their parent, siblings, relatives, neighbors, and other friends)?

8. Have children (at their developmental level) developed a viable pattern for linking up with the community through meaningful recreational, civic, and work prospects?

9. What are the inter-relationships between these ecological events and what can we learn from them in terms of planning family-school programs?

10. In viewing families from an ecological perspective how can educators use this process to organize productive modes of parent involvement?

Family Assessment: Implications For Parent Involvement

In seeking answers regarding children's success or failure in school we have often confined our study to localized situations in the classroom or attributed the problems to negative family syndromes. The use of an ecological assessment approach provides us with a more comprehensive way of understanding human development and learning in home, school, and work/community settings. By using family assessment data from ecological studies we conduct in our communities, we can begin to get answers to some of the following questions.

— What factors in the family influence a child's learning and development and how can we facilitate the family in organizing their system to generate these interactions with children?

— How do family support systems interact to influence parent-child relations in positive ways and how can we generate activity in home-school contacts that will encourage the development of such supports?

— What kinds of family-school interactions promote positive functioning of children and parents and how can we generate activity toward accomplishing such programs?

As data is gathered on the family at various levels of social functioning a profile of family behavior can be developed. This profile need not be highly complex but rather a clear picture of how the family interacts within various environments and a sense of its' overall effectiveness. For example, a family in which productive relationships exist and a high support system is available may well prove to function quite effective in home-school relationships while a family that has a few social supports and a history of negative interactions will find it difficult to establish productive linkages with the school.

By acquiring a broad picture of the family, educators of young children can plan parent involvement experiences pertinent to supporting and involving families in meaningful ways. In some cases families may need more support services from the school than involvement opportunities. In other cases family talents will prove useful in building school curricula and in improving other aspects of the home-school relationship.

Family assessment data, when combined with school planning information, will give us a basis for establishing an understanding of the family-school planning process. Further, when this information is used in productive planning by parents and teachers it can aid in forming specific objectives for parent involvement.

CHAPTER EIGHT
PARENT EDUCATION:
FOCUS ON NEEDS AND RESPONSIBILITIES

Current attempts to develop parent education programs have focused on a variety of objectives and populations. For example, programs have been developed to serve teenage parents, parents of exceptional children and parents in trouble. Most such efforts have focused on providing parents with information on topics such as child care and/or have attempted to heighten public awareness of the significance of parenting as a societal role (Swick & Duff, 1982). Yet within the context of most existing parent education programs the processes which occur within parenting have received little attention. This is especially pertinent to the education of parents during the early, formative years of the family (White, 1981). For example, while the content of a variety of parent education programs which focus on the preschool years may deliver information on the learning and development of children, these same processes as applied to the parents too often are neglected (Galinsky, 1981).

Initial Thrust of Parenting Programs

The initial thrust of parent education should be on the "personal" dimensions of the parents' developmental stage and the related issues that will help them be effective in both personal and parental roles. For example, White (1979) has identified some critical components of the parenting process that should be included in parent education programs.

1. *The ecological influences* impacting the lives of parents and children should be studied and used as a basis for selecting program content. For example, what kinds of support systems exist for families to use in carrying out their roles? What are some of the unique problems confronting parents in your community? Ecological research on families indicate this kind of data is critical to have as we design programs (Bronfenbrenner, 1979).

2. *The developmental needs of parents* should be addressed at the outset of educational programs for parents. Emphasis should be placed on helping parents realize they have "new" needs as they take on the responsibilities of parenthood and yet have personal development needs that continue to exist regardless of their new role as parents (Jaffe & Viertel, 1980).

65

3. *The initial focus of programs should be on "first time" parents,* their infants and the forces that affect the family as it encounters many new experiences. The first three years of the parent-child relationship provide parent educators with a "prime time" for establishing productive, positive behaviors among parents (White, 1975, 1981).

4. *Preventive approaches to educating parents* (methods that reach parents before they establish negative or even pathological syndromes) *are most effective when they focus on the positive aspects of parenting.* The use of "talk down to" or "sermonette" approaches will only serve to reduce the confidence level of new parents. Methods which focus on "sharing," "using personal resources" and capitalizing on the skills new parents have can provide the basics for a growth-oriented approach to parent education (Gordon, 1976).

5. A major focus on parent education programs should be on guiding parents toward the notion that children and parents learn from each other and do so — if intentionally pursued — in a developmental, almost rhymic manner. For example, Stern (1977) asserts that even at birth there is a crude form of learning existent in the mother-infant relationship.

As parents grasp the dimensions of parenting — both personal and parental roles — they can shape more of their behavior toward constructive ends. For example, parents who, from an early point in parenting, understand themselves and the changes they are experiencing, will be more apt to design learning experiences to nurture their children and themselves.

Insights on Program Design

As parent educators design programs for parents the following insights should help them focus on basic knowledge, skills, and attitudes that parents need to be aware of in their quest for personal — familial success. In examining these points, teachers of young children will want to think about unique aspects of their community that should be integrated into the planning process.

Insight One: Just as children function at different levels of development so it is with parents. Unfortunately, many parent education programs are geared toward meeting group needs instead of individualizing the content and process of the program to meet specific needs of parents and their children (Swick and Bollinger, 1980). For example, while some new parents may have a history of positive experiences with children (possibly through teaching children or through their own intergenerational family experience) others may find this "new" experience a foreign intrusion

66

upon their lives. After interviewing many different parents (who were obviously functioning at varying developmental levels) Jaffe and Viertel (1980) exclaimed:

> If one general theme did seem to recur in our interviews, it was a very broad one, and a difficult one to talk about: the maturation process. The struggle to become parents is a struggle to become grown (p. 319).

Parent educators can facilitate parents best when they design and implement programs which foster individual growth in each parent.

Insight Two: The context in which parents and children function needs to be considered when organizing parent education programs. For example, the single parent who is the only source of economic support for the family may have a different effective style than a parent who has access to a plethora of family support services. Isaacs and Keller (1979, p. 150) list other contextual situations such as loneliness, marital disintegration, financial crisis, unwanted pregnancies, family illness or death and repeated personal failures that have a dramatic influence on parental effectiveness. Parent educators must relate program substance to the divergent contexts of parents if they hope to have a successful venture. Otherwise program content will fall on dead ears as parents must be functioning effectively before they can grow toward their personal-familial identity (Bronfenbrenner, 1979).

Insight Three: The hierarchy of human needs as presented by Maslow (1959) must be incorporated into parent education programs. While it is essential for parents to learn about the "needs" of the child, even more significant is their learning about their needs as human beings. First time parents who have actualized (to some degree of success) the basic needs of love, security and related needs of body synchrony (through proper rest and diet) and emotional support (with their husband/wife or other friend) are more likely to handle the process of parenting more effectively than parents whose basic needs have gone unmet (White, 1979; Bronfen brenner, 1979).

Jaffe and Viertel (1980, p. 319) report that "the growth spurt associated with the first year of parenting is probably the most intense, compact and pressurized period of growth in a young adult life." To meet the demands of this new, intense life style (parenting) these young adults must be secure in their personal selves. Indeed, data from two areas of study on parenting support the assertions of Maslow (1959) and Jaffe and Viertel (1980). Kempe (1978) reported that, in his studies of parents who abused children, he found them (the parents) to be insecure, lonely and in general to be deficient in meeting many personal needs and lacking in what we might term "meta-cognition" skills. On the positive side, White (1981) has noted effective parents exhibit a personal sense of control over their lives and this affects their family relationships in a positive manner.

Parent educators can assist parents in developing a self-examination by which they (the parents) assess their personal lives to see where they are with regard to meeting personal needs such as rest, security, social contacts (so vital for mental health) and general health status. It is advantageous for those anticipating parenthood to think through these personal needs and to consider how they can meet such needs within a new life context — parenthood.

Insight Four: Parents must have adequate support persons and resources by which they can grow and develop as parents and as unique individuals. Early in the formation of mother-infant relationships the reciprocal supportiveness (or lack of) between mother and infant has been noted. This initial thrust toward bonding is repeated and in healthy individuals it is translated into a trusting life style (Stern, 1977). Parents who have developed and nurtured a supportive relationship in their marriage are likely to exhibit this with their children. Parents who have adequate external supports are more likely to function effectively than parents who lack the external resources to provide a coherent and secure home life for themselves and their children.

Two examples of this phenomena are cited by Bronfenbrenner (1979). The first deals with single parents who have support systems as opposed to those who lack them. Supportiveness enhanced the single parents' functioning, whereas a lack of support played a part in decreasing it. The second related how parents react to the adequacy of support systems. Parents who viewed their children's day care arrangements as adequate, for example, were also more positive in their overall view of their children.

Parent educators, by enabling parents to see the significance of internal and external support systems, can provide a source for parents to use in building a basis for positive parent-child and parent-parent relationships.

Insight Five: First-time parents, if highly attentive to their new status in life, can be most open to learning basic parenting behaviors. New parents are generally eager to do what is best for the child (White, 1975). There is considerable evidence to indicate that during the child's first year of life, first time parents form behaviors that have a lasting effect on themselves and their children (White, 1981).

This part of parenthood includes the most emotional upheaval that parents ever experience. The exhilaration of being involved with new beginning and the often depressive periods of recognizing the immense journey ahead literally shake the foundation of many marriages (Jaffe and Viertel, 1980). In addition, the life style changes that accompany this stage of life are most dramatic. Preparation for dealing with this experience by re-organizing schedules, arranging a positive home setting, securing strong marital relationships, becoming comfortable in an anticipated new role and acquiring some basic understanding of the needed support systems for nurturing a young child are all vital components of a curriculum for first-time parents.

Parent educators need to include these psychological facets of parenting as vital elements of programs for parents. All the behaviors performed by parents must be based on healthy interpersonal relationships among the parenting partners.

Insight Six: Most parents are reactive instead of being proactive family leaders. A major gap in the parent education literature exists in this area of parent control. In his work with parents Gordon (1976) noted that parent education not only improved the behavior of the children but enhanced the parents' self-image. It is essential that parents establish control and direction relative to their personal and family lives early in their parenting career. One of the correlates of ineffective parents is their sense of a lack of personal control over their lives (White, 1979).

Maintaining a sense of control involves planning, organizing, assessing and refining personal values as related to family life. Learning to manage time, establish priorities and use human resources to enhance the entire family are most important skills parents need to be successful. Parent educators can incorporate these family planning and development skills in programs for parents. The use of real life examples of how parents have successfully managed their families will be especially pertinent to new parents.

Parent education programs should emphasize the need for parents to understand their individual and marital needs as well as their parenting responsibilities. This topic is rarely dealt with until it becomes a focus of some family therapy process. Preventive approaches to dealing with child abuse have found the most success when parents have developed a sense of internal focus of control (Jaffe and Viertel, 1981, p. 316). Education for parenthood must begin with some form of educating parents about developing a sense of personal control they can use in dealing with the challenges of raising children in a very complex culture. Individuals who lack this sense of control over their lives will have a difficult time being parents.

A Team Approach to Parenting

Parenting must be a part of a team approach if families are to be productive social systems. Parents need to know that it is a positive approach to involve relatives, friends and community resources in developing their family. They need to know what and where these resources are and they must become skillful in organizing them. As Bronfenbrenner (1979, p. 7) states:

Parent's evaluations of their own capacity to function, as well as their view of their child, are related to such external factors as flexibility of job schedules, adequacy of child care arrangements, and the presence of friends and neighbors who can help out in large and small emergencies, the quality of health and social services, and neighborhood safety.

A major resource for strengthening parents exists within the context of the family itself. Where two parents are present, the use of a partnership system can go a long way toward meeting the practical demands of the newborn such as feedings, usual sleeping patterns, cleaning and maintaining family schedules. Where older siblings are present, families can involve them in helping with various activities such as having them clothe the infant and doing other nurturing type tasks (Swick and Duff, 1982). This is a good way of introducing children to caring roles and to their part in family and community life. In one-parent families, the use of friends or relatives and intimate partners can and should be used to foster reciprocal patterns of family living (Hetherington, 1977).

Significant resources external to the family include community agencies, business, industry, religious and other groups that have a direct bearing upon the status of the family. For example, business leaders need to consider how their working practices effect the lives of parents and children. The use of well planned maternity and paternity leave policies as well as the use of flexible work scheduling can enable parents to be effective in establishing positive family settings. Parents, in many cases, need a knowledge base for planning the "match" between home and work place (Swick and Rotter, 1981). Parent educators, by incorporating content on these issues of dealing with family and community resources, can provide parents with needed skills for handling the delicate balance between family life and work place.

A factor that must permeate all aspects of parenting is the attitudinal focus of the parents. A positive psychological view of life and of the parent-child relationship can establish a setting where minor problems and normal conflicts are solved in a productive manner. Researchers have confirmed that parents who have developed a healthy psychological perspective about themselves, their families and their work are more likely to have a positive effect on children than parents who are insecure and negative in their daily activities (Gordon, 1976; Bronfenbrenner, 1979; White, 1981). Parent educators need to help parents in realizing how their psychological composite permeates everything they do with children. In addition, parenting programs should include content that informs parents of resources and strategies they can use in fostering positive mental health in themselves and family members.

Guidelines for Parent Educators

The focus of parent education needs to be expanded and/or refined to include the realities of parenting that are so often neglected or ignored in parenting programs. While many programs have been successful in helping parents understand the child in their family, there has been less success in helping parents develop an understanding of themselves and their needs and responsibilities as parents. The following are some guidelines parent educators should adhere to in the development of programs and practices they use with parents.

1. Begin with the premise that parents are learners. That is, they act and want to add to their information base on a variety of parenting issues. Unfortunately, too many programs are founded upon the idea that parents are ineffective people.

2. Parenting behaviors are developed early in the parenting process. The most effective parent education efforts have been with first time parents and have focused on the total family context in the first stages (B–3 years). This preventative approach should be a part of all parent education programs.

3. While parent education should begin with the early stages of parenthood, it should be continuous and based upon a developmental approach which attends to the unique needs of parents as they proceed through various life stages.

4. Effective parenting programs should involve parents in planning the content and process of the programs. Parent educators need to consider the substance of parenting in developing curricula. The dynamics of personal and parental roles need to be included in program formulation.

5. THE PSYCHOLOGICAL FACETS OF PARENTING SHOULD BECOME THE PRIMARY BASIS UPON WHICH ALL PROGRAMS ARE DEVELOPED. For example, most parents are successful in handling the parent-child relationship if their personal life is basically positive and if they prepared psychologically for this added dimension of life.

While many parent educators have been effective in helping parents with the child's growth and development, they have been less successful in helping parents deal with their own development and learning. It is possible that parent educators have missed the key ingredient in having productive families; healthy parents.

CHAPTER NINE
CRITICAL ISSUES IN PARENT EDUCATION

The idea of continuous education and renewal for parents is ingrained in our history. While parents during the early American experience relied primarily on the Bible, they were politically adept at drawing up community norms related to parental responsibilities. Just as parents were held accountable by community norms their independence was respected except for extreme neglect. As our society became more complex parents began to seek assistance in improving their effectiveness. The first White House Conference on Children, was in part, prompted by the concerns of parents as well as social workers and educators. With increased knowledge on how children develop and information on effective parenting gaining substance the "modern" parent actively pursues ideas relative to the performance of their many roles.

There are three historical trends that have shaped the parent education movement: (1) the evolving complexity of society, (2) the increase in knowledge related to child development and learning, and (3) the recognition of the critical role parents play in the development and learning of children.

The increasing complexity of society spawned a rich diversity of life styles and increased the level of human functioning necessary for successful involvement in the community. For example, parenting in a rural, homogenous world required simple skills of monitoring the child's development to accomodate a corresponding fixed community. The idea of "maximizing" a person's development was not accepted, thus parents were not concerned with the full development of the child. Moral values, job skills, and family-community education was carried out in the home and to a lesser degree in the school and neighborhood.

With industrialization (and later the emergence of the information age) came new jobs, increased mobility, and the need for a more advanced education among the citizenry. A part of the trend included the belief that children's development could be maximized under the proper conditions. The parenting role, by necessity, quickly evolved into a more challenging and demanding task. Suddenly parents and children were faced with increased societal expectations. No longer could an individual accomplish their development and learning within a simplistic system but became involved in extended education and job training beyond the home and immediate community. Parents, who at one time needed children for operating the family system, now found children as "social dependents" who would spend extended time periods in the home. By the very nature of this increased complexity of society, parent-child interactions became more complex — thus requiring more parental insight into their role. As the parenting role became more sophisticated the education and renewal of parents evolved in many different ways.

The development of a knowledge base regarding how children learn and function increased the need for sophisticated parents. While parents have always used some "knowledge" system to care for children, it is only in recent times that they have had access to a comprehensive body of information on children's learning and development. For example, the medical, educational, social, and psychological information available to parents regarding children is voluminous and significantly influences the way parents and children conduct their lives. With this increment in knowledge has come an increase in the amount of time parents spend in learning how to carry out their tasks and remain as effective agents for educating and socializing the child.

The recognition of the critical role parents perform in educating children has increased the social awareness for having an educated parent. Studies conducted by psychologists, pediatricians, and social workers have documented the negative impact abusing and neglecting parents have had on their children and themselves (Green, 1982). Other studies have shown how productive parent-child interaction can positively influence the child's development and learning in many modes including language acquisition, socialization skills, intellectual, emotional, and spiritual development (White, 1979; Gordon, 1977; Stinnett, 1979). Parents have become sensitive to their influence on children and sought more involvement with the educational process. Likewise, professionals who work with children and families have recognized the critical role of parents and attempted to provide for this need in their designs for educating young children.

The emergence of a formalized body of information on parent education has raised some significant issues relative to the effective development of parents. Questions such as the following are symbolic of the issues and represent the kinds of concerns educators of young children need to examine as they develop programs aimed as fostering effective parenting.

- What is meant by parent education? What does it include and what is the intention of this focus of study?

- What is meant by parenting? What is the parental role and what is the educator's role? How can role confusion be avoided by parents and teachers?

- What is the role of the parent educator? Given the diversity of parenting styles how can parent educators carry out an educational program effectively?

74

— Is there public support for enhancing the role of parents? How can public policy be influenced toward recognizing the need for educated and involved parents?

— Given the rapid increase in "teen parents", child abuse, and related family issues how can parent educators be effective in designing programs that are of value to parents in these situations?

— How can parent education programs be organized and implemented to meet the many needs of parents who are in divergent situations?

Each of the questions asked in the above listing is pertinent to any discussion of parent education in the 1980's. These issues are discussed in the remaining sections of this chapter.

Parent Education: Meaning and Focus of Concern

Any definition of "parent education" must be comprehensive in order to reflect the varied roles parents perform and the multiple methods they can use to increase their effectiveness in carrying out their roles.

> **PARENT EDUCATION IS ANY** effort designed to increase the development and learning of parents in carrying out the diverse roles they perform.

Specific components of parent education are organized to reflect the needs parents have in meeting their role requirements. Thus, specific components usually include the following: (1) information on the personal dimension of marital roles and relationships, (2) information on skills needed in the parenting process, (3) knowledge regarding child development (including parent-child relations), and (4) specific skill development in parents to perform tasks that arise in special or exceptional family situations (Land, 1983).

The focus of different parent education efforts reflect the existence of these components in programs. For example, many media based programs are aimed at increasing parental awareness of certain child needs and the importance of their attention to meeting these needs. Other programs may have specific skills for parents to grasp and thus use training modes to accomplish the desired outcome. Knowledge based programs (such as informing parents of child care techniques or the offering of personal renewal experiences) may use a combination of approaches to goal achievement (Hanes, 1983).

The basic premise of all parent education programs is (or should be) that *parents are learning and developing human beings.* This positive approach capitalizes on the strengths of parents and involves parents in

75

developing their skills within a life span perspective. The integrity of the family is valued and educational efforts are directed toward strengthening that integrity. Even where major parent rehabilitation efforts are necessary, decisions are made with respect to maintaining family stability wherever possible (Schaefer, 1983).

Parenting, Parent-Professional Roles and Conflict Avoidance

To be a parent may appear simple at the outset, yet research indicates the complexities involved in the process are at the core of many parent-child and parent-teacher conflicts. Parenting involves four key roles: (1) nurturance, (2) guidance, (3) education, and (4) modeling (Swick & Duff, 1982). Each of these roles is developed and used by parents in their encounters with children, spouses, teachers, and indeed all individuals directly involved in the family. Obviously, parents need assistance in carrying out these roles and that is where their support system of neighbors, relatives, teachers, and other helpers must be in place (Swick, 1983). Thus a parenting team concept is the most effective way to view this process of nurturing and educating young children. The parenting team is comprised of parents, professionals, and helpers of all sorts who work jointly to foster the healthy development of children.

> **PARENTING TEAM** members may include pediatricians, teachers, child care professionals, counselors, ministers, home makers, social workers, and many others who support the development and learning of young children.

This view of parenting places the parent-professional role relationship within the context of a positive paradigm. Such a paradigm advocates an interactive relationship between parent and professional as well as an expanded role for other parenting team members such as neighbors in supporting total family development. A mutual respect between parent and professional is essential to the formation of a productive relationship. The professional understands the parent as team leader and utilizes parental skills in carying our major efforts directed toward child and family improvement/refinement. The parent sees the professional as a skilled helper in expanding family effectiveness.

INDICATORS OF A POSITIVE
PARENTING TEAM PARADIGM

1. Parent is viewed as team leader.

2. Parent is considered skilled in their personal/parental roles.

3. Professional is viewed as a skilled helper.

4. Professional is considered skilled in specific areas of human development that extend family effectiveness.

5. Parent-professional relationship is interactional; parent and professional learning from each other, supporting each other and thus forming a team approach to supporting the children's development and learning.

Professionals can avoid role conflicts with parents by articulating their role, helping parents see their role as facilitative of family life, and spending time in continuous communication with parents on the services they are providing. Schaefer (1983, p. 11) provides the following role clarification matrix.

A MATRIX OF CHILD CARE SETTINGS AND OF PARENT AND PROFESSIONAL ROLES		
	Family	*Institution*
Parent Roles	Caregiver Teacher Model	Volunteer, fund raiser, paraprofessional, observer-student, decisionmaker
Reciprocal Roles	Advocate Planner/Organizer Case Manager/Coordinator Collaborator	
Professional Roles	Family Helper Parent Educator Parent Consultant	Caregiver Teacher Model

Schaefer's matrix on parent-professional roles can be used in parent-teacher discussions regarding the need for an understanding of their helping relationship. Parents and educators may use this as a beginning place for developing their own role clarification guide.

Parent-Educator Role,
Being Effective In Meeting Diverse Parent Needs

The formalization of the person-role identified as *parent-educator* implies the emergence of a professional who is skilled in guiding parents toward maximum use of their skills. The focus of parent educators is on organizing a design for influencing parent behavior in positive ways. Within the generic design of promoting parent effectiveness, parent-educators perform diverse tasks that focus on specific parent needs. Hanes (1983) gives a comprehensive picture of the "training needs" parent-educators attempt to use in program implementation. Gordon (1975) presents "educational, social, and support" roles often performed by parent educators. A synthesis of roles performed by parent educators is presented.

78

PARENT EDUCATOR ROLES

1. Helping role as indicated in parent counseling activities, parent support services, and continuous communications with parents.

2. Educational and training role as indicated in performance of parent information sessions on topics such as child development and "training" activities where parents are taught specific skills such as how to care for a handicapped child.

3. Resource coordination and liason role as indicated in performance of program coordination, linking parents up with key supports such as teachers and social work personnel or in the activation of a neighborhood resource group.

It is in the implementation of these roles that parent educators face the "matching" of services to the divergent needs of parents. Fantini (1980) reviews the cultural differences in parenting and notes the importance of understanding these differences as parents and professionals attempt to function in joint capacities. Swick (1983) examines the many different styles of parenting and advocates the involvement of parents in planning educational programs so the content is reflective of true needs parents have in their family situation. Thus parent educators can maximize their effectiveness by assessing the makeup of the parents they work with and through integrating parent needs into the program plans. The presence of parents on planning teams will assure the development of viable programs. Further, the cooperative efforts of parent-professional teams will provide a basis for implementing a plan that is supportive of both groups' ideas and objectives.

Public Policy, Parenting, And Parent Education

With the exception of a few programs (Head Start, Title I Parent Advisory Councils, and State Mandated Parent Involvement) most public sponsored parenting programs have been designed to alleviate a critical situation such as child abuse, teenage parenting, and other individual family crisis situations. Until recently the attitude has been that parental concerns were private matters and not the concern of the larger society. Two factors have altered this cultural premise: (1) a dramatic increase in parent-family problems — generally resulting from major socio-technical shifts in our culture; and (2) increasing evidence that effective parents have impacted the entire family in positive modes.

The development of public policy that supports parenting and programs that effectuate positive changes in parental behavior is viable as the efforts in Head Start indicate. The challenge lies in formulating planning mechanisms that utilize community leadership in promoting parenting needs and parent-professional efforts to facilitate family development in a variety of educational and social programs. Public policy leaders have been favorably impressed with the "cost effectiveness" of parent oriented education programs such as child and family centers, home-based intervention programs, and parent-professional medical support programs.

The objective of educating policy formulators toward supporting parenting and parent education programs can be accomplished by using research supportive of this paradigm in contacts with legislators and other leaders who influence public policy decisions.

STRATEGIES FOR INFLUENCING POLICY FAVORABLE TO PARENT-FAMILY DEVELOPMENT

*Clear statement of parent needs to function effectively for dissemination to policy makers.

*Establish data base on positive social effects of productive learning.

*Clear statement of role parent education programs have played in improving parent functioning and thus enhancing child and family development.

*Organize "policy influence networks" that impact decision makers with information such as economic viability and social value of parent education programs.

Parent Educators: Responding to Pathological Family Situations

Parent educators have a role in aiding families that have serious problems. The clarification of this role is significant to the development of a productive parent-professional relationship. Six components to the parent educators role in working with pathological family situations are discussed as follows.

Awareness Component: A major contribution parent educators have made to family and community development is enlightening the public about the existence of family pathologies and the effects of negative family dynamics on the community. This awareness function serves two purposes: it expands citizen understanding of family life, and it increases public support for family support services essential to the maintenance of healthy families.

Prevention Component: Parent educators can attempt to prevent family pathology by combining parent education/training with support services to target groups that need these services. Contacts with first time parents early in family development can influence the formation of productive behavior and thus minimize the emergence of pathologies. Parent education programs that have focused on reaching parents early in their parenting are effective in directing parental efforts toward constructive family outcomes (White, 1979).

Diagnostic Component: The early identification of specific family pathologies can lead to effective treatment and the restoration of the family to a state of health. Researchers have identified characteristics of families who are victims of various pathologies. Parent educators come into contact with parents often and thus can (if informed) identify "high risk" parents and then attempt to help them acquire appropriate professional services. It is essential for parent educators to become knowledgeable of the characteristics of "high risk" families and to utilize the knowledge in their relationships with parents.

Referral Component: Parent educators, once they have identified a critical family need, can "match" the need with appropriate community services. Awareness of various counseling, medical, and educational professionals in the community is an important part of the parent educators "tool kit". Helping families find useful services is a first and major step toward moving the family toward rehabilitation.

Support Component: The road to positive mental health among families is only possible when support services enable them to regain dignity and self reliance. Parent educators can be a "significant other" in this family support team. For example, they may visit the home on a regular basis to build confidence in family members, carry out training sessions geared toward parental rehabilitation, and act as the family's liason with school and community agencies during the family's rebuilding period.

Follow Through Component: As the family regains self direction, continued support is essential to assure long term health. Continued contacts with the family, encouraging family contacts with the community, and supporting family development along healthy lines are tasks the parent educator can perform. Follow through support to families is the most effective way to prevent future problems.

Involving "Hard To Reach" Parents

A major difficulty facing parent educators is reaching the parents really in need of their skills and services. Typically, large group parent education programs are attended by parents who identify with the goals and values of the sponsor. Parents who, for various reasons, are at odds with the value base of the sponsor or who have had negative experiences with the sponsoring agency tend to isolate themselves from the activities of the association. While the program certainly has value for whoever participates the group most in need may not be reached. Successful parent education programs have used the following approaches to reach parents who usually lack inherent motivation to participate.

TECHNIQUES FOR INVOLVING HARD TO REACH PARENTS

1. Utilize "neighborhood aides" to visit parents and encourage their involvement in parent education programs. Ira Gordon (1976) used a "each one reach one" approach in his parent training project. He noted that parents were able to identify with the trained aides and involvement increased as a result of this process.

2. Parent education media packages such as "Footsteps" (1979) and "Promises" (1982) are excellent in reaching large parent audiences. Both television series are broadcast regularly on National Educational Television. Local television stations have used supplementary materials for parents to use in addition to the programs.

3. Church sponsored parent education programs often attract parents who identify with the values of the church but would not attend similar school based programs. Head Start practitioners found church sponsored activities to be effective in reaching many parents who otherwise remained isolated from the mainstream of events.

4. The use of parent education materials in pediatric care centers is an excellent way to reach "first-time parents". Pediatricians have access to parents during the formative years of the child's life and the parents' early parenting life.

5. Home visitation programs conducted during the preschool years have proven effective in helping parents establish a basis for continuing productive family relationships. Levenstein (1971) used home visitation to alter parent-child interaction and thus increase the language base of the child's home environment. Early contacts with parents help build bridges between the home and school.

The key to reaching parents who are isolated from community activities is involving them early in their parenting lives and designing activities of value to their family.

Parenting And Parent Education:
Building A Community Support Base

While there are signs of increasing social concern about parenting, very few significant steps have been taken to alter our society in terms of valuing parenting. We have kept the same social structures in place while the lives of parents have changed. Today's parent, for example, functions in a socially complex situation with few supports and more demands within the family and the community. Family situations are more divergent and the needed skill levels of parents has increased.

A community support system for parents is needed to validate a social caring for the value of parental roles and to sustain parent efforts made in the home. Examples of substantive community support efforts are described as follows:

1. Business/industry efforts supportive of parenting such as sick leave and maternity/paternity leave policies which allow for maximum family development.

2. Church and civic agencies that sponsor family support programs such as day care, counseling services, parent education programs, family resource centers and ther practices promoting family stability.

3. Schools that focus on the family as the primary environment for learning and development by providing programs such as extended day activities, flexible academic and support programs for teenage parents, and continuous communication modes such as conferences, home visits, and parent programs.

4. Professional teaming among medical, social, and educational personnel in planning and implementing parent oriented education and support efforts. Multi-disciplinary teaming is not only efficient but expands our bases for involving community in the parent support effort (Swick & Bollinger, 1981).

The involvement of community agencies in parent/family programs tends to accomplish two objectives: (1) it increases our cultural context for expecting quality parent-child relations, and (2) it promotes a community team sensitivity to the significance of parenting and the need for a total family support system. For example, the involvement of business/industry leaders in adapting the work place to the legitimate needs of parents has increased worker productivity and business' sensitivity to the role of quality family life in promoting quality workmanship (Swick & Rotter, 1981).

The focus of the issues discussed in this chapter are on improving the quality of parent-child interactions. Parent education is a process used to improve the possibilities of having quality families. In developing useful parent education programs for today's parents the following guidelines are an essential beginning point.

1. Societal values toward parenting must be made more positive through substantive changes in our taxation policies, health care approaches, work place functions, and overall contextual situations in which parents and children operate.

2. Parent education and education for parenthood efforts must be integrated into the entire community arrangement rather than isolated into courses of study and periodic efforts through the media.

3. The significant changes in family life as well as the unique challenges facing parents must be incorporated into parent education programs. This can be accomplished by involving parents in the planning stages of the program.

4. A teaming mentality must emerge in our cultural system (especially in the helping professions) to capitalize on the talents and resources available for educating and supporting parents.

5. Community awareness of the importance of every citizen's participation in the nurturance of young children is essential. With an increasing number of people electing not to be parents, it is critical for non-parents to understand their roles in being a part of the child development team.

CHAPTER TEN
THE HOME LEARNING ENVIRONMENT

The significance of the home learning environment in shaping the educational and social behaviors of young children is finally receiving the attention it deserves. With renewed interest in improving educational quality the initial "school" the child attends is surfacing again and again as the logical beginning point in any quest for excellence in education. Any serious examination of parent involvement as a viable concept must include the parental role in desiging the home learning ecology to maximize the child's development.

In addition, recent technological developments indicate information is becomming highly portable — making it quite simple for families to acquire materials and resources that were once the province of a few select scholars. The "computer revolution" along with the mass media technology already in homes, transforms — indeed revolutionizes — the way we can conduct the teaching-learning process. Beyond the "information processing role" that can now be carried out in the home is a far more important process — *that of building the human identity of each family member toward productive ends.*

Three trends have evolved through social science and educational research are at the basis of the current focus on the home learning environment as an effective instructional setting.

Data regarding the *influence of the home environment on childrens' development is substantive* and conclusive in that the home is a truly powerful educational ecology. Studies comparing children's functioning in home versus institutional ecologies (i.e.: orphanages, prisons) indicated productive home settings were far superior to institutional arrangements. The security, developmental stimulation, and human identity that is potentially available in the home setting is often impossible to replicate in large, systematic institutions (Hunt, 1964; Bloom, 1981). Schaefer (1983) synthesized major studies carried out on the home environment and conceptualized that the home ecology — when designed properly — impacted infants and young children's intellectual, social, language, motor and emotional development in productive modes. In his own research efforts Schaefer (1983) has identified specific characteristics of parent-child interactions favorable to maximizing the family's learning potential.

The emergence of *information on parental skills in designing effective home learning environments is a second trend.* Observers and researchers studying children's development over extended time periods note that as children reached age 3 some were far superior to others but not necessarily because they had innate abilities (Frailberg, 1977). Investigations into the natur eof these observations led researchers to what was happening in home learning settings. The role of "parent as educator" emerged as a significant variable influencing infant and child development/learning patterns. The parent as designer of learning ecologies emerged as a role that apparently made the difference in having a highly competent 3 year old or a less effective child. Particularly significant in this regard is the work of Burton L. White (1979). White believes that parents perform at least three critical roles within the home that impact the child in significant and long lasting ways: (1) educational role, (2) designer of environments role, and (3) nurturance role.

Parental nurturance of infants, for example, has been noted to stimulate infants developmentally (Brown, 1981). Stern (1977) noted that "bonding" between mother and infant took place at or soon after birth and that this was related to the child's development. The parent as educator has been studied by many researchers. Gordon (1975) found success in helping parents enact this role by involving them in home visit instruction programs. As parents implemented their skills they found their relationships with children strengthened and researchers documented improved language functioning in the children. Levenstein (1970), Schaefer (1983), Swick (1979), and Watson (1983) are examples of scholars who have substantiated the impact of the "parent" as educator on the family ecology.

Ultimately parents are designers of learning experiences for children. Beginning at birth parents develop, implement, and continually refine the home learning environment. They organize a life schedule, arrange the physical setting in which the child learns, and establish a learning model for the child through their transactions with each other and with the child. White (1979) in studying parental skill in designing home learning environments found marked differences among parents and varying influences on children especially with regards to the development of social competence in children.

A third trend in the development of our perceptions of the family as a learning ecology *is the research on the interaction of effective families in the larger society.* A central theme emerges from the research on this subject: children who benefit from experiencing a productive home learning ecology perform more effective in school than their less fortunate peers (Lazar, 1976). For example, children from productive home settings were more likely to succeed academically in school, complete high school, and acquire meaningful employment than children from less effective homes. There appears to be a reciprocal process at work in productive homes: namely that positive parent-child interactions influence both children and adults to perform effectively in their efforts in school, work, and the community. The significance of the home as a learning environment leads to a close examination of the major features of that ecology.

The Home: A Learning Environment

As a learning setting there are at least four critical human functions that take place in the home which impact the child's learning style. The kinds of *behavior models, interaction patterns, physical settings,* and *guidance behaviors* parents formulate and use in their home have important implications for what educators do (or should do) in the school setting and in their interactions with parents. The continuous use of parenting behaviors that promote positive development and learning in children are the focus of this conceptual view.

Behavior Models in the Home: Implications for the School

The performance of parents in regards to the behaviors they model for their children is more important than any other learning experience in which the child might become involved. Many teachers of young children often comment on the resemblance of the child to parent. Indeed, children do internalize many of their parents' traits. At a young age the child will mock parent behaviors and in many situations they acquire parental values — albeit in modified form.

The continuous influence of parent behaviors upon the child come to fruition as the child organizes a life style. The aggressive child, the gentle child and the myriad of other behavior styles children acquire originate during the early years of life. What happens within the family is critical to the shaping of self concepts in both children and adults (Yamamoto, 1972; Purkey, 1984; Bell & Harper, 1980).

For example, parent interactions with their children regarding what is happening in the environment and their involvement in the world is influential in aiding children in developing a proactive life perspective. Dialogue between parents and children provides a basis for them to interact within their respective worlds. Language development, social learning, and individual security are above all the outcome of the kinds of parenting models children veiw and relate to in their life context (Markun, 1973).

Specific examples of parental influence on children is evidenced in the area of language development. Children who enter school with an elaborate language base are usually the products of homes where parents have designed learning situations that stimulate such experimental development. Additional examples of parental influence are found in the formation of productive social behaviors in children such as sharing, proactive involvement in school learning situations, and reciprocal social involvements with other children and adults in various community arrangements (Solnit, 1976).

Specific forms and modes of parent-child interactions in the home are of importance to the types of socio-emotional behaviors children develop and apply in other ecological contexts (Schaefer, 1972). These parent-child interaction patterns can be grouped into three response syndromes: authoritarian, chaotic, and compromising. Each of these patterns presents a style of functioning which the child internalizes as a way of approaching life in and out of the family system.

For example, the aggressive child is often the product of an aggressive home setting. The child who is unable to relate to others without fighting has learned such behavior in the early years of life. Likewise, the "chaotic child" is often the outcome of a badly disorganized home arrangement (disorganization here refers more to the psycho-cognitive structure of human interactions than the physical environment although both factors are usually present). In such environments the child has no structure to use in forming response patterns to varying social situations. The compromising child, the child who cooperates and reciprocates with peers and adults is usually the result of a high quality home environment (Weikart, 1975).

The development of a framework for positively influencing children's social behavior in the family ecology is delineated by Swick and Duff (1982). The focus is on parental use of nurturance, guidance, modeling, and problem solving behaviors that introduce children to concrete modes of human interaction.

The Physical Setting of the Home: Implications for the School

The physical setting of the home, the way objects are arranged and are organized influence not only what the child can learn but how he will process it, act on it, and eventually internalize it. A home arrangement that is lacking in organization and contains few learning objects is not conducive to the kinds of exploring and grasping of things the young child needs to do as he learns and develops. The environment in which the child can move about *safely,* reach and manipulate objects, participate in family activities and have access to personal space is a productive place that enhances the child's development (Gordon, 1972).

Children learn from their involvement with the "substance" of their environment. Parents are the key resource people in the child's life. Their design of the home toward maximizing the child's functioning will include selection of developmentally appropriate toys and materials the child can use in acquiring language, social, cognitive, and motor skills. For example, in infancy the home environment should include mobiles and other objects that prompt the infant to engage in sensory learning and development. As the child develops parents can select more advanced items for involving the child in learning. Many items such as pots and pans are common household equipment. The physical environment of the home should prompt the total development and learning of the child in a safe, sequential, and meaningful manner (Swick & Willis, 1973).

Ideally, the classroom should be an extension of the home learning environment. Unfortunately, too many classrooms are arranged without regard to what happened to the child in his primary socializing environment. The child who has never been exposed to books, pictures, and other elaborating language development experiences will have difficulty in dealing with these materials and related concepts unless he receives sensitive guidance from a teacher. Parents and teachers must continually attempt to improve the learning arrangement in which they introduce the child to life (Graham, 1974).

Parental Guidance in the Home: Implications for the School

Young children are not only in need of guidance but they seek it out by the way they form attachments to parental life styles. The way in which parents involve their children in handling different tasks influences the total learning style of the children. For example, children who are encouraged to be proactive in shaping their part of the home environment are usually proactive in other social settings (Swick & Duff, 1982). The manner and form in which the child is corrected for inappropriate behavior sets a style of acceptable behavior for the child (White, 1979). The training acts (learning to talk, walk, eat and sleep) and the ways in which parents handle them are significantly related to the child's behavior in various settings.

Parents are the most influential persons in terms of helping children learn and actualize guidance skills. As parents reveal a positive understanding of human development thay are setting the stage for fostering similar understandings in children. The intervention modes used by parents will be perceived as "the way to do it" by children. Gentle, responsive behaviors with infants, for example, is the parent's way of saying "this is how we learn". Similarly, and unfortunately, when parents act out aggressions toward children they are promoting an inadequate basis upon which children develop a distorted view of self and others (Olmsted, et. al., 1980).

In order to guide, one must be able to communicate effectively. Parents who actively listen to their children and respect what they have to say are encouraging them to take part in the family's total functioning. Helping children to establish and follow through on limits they set is another way of providing a fair and consistent setting for growth. Responsible children have internalized a concept of behavior that is responsive to their own needs as well as the needs of others.

Teachers play a major role in helping children extend and refine their self-social skill kit. Hopefully, this process is enacted by parents and teachers as a joint venture. When children come to school lacking in the social skills necessary for group functioning the teacher must help them learn new behaviors. Such a process can only be effective when carried out in a positive manner. A true guide is one who first acquires an understanding of the situation. The teacher-guide must know the home learning environment and relate the classroom social setting to it in a useful way. The ideal arrangement is where parents and teachers work together (beginning in early infancy) as guidance partners who cooperate in facilitating the development of the young child (Swick, 1975).

Parents and children as they function in the home environment establish a great deal of social, emotional, and intellectual behavior they will use once in the school ecology. The origins of school success are certainly rooted in the home (Watson, Brown, & Swick, 1983). Educators need to focus more on the home as a learning environment. Model programs exist such as the "Saturday School" project (Ogg, 1975) and Gordon's (1976) home visitation program.

Technology and the Home Learning Environment

The home learning environment is being transformed by technological innovations. Television, computers, space age appliances, and highly sophisticated toys all combine to influence the nature of human learning in the home. In many cases today's family is overwhelmed by the availability of information and instant learning modes such as the microcomputer. In addition, many modern home appliances actually discourage parent-child interaction and encourage a passive, reactive style of learning in the home. Parent sophistication in the use and integration of technology into meaningful home learning arrangements is critical to having successful developmental and educational ventures in-and-out-of-the-home (Moore, 1983).

Parent selection of home learning technology is the initial step in their designing today's home setting. Poor selection of computer technology and chaotic use of media such as television are current problems. In designing home technology parents need to ask several questions of which the following are certainly included.

1. What purpose can various technological tools serve in enhancing family learning and communication?

2. What criteria should I use in selecting sophisticated technology such as microcomputers?

3. How can I integrate these technological devices into the home learning process to promote my child's cognitive, social, emotional, and sensory development?

4. As a parent how can I become knowledgeable about the full range of technology influencing my family and become literate in using it to our advantage?

5. What guidance should I use in monitoring the home setting to calculate the influence of technology on my children and how can I intervene to orient the family-technology relationship toward productive outcomes?

Unfortunately, too few parents are asking these questions and little guidance has been forthcoming from educators to assist them in making sound choices on these issues. Teachers, parent educators, and counselors have a major role to perform in helping parents arrive at an effective approach to the use of technology in the home. Indeed, this issue alone merits contacts between home and school from birth on through the child's years of schooling. This issue also validates the need for a life-span view of the learning process.

Some approaches educators can use include cooperative programs with instructional television stations, parent education programs on technology in the home, availability of counseling services for parents regarding their interests on this topic, and involvement of parents in school-based technological education efforts. Further, more refined school-community education efforts may focus on "home learning management skills" for parents (Shane, 1983). Attempts to facilitate the use of home learning arrangements by parents and children can begin with the following items.

1. Assist parents in selecting technology appropriate for home learning.

2. Assist parents in developing home learning management plans that place technology in a facilitative role and not in a domineering role.

3. Assist parents in organizing family perspective toward balancing childrens involvementin technology with more critical involvements such as creative arts, language experiences, parent-child activities, and peer relationships.

Television, microcomputers, and robotics have impacted the home learning environment in revolutionary ways. The family, as a social institution, faces the challenge of selecting viable modes of utilizing these tools for productive learning and development. Educators, through parent education and community involvement, can influence the development of productive home learning by assisting parents in proactive family designs for integrating technology with critical family developments such as identity building and problem solving. A positive outcome of home learning arrangement is our increased awareness of the role parents can perform in educating their children (Holt, 1983).

While specific family pathologies are dealt with in another section of this book, three impediments to effective home learning are examined for their influence on how families are coping with existing cultural conditions related to family functioning. These three factors are: *time, resources,* and *relationships.*

Time is an essential ingredient in forming effective home learning arrangements. With major changes taking place in the society many families find themselves with little "home learning" time available. Yet the need for establishing effective relationships within the family require significant segments of time spent in human interaction. Indeed, family researchers have found "time spent together in meaningful activity" to be a major feature of healthy families (Stinnett, 1980). Maximum facilitation of home learning can be achieved through community supports such as flextime in the work place and through parent education programs on time management.

Lack of essential resources may be the major impediment to effective home learning environments. While economically secure parents may be able to acquire needed learning resources, a large segment of families are unable to meet even the minimum needs of their children. Psychological and cognitive abilities of parents are key resources in this regard. Financial and material resources are also essential ingredients in having an effective home learning system. Community supports in the form of education, health, nutrition supplements, medical care, and additional resource modes are critical to helping families establish viable learning and working patterns in the home (Green, 1982).

Pathological relationships within the family context prevent meaningful interactions which are essential for the learning process to occur. For example, children who experience severe neglect during the early years often fail to develop productive cognitive, language, and social skills — all of which require meaningful parent-child interactions in the home. Lack of knowledge regarding the parenting process, a shortage of time and insufficient resources are some of the major conditions contributing to various family pathologies. Enabling parents to acquire basic cognitive and human development skills for organizing effective home learning environments in a major objective of early childhood programs (Quisenberry, 1983).

Strategies For Influencing The Home Learning Environment

Early childhood educators are making progress in promoting home learning arrangements. While specific activities for preschool settings are discussed in this chapter, several strategic ideas on influencing home learning arrangements need further development.

Technology provides an opportunity to support the formation of productive home learning environments in many ways. The use of television for parent education efforts is one example of the unlimited influence the media can have on the family. Programs such as Footsteps (1979) reach millions of parents with information on child development, family relationships, and critical periods families experience over the life span. These "media-based programs" are usually designed so they can be adapted to meet local community needs with minor adjustments in the content. Additionally, media efforts on children's programs and family hour programs are small but positive steps toward using technology as a family learning tool.

School-based parent-oriented-education programs and family learning centers are additional examples of efforts being carried out to impact the home learning arrangement. The South Carolina Program uses content on children's development and learning as the basis for school-centered parenting projects.* Most of the broad based programs aim to influence large numbers of "functioning" parents in the direction of improving on what they are already doing with children. "At risk" families present a different and more complex situation. Early identification (during pregnancy or at birth) of "high risk" parents is one successful effort to prevent the development of pathologies in parent functioning. Diagnosis of parent situations usually reveal a syndrome of behaviors that indicate functionality or pathology. Where the pathology is obvious, preventive measures in the form of parent education and family supports can be taken to rectify the ecology so productive family development can occur. In some cases the effort may be in simple support mechanisms (health care, home assistance) and in other cases the severity of the predicament may call for major efforts such as family therapy (Kempe & Kempe, 1978).

The home learning environment is part of the larger culture and requires continuous support if it is to be an effective educational and social institution. Specific supports needed for effective home learning include adequate economic resources, access to educational ideas and materials, psychological validity gained through community recognition, and meaningful linkages to the community. Strategies for accomplishing this support function are exemplified in communities that sponsor parent-child health care, foster family togetherness through recreational opportunities, day care, and community education programs (Bronfenbrenner, 1979).

One particular strategy that carries major significance for children and families is preschool care. With two-thirds of the nation's families working full time outside the home, major attention to quality child care is critical

---

*Materials on the South Carolina Parent-Oriented-Education Program can be obtained from the Department of Education, Early Childhood Consultant, Rutledge Building, Columbia, South Carolina.

to having productive home settings (Clarke-Stewart, 1982). Bronfenbrenner (1979) noted the significance of quality day care for parents when he stated that parental attitudes toward their children were dramatically influenced by what happened to the child in the day care setting. Further, as Galinsky and Hooks (1977) have noted day care centers can serve as "extended family" in terms of meeting the psycho-social needs of parents and children as well as engaging families with other families in exploring some common developmental milestones. This support system can be continued in the elementary school years through various parent-teacher contacts and by using "extended school-day" programs to meet unique needs of the total family-community system (Nieting, 1983).

The home learning environment provides a setting in which our "future parents" are developed. The experiences children have in home and school shape their view of what it is to be a parent. Beyond influencing parent behavior there are efforts we can make to provide children and young people with productive interactions regarding their emerging view of parenting. Swick and Duff (1982) describe curricula experiences that can be integrated into early learning programs that focus on the development of nurturant, problem solving, self disciplined learners. The objective is to enable children to acquire a "caring skills kit" they can use in various helping roles of which parenting is certainly included. In middle and high school programs Ogg (1975) provides many ideas for the development of instructional units that engage learners with all aspects of the life span.

Linking Home And School: Learning Experiences And Activities

"Nancy goes to school next year." This phrase is repeated by many parents and experienced by all children every year. The excitement of small children running to meet buses and new teachers is common place in our culture. Unfortunately, (and illogically) the excitement over the formal education of children is not matched by a corresponding zeal during the preschool years. While parents are becoming increasingly aware of their role in educating infants and young children, they often fail to integrate this concern with family actions. Even when the concern is activated it is too often sporadic or mis-directed toward highly regimented teaching which, of course, is undesirable for the very young child.

Even after the child has entered school there is often great disparity in the home-school arrangement. Home learning, while carried out in some family interactions, is absent in most home settings. Educators have always been superficially interested in what happens to the home but have not matched that interest with meaningful action. Parents and teachers can develop useful home learning arrangements that help the child initiate self development skills (during the preschool years) and extend the child's learning and development throughout the formal school years.

94

Preschool Based Home Learning Experiences

The preschool years provide a time span where parents (supported by a community team) can establish within the child a productive approach to living in the world. All professionals who work with young children and families can influence the home ecology in positive dimensions. Some techniques that can be used in this endeavor are the provision of parent education programs, dissemination (with training) of basic learning materials to parents, accessing family services in health and nutrition as needed by parents, and by making available supplemental child care to free parents to carry out needed family and personal sustenance tasks (Butler, 1976).

Parent education programs designed to influence home learning through parent awareness and skills in working with infants and toddlers is one way of improving parent-child relations. Experiences offered through various parent education efforts include the following.

- Courses on child care practices, family management techniques, marriage and family life, and nutrition and meal planning.

- Resource persons such as pediatricians, counselors, social workers, family service workers, child care personnel, and other family support persons.

- Direct instructional programs for parents that focus on helping parents assist children in learning about their environment, themselves and others in their world.

As parents acquire an understanding of the way young children learn they seek additional materials and resources for use in the home learning environment. Most parents will participate in programs that make available toys, games, books, and other educational resources to the family. With knowledge of how to use these resources parental involvement in the child's preschool education generally increase in quantity and in the quality of family interactions (Swick & Duff, 1978).

The dissemination of home learning materials can be accomplished in many ways. In selecting a way of accomplishing this task keep in mind major parent needs, local resources that can be easily used, and the nature of the community in which you hope to carry out the program. In all cases the dissemination of home learning materials should be accompanied by parent training sessions.

One approach used by some school districts involves the development of a parent-child lending library. This usually involves the organization of materials that suuplement regular classroom instruction. The materials are made available to parents and children on a loan basis. Lending libraries can be very simple in design (such as those developed in the classroom) or more elaborate programs where an entire community is involved in organizing a large facility in which thousands of pieces of learning materials exist.

An extension of the lending library concept to include parents of preschool children is most desirable as learning habits are formed early in the family's life cycle. Parents will participate in this type of program when the materials are accessible and the atmosphere in the school or center is conducive to their involvement. By involving parents of pre- schoolers in utilizing school-sponsored resources, teachers can forge a partnership with the home before negative perceptions emerge and dissipate the educational influenceof schooling (Duff, Heinz, & Husband, 1978).

Other modes of disseminating materials and learning activities to parents of preschool children include the use of television specials, local library usage, civic group involvement, family service programs, and local medical and dental professionals who are willing to participate. The early prevention of school failure can be initiated throught the develop- ment of programs where parents have access to education and materials to use with their children in the home setting (Weikart, 1975).

The general health of preschool children is of extreme importance during the preschool years. Interagency efforts directed toward a com- bination of preventive medical care and on-going health education are desirable goals. Unfortunately, the significance of health and nutrition are left to random happenstance during the preschool years. Recent Pediatric Roundtable Seminars promoted more attention to the develop- mental enhancement of young children through early and continuing medical/health education efforts (Sasserath & Hoekelman, 1983). Several states are utilizing educational media packages to enlighten future and recent parents regarding the importance of this facet of the child's development.

By working closely with family service groups the educational com- munity can plan and implement programs that assure each child is given proper health care. Specific components of these programs include the use of materials on infant care with new parents, community sponsored immunixation efforts to protect children from killer diseases, passage of legislation to secure safety techniques are used in making children's toys, and citizen involvement in providing for child abuse and spouse abuse cases. Professionals designing such programs will find the *Center for Parent Education** a valuable resource center in acquiring materials and ideas for sharing with parents.

Technology is impacting the home environment in dramatic ways; transforming the way we learn and the way in which human interaction

---

Center for Parent Education. Newton, Mass., 55 Chapel St. Directed by Dr. Burton L. White.

occurs. Parents need and seek information on how to cope with the many issues that emerge from the complex mix of human development and technology. This single issue offers teachers of young children a chance to initiate contacts with parents during the early years of family development. For example, a component of preschool parent education programs should be devoted to managing home technology to the family's benefit. Guidelines for selective use of television and effective management of microcomputers are two examples of content and can be integrated into such programs.

The family today needs much help and support. The home learning environment needs *an extended arm* in the form of quality child care. These centers must not become home learning substitutes but rather be extensions of the family (Galinsky, 1977). The "family learning center" concept as conceptualized in the Head Start design is viable because it involves parents and citizens as well as teachers and other helping professionals in the full range of activities inherent in quality programs (Swick, Brown, & Robinson, 1983).

School leaders have a tremendous responsibility and opportunity to initiate the beginnings of these programs within the confines of the school. There are additional opportunities for cooperative school-community efforts at developing community based child care centers. The education of parents about parenting and the provision of the needed materials, services and quality child care facilities can improve the foundation of children's development and learning.

School-Based Home Learning Activities

The home-school partnership can be enhanced and strengthened through the use of home learning activities. The usual mechanism for maintaining or extending student progress made in school is the home-work mode. Yet as "home-work" has been utilized it has defeated the original purpose of extending and reinforcing knowledge and attitudes acquired by children in the classroom (Swick & Dennis, 1973). Too often home-work is assigned to students without any direct relationship to the learning in school or the progress already made by individual students.

Home learning is designed to "match" the learning situations in the school with the life context of the child's home ecology. Home learning is the most powerful type of learning we experience and current study of positive uses of this environment indicate that disregard for it as an instructional setting is costing educators additional remediation efforts in the school (Holt, 1983).

The concept of home learning is built around the idea that since learning is continuous and most meaningful when it is relevant to the lives of children the home and the school should incorporate positive modes of involving children in mutually satisfying undertakings. Thus both parents and teachers need to be involved in designing home learning activity packages. The critical difference between home learning and home-work is the attitude among teachers, children and parents about the entire process of growth, development and learning. Home learning advocates are convinced that as partners involved in teaching and learning they can and must plan experiences for the growth of the child and themselves together. Home-work is simply a teacher assigned duty which is made without concern for the child or the parents. *Home learning is a process (begun initially during the infant years) that involves all members of the teaching-learning team in designing and implementing activities* that promote the development of everyone involved whether in home or school situations.

What is home learning? The following examples provide some idea of how this concept can be utilized to extend the instructional gains made in the classroom into the home in a positive way.

Communications: The communication arts are a vital part of the early learning context in which children become involved. The home is a logical place to begin such an investigation.

For example, the children can study the non-verbal modes of communicating that are so abundant in their homes. They can examine various aspects of the topic in school before they go home and set up ways in which they will observe gestures, walking styles, silences, laughter and other non-verbal happenings. If one of the children had a baby brother or sister, he could list ways in which the infant communicates. Another child might live in an extended family and desire to compare the nonverbal behaviors of the different family members. These activities could be implemented by having students study the varying non-verbal behaviors of families from different cultures in the classroom.

Environmental Studies: Parents and children do many things to maintain or delibitate the environment. The classroom teacher can design home learning and community learning situations where children actively participate in developing productive settings in which to live. Activities like collecting glass, cans and paper for recycling, cleanup and plant-a-tree days nd beautification weeks are extremely helpful in developing children's concept of service.

The diversity of such activities include having children and parents examining their neighborhood settings to see how they can be improved, studying the ways in which the environment affects the way they live and discussing how the family, school and community can become a team of people who work together to make the settings livable.

Social Studies: Social studies, in the broadest sense of the term, involves the study of the activities man performs. People in all cultures use different modes of transporting themselves and goods and services to different places. Transportation is simply one area of social studies in which children and their parents can study the rapidly changing nature of social and cultural behaviors.

Many different home learning activities can be used to involve children in the study of transportation. They can, for example, find out how their parents traveled to school, what cars looked like when they were first built and what air travel was like years ago. Some parents may have traveled to different places and would be willing to share their experiences with the children in the classroom. Aunts, uncles and grandparents also can be a source of information on this topic. Together, parents and children can 'dream' about how transportation modes will look like and function in the future.

These are some examples of home learning activities that can be used to constructively involve parents in the school learning events of their children. In order that the children may gain maximum benefit from these experiences, and through them both parents and teachers as well, try as often as possible to let the parents know *what you are doing, why you are doing it,* and *how they might help* make it a success.

It makes sense to give the children as much freedom of choice as possible sot that they are not put in the position, even unwittingly, of exposing themselves to difficult or embarrassing situations. Teachers need to be aware that not all children have the easy access to parents or the materials tha middle class homes accept as a matter of course. The home-learning environment in conjuction with home-school, teacher-parent designed learning activities play a major role in the development and growth patterns of infants, toddlers and young children.

CHAPTER ELEVEN
THE HOME VISIT:
EDUCATING AND SUPPORTING FAMILIES

The basic concept of the home visiting process is to promote positive family development and strengthen family-school-community linkages. The use of home visits implies some common purpose exists between the family and the agency conducting the visitation. It also carries the connotation that the welfare of the family is paramount amoung the individuals designing and implementing such programs. The common purpose which is to promote family development has been the basis for past success stories regarding home visit programs. Home visitation programs, for example, were successfully carried out during the early part of this century in conjunction with agricultural extension projects. Within the parameters of these projects parents (mostly mothers) received government publications on child care, home management, and health care (Osborn, 1980).

Additional examples of the "visitation" practice include visiting nurses who provide families with health education and medical attention and home visits made by teachers in rural America. The fields of social work and medicine have used the home visitation process to support their involvement with families.

The development of a systematic approach to conducting home visit programs was developed during the 1960's. Family intervention programs which focused on increasing the functionality of families used the "home visitor" as a conduit to accomplish their objective. For example, a major component of Head Start was the development of home-based educational practices including home visitation learning materials. A team approach was used in the visitation practice where educational, social, medical and health care needs of families could be addressed in a productive manner (Nedler & McAfee, 1979).

As the popularity of home visitation programs increased the need for training parent educators to accomplish this task surfaced in many early childhood programs. Research and development efforts on carrying out the home visit practice were conducted by leaders in the early childhood and child and family fields of study (Gotts, 1977; Gordon & Brievogel, 1976; The Portage Guide to Home Teaching, 1976). Training programs for educating "home visitors" and "parent educators" were developed to improve the effectiveness of professionals and paraprofessionals working with families in home-and-center-based programs.

Functions of Home Visitation Programs

Home-based early childhood education programs gained in acceptance as the impact of the early years of development on children and families became apparent (Gordon & Brievogel, 1976). During the developmental stages of Head Start the philosophy that one must "teach" the family and not just the child became a major focus for all early childhood educators. While the early efforts in home visitation programs were directed to parents of preschoolers who were not in day care the focus of the programs have expanded to center on parents and children in various settings and situations. In a similar fashion, the goals of the home-based programs have broadened to cover not only "at risk" or "disadvantaged" families but to reach as many families as possible. Thus the functions of home visitation programs include the enhancement of the home learning environment of families from different cultural backgrounds as well as improving the interface between the family and learning settings beyond the home (Morrison, 1978).

Early childhood education home-based programs include at least the following goals: (1) to improve parent skills in educating children within the home environment; (2) to improve parent sensitivity to the developmental milestones children experience; and (3) to improve the home learning environment. Additional objectives of home visit programs emerge from the context and purpose of specialized projects. For example, schools often carry out home visits in advance of school opening to orient parents to the program and to introduce the teacher to the child in the family ecology. Home visits are used to reach perants who are not a part of the regular parent involvement program and, in some cases, to solve problems best dealt with in the home. Home visitation programs have been successful in accomplishing many other things such as monitoring family development, providing parents with a social linkage to the outside world and introducing parents to aspects of child care they were unaware of in their cultural setting.

In order to accomplish the various functions of home visitation programs the following components are essential: (1) clearly specified objectives, (2) an organized body of content to use in program implementation, (3) an organizational process for carrying out the visitation program, (4) a staff design for home visitor roles and for coordination purposes, and (5) a process for continual assessment of program achievements and necessary revisions in the program (Swick & Duff, 1978).

Considerations in Organizing Home Visitation Programs

Effective home visitation programs are the result of advance planning and careful development of all components (Gordon & Brievogel, 1976). Often times home-based programs that fail to bring about expected results lack the training and planning necessary for achieving desired outcomes

(Land, 1983). Advance planning is a key to organizing home visitation programs.

Planning home visitation programs involves the articulation of desired objectives, selecting content and procedures appropriate to goal attainment and selecting and preparing personnel to implement the program.

Goal development should evolve from assessments that reflect specific needs that can be addressed through the home visitation process. For example, a typical need being met through home visitation programs is the training of parents in educational skills they can use with their children. Additional goal areas include doing assessments of children regarding their developmental status, assisting families in dealing with intra-familial stress, and supporting families in developing effective home learning environments. Some schools use home visits to complement their instructional program. In so doing they establish a corresponding set of learning activities for use in the home. The important point here is that specific goals can give direction to program efforts (Swick & Duff, 1978).

The selection and/or development of content and procedures for use in the home visit process is critical to successful home-school efforts. Content selection will emerge from the objectives of the program. For example, Levenstein's (1977) program focused on stimulating verbal interaction between mother and child. To achieve the goal of mother-child interactions materials were selected that would stimulate exchanges between mother and child. Other programs have developed learning packets on language development or used home utensils as materials for advancing the parent-child relationship. When home visits are used to report on pupil progress the child's school performance becomes the substance of the visit. Various procedures are used to conduct home visits. Typically a team of at least two "visitors" conduct the visit. In advance of the visit they plan their agenda, assess the needs to be addressed, and prepare needed materials as well as explore various issues relative to the visit. The implementation process is focused on carrying out the agenda and yet leaving room for parents to ask questions and respond to the materials presented. Following the visit an assessment is conducted to explore what worked and to locate areas that can be improved in conducting future visits (Swick & Duff, 1978).

Parents who are to be a part of the home visit program need a comprehensive orientation. This can be accomplished in a group meeting or by utilizing the initial visit to clarify the purpose of the program and the expectations parent educators have for the parents. During this orientation parent questions can be answered, the framework for each visit explained and a schedule of visits established. Parent participation in advance preparation to the actual visits will increase the effectiveness of the program (Land, 1983). It is desirable to ask parents for input on the usefulness of the various visits and for their suggestions for making the activities applicaple to their home setting.

Like any educational strategy the home visit program needs continuous monitoring. This role is usually performed by a parent involvement director, parent education leader or a person assuming the role of program leader. Problems emerge in any home-school program and thus the need for on-going coordination. For example, a typical problem is the parent not being home at the agreed upon time. A parent coordinator could minimize this problem by telephoning each parent the day before the visit. Where the problem becomes serious the program leader could intervene to resolve the issue. Additional issues in need of continuous attention include program effectiveness, personality clashes that may occur, and other issues dealing with the substance of the program.

The following are some additional considerations to examine in conducting home visits.

1. Is the rationale for the visit clear to the parents and of significance to them within their family ecology?

2. Have clear and continuous communications been established with the parents? Were the parents involved in the planning of the program and are parents and teachers in touch with each other on the significant issues involved in their partnership?

3. Have the home visitors prepared themselves to have meaningful involvement with parents? Have they acquired needed skills and prepared themselves attitudinally to make the visits productive experiences for everyone involved?

4. Are the instructional materials prepared in advance of the visit?

5. Have the details of the visit been reviewed by the people responsible for conducting the process?

Follow-up and evaluation are essential to the continuous development of productive family-school programs. What happens after the visitation is critical to making the purpose of the visit a reality in both the home and the school. There are two post-visitation activities the early childhood educator should undertake; follow-up contact with the parents and an evaluation of the home visit as it was implemented (Hanes, 1977). Provide parents with immediate feedback on their involvement in the activity undertaken. If the visit focused on parent training let them know how you felt the activity went. If the visit focused on some aspect of the child's development inform the parents of your response to the situation along with additional discussion of any concerns they had. This immediate and pleasant feedback to the parents will show your sincerity and strengthen the family-school bond.

In addition to the follow-up activities the visitation process needs to be evaluated. The following are some questions parent educators can use in evaluating the substance of their home visit.

1. Did the visit accomplish the objective it was designed to achieve?

2. Was the visit pleasant and productive in terms of strengthening the family-school relationship?

3. Was I prepared for the visit? Did I have the needed materials for making the visit a success?

4. Was I a good listener and was I communicating clearly with the parents and children?

5. Was I responsive to the parental concerns in a positive and accepting manner?

Training Home Visitors

A major weakness in many home visitation programs is a lack of training for personnel involved. The training of parent educators (especially regarding their roles in home-based programs) and paraprofessionals involved in home visit programs includes the following components: (1) orientation to the goals of the program, (2) clarification of home visitor roles and tasks, (3) training regarding various aspects of the home visitation process, and (4) involvement in developing the qualities of effective home visitors (Morrison, 1978).

Home visitors need a thorough knowledge base in child development, family dynamics, communication skills and home visitation techniques. While many potential home visitors will have acquired these skills in their early childhood training, some applicants will need all or part of this knowledge/training component. An understanding of the various cultural influences on family dynamics is essential. A working knowledge of instructional training and planning and human relations skills are also requisite skills. The following objectives reflect the kinds of skills needed by home visitors.

1. To assist home visitors in acquiring a knowledge base of children's social, emotional, cognitive and physical development.

2. To assist home visitors in developing a sensitivity to the special needs of the families they serve.

3. To assist home visitors in acquiring home visit techniques and instructional skills for use in visitation sessions.

The attitudes of home visitors must be of a positive nature regarding the process and substance of working with parents and young children. Morrison (1978) identifies desired qualities of effective parent involvement leaders: honesty, trust, compassion, caring, courteous, motivated, tactful and other such descriptors. While training programs may not be able to instill these skills in home visitors, they can nurture them by

105

including experiences where personnel are reminded of the psychological impact on parents and children.

A Case Study in Home Visitation:
The Learning Assistance At Home Project

The Learning-Assistance-At-Home program was developed by the Community Care, Incorporated of Columbia, South Carolina. The goal of the program was to enhance parent-child interactions through home-based instruction with parents in educational activities they could implement as a natural part of the home learning arrangement. Several urban elementary schools agreed to participate in the program. Program objectives were carried out through home visits which focused on parent education activities, positive parenting workshops, communication training sessions, a home-school newsletter, and through a radio program.

Program coordination was handled by a parent involvement director who was assisted by a home-based educator. Coordination of visitation schedules, organization of training for home visitors, and planning, implementing, and evaluating program components were handled by these two people. *Participating families were selected* based upon the following criteria: (1) identified as needing assistance by the classroom teacher and the principal, (2) had a child in the elementary school years, and (3) where possible had a preschool child in the home. The rationale for these criteria was that the families most in need would benefit and if a preschool child was in the home, parents would transfer new skills to their relationship with the younger child and thus have a positive effect on his school readiness.

Once the families were identified the home based educator and social worker made home visits to determine the various needs of the families, to find out if the parents would participate, and if so, to prepare them for the ensuing visits. These initial visits provided program leaders with a chance to set the stage for having a successful program.

Students in early childhood education programs at universities in South Carolina *were selected to conduct the home visits.* A training program was designed to assist the students in becoming proficient in home visitation skills. One of the goals of the program was to broaden the student's cultural understanding of people. Thus the students conducted the visits in pairs and every attempt was made to "mix" the students in terms of the personal-cultural backgrounds.

The training sessions included information such as the following: historical overview of the project, information regarding the participating families and schools, background information on situations they might face and how to deal with them, the mechanics of conducting the actual visits, exploration of lesson plans and materials used in the home visits, directions on how to conduct pre-and-post assessments, and mock home visits so the students could simulate some effective interpersonal skills for use with parents. During the training sessions the students had a chance to meet the people on the staff, their team member, and time to work out details on travel arrangements and to ask questions regarding home visit instructional strategies. Building from this initial basis the students had formal seminars related to their home visits throughout the school year. At the end of the initial training session, the students were given the home visit packets. These packets include a lesson plan (flexibly designed) built around a theme and actual teaching materials (often in the form of a learning game) for use with the parents and then to be left for parents to use in the home. While this particular training process was very specific, there were many opportunities for home visitors to be creative in the actual use of the materials (Swick & Rotter, 1980). A sample home visit instructional plan is described as follows.

Sample Visitation Plan: Learning Through Home Experiences

Main Goal: Parents will become aware of the multitude of opportunities that are available in the home to enhance their child's learning. Parents will realize that helping children structure their time will aid them in having time for school, homework, and play. The concept of parents being the most important teacher and model for their children will be enhanced.

Materials: Clock, "Your Home Is Your Child's First School" and two calendars and a letter to parents.

Behaviors To Be Encouraged: The following are specific behaviors to be encouraged in the parents.

Asking questions: Parents will be encouraged to ask questions of their children and answer questions for their children.

Praising: Parents will be encouraged to reinforce appropriate behavior of their children by praising them.

Encouraging participation in meal preparation: Parents will be encouraged to allow their children to participate in preparing food for meals, setting the table and cleaning up after meals according to their ability.

Assisting with homework: Parents will be encouraged to provide a place and time for homework each day.

Implicit Objectives: Parents will become aware of how important they are as teachers of their own children.

Attitudes that parents have about school and education will be examined.

The importance of asking and answering questions to facilitate cognitive growth will be fostered.

Parents will be helped in becoming aware that very important learning opportunities are available in ordinary activities and play situations as well as in school.

Home Visitor Activity Plan: Read carefully the "Introduction", "Daily Experiences that Can Be Shared Between Parents and Children", and "Your Home is Your Child's First School."

Before you begin discussing "Home Experiences" with your parents, present them the clock. This is a gift to the family and will be left in the home when you leave. As you present the clock to the parents discuss with them the importance of children being award of time. Suggest to parents that they use the clock to reinforce the children different times that events happen during the day.

Begin talking with parents about home experiences using a statement like:

> "I'd like for us to talk about different activities that happen in the home each day and how we can use these to help the children learn."

Now mention individual activities that take place in the home. You can use your letter to parents and the brochure as a guide. Go over them with the parents.

Let parents tell you how they feel their children can learn from these experiences. Listen to the parents!

Share your ideals with them. Suggest to them that touching, holding, looking at eyes, smiling are important ways to communicate with children. Try to leave them with the feeling that showing their closeness and warmth is the best way to help their children learn.

Give the parents the calendars. On the calendar write the dates and times of your visits, the time for parent-teacher sessions, and happy home club meetings. Feel free to include any other items on the calendar that you think are appropriate. Go over the other calendar and a few of the suggestions for parent-child activities.

Parent-Teacher Communication: In concluding your visit with the parents encourage them to make direct teacher contact regarding any specific problems or concerns they may have about their child and/or school. Remind them of the happy home club meetings and the parent-teacher sessions that are pertinent to them.

Additional Issues To Consider

The use of home visits is not without its' problems. Some of the common problems that evolve in conducting home visits include: (1) parent absence from the home at the agreed upon time, (2) tardiness on the part of the home visitor, (3) personality clashes between home visit team members, (4) cultural misunderstandings between parent and home visitors, (5) lack of implementation of the home visit plan, and (6) misunderstandings about the role of the home visitor. Each of these problems and possible solutions are the topic of the following discussion.

Parent absence from the home at the agreed upon time is a common problem in many programs. In some cases there are valid reasons for parents to miss the home visit such as when the child is sick. One way to prevent this from happening on a continuous basis is to telephone the parents and remind them of their committment. If the problem becomes serious the parents may have to be dropped from the program.

Tardiness on the part of the home visitors should be dealt with during regularly scheduled training sessions. The importance of scheduling and following through on home visits needs to be continually emphasized. The parent involvement coordinartor can monitor this area on needed improvements. For example, if home visitors are scheduling visits too close to allow time for maintaining their schedule they need to deal with this issue in one of their training sessions.

Learning to "team" on various teaching projects is a developmental process. When home visitor teams experience personality or philosophical clashes they need to be encouraged to examine their skill base for collaborating with each other. Many of these "clashes" can be prevented by incorporating sessions on teaming in the training component of the program. A useful technique is to "match" an experienced and successful home visitor with an inexperienced person. Where team members are unable to solve their problems they will need to be reassigned to other home visitors or dropped from the program.

Home visitors should be versed in the multicultural orientation of the families they visit. The value orientation and cultural identity of parents influences their involvement in the home learning process and advanced knowledge of these factors can aid the parent educator in organizing the visitation with these issues in mind.

For a variety of reasons many home visit plans never get implemented. The home visitor or the parent may go off on a tangent totally unrelated to the plan. The home visitor may have failed to prepare for the visit and end up discussing with the parent about other issues. While there may be legitimate reasons for abandoning the plan, home visitors should be encouraged to stay on course in implementing their program. If significant needs arise during the visit these can be identified and dealt with in a follow-up to the visit.

Conflicts can also emerge when the "roles" of the home visitor are not clear. Parents need to know what to expect and what not to expect from the home visitor. Parents should have a clear picture of their part in this endeavor if the program is to succeed. For example, parents may not see their role as educator but view the home visitor as the person to "teach" the child. Orientation sessions for parents and training activities for the home visitors can focus on the appropriate roles for all individuals involved in the visitation process.

The following are some suggestions for making home visits successful.

1. Arrive at the home on the appointed time!

2. Begin the visit in a cordial and positive manner reiterating the purpose of the visit.

3. Keep the discussion brief, relaxed and focused on the topic of the visit.

4. Be a good listener, responsive to parental questions and concerns. Let parents share memorabilia of the family with you but avoid spending the entire visit this way.

5. Focus on the positive aspects of the child and the parents but be honest about the child and his school or center behavior.

6. Show your concern of the family by being sensitive to the various problems they face.

7. Be flexible and composed in dealing with family behaviors that may be at variance with your ideas about family life.

8. If appropriate involve the children in the visit. Young children are impressed when the teacher visits their home so take an interest in them.

9. Avoid conducting home visits during meal times or other peak busy hours of the family unless invited by the family.

10. If the visit concerns a serious issue be reasonable and approachable, entertain ideas of the parents on solving the problem.

Research Findings on Home Visitation Programs

The influence of parent behavior on the child has been established by various studies. For example, White (1979) examined the infuence of parenting processes on children's development during the first three years of life and found a high correspondence between competent parenting and healthy development among children. White identified three key roles parents perform: (1) educational, (2) facilitator, and (3) designer of the environment. Home visit programs have incorporated these roles in their planning and implementation efforts (Swick, 1979).

Specific traits of parent effectiveness have been correlated with the positive functioning of children over extended time periods. For example, Schaefer, Edgerton and Hunter (1983) found a high correlation between the mother's focus of control and the child's performance on competence scales of curiosity/creativity and verbal intelligence. This correlation remained constant from early infancy through kindergarten. It is clear

110

that parental competence impacts the functioning of the child and that this process is a continuing one which has long term effects on the entire culture.

Given the significance of parental competence as related to children's performance in school, it is disappointing that many teachers continue to teach the child in isolation from his family ecology. Ira Gordon (1977) puts it candidly when he urges educators to teach the family instead of limiting our focus to the child. It was in this context that Gordon designed and implemented various forms of parent education designs. Additional parent education/training projects have been used to assist parents in improving their competence to deal with children and related family situations. Hanes (1983) reviews the major training programs used with parents and discusses their impact on parents. The results of parent education studies indicate programs have influenced parents children in positive ways (Swick, Duff, & Hobson, 1981, chapter 15).

Swick and Duff (1979) point to the following as influences effective programs have had *on parents.*

1. Improved their relationship with children.

2. Enhanced their self image as parents and as individuals.

3. Increased their knowledge of parenting.

4. Increased their involvement in schools and with their children at home.

5. Reduced the amount of negative interactions they had with their children.

Further, the following are influences these programs have had *on the development and learning of children.*

1. Improved relationships with parents.

2. Enhanced their self images.

3. Increased their language, social and cognitive skills.

4. Improved their school performance and attitudes toward school.

5. Decreased their chance of developing learning deficits.

Home visitation programs have had positive influences on parental ability to relate to their children as well as other positive outcomes. A classic study in the field of home visitation was conducted by Ira Gordon at the University of Florida. An important part of Gordon's (1977) work involved training low-income parents as paraprofessional home visitors in teaching child care skills to other low-income parents. Some of the major research findings were: (1) children of parents involved in the program gained in intelligence quotient scores; (2) there was a relationship between maternal language behavior and child performance on language related activities; and (3) parent training in home visit settings could affect changes in the development of infants and young children.

Gordon's work on home visitation programs revealed additional items of significance for planning such programs. The following are key points Gordon (1977) noted for those professionals planning to use home-based, parent oriented education programs.

1. Incorporate the cultural and individual needs of the parents you plan to serve in your program.

2. Develop specific objectives for your program and relate all of your program activities to these desired outcomes.

3. Training home visitors in the desired "parent educator behaviors" is essential to the success of the program.

4. Continuous assessment of the effectiveness of the program is critical to having long term results in influencing parent-child interactions.

5. The content of the program should be developmentally based; using the natural learning tools of the home environment as keys to unlocking the "teaching and learning" potential of parents and children.

The expansion of home visit program to include community supports is an effective way of assuring permanent changes in parental behaviors. A "ripple effect" has been noted in various parent education programs. For example, Kempe & Kempe (1978) noted that the mere presence of a "support system" for abusing parents reduced their anxiety level and improved their parenting competence. Bronfenbrenner (1979) cites several studies that support the paradigm of combining education, support system resources and other proactive efforts in our work with families. Home visitation programs, when designed and implemented properly, can influence the development of healthy families.

CHAPTER TWELVE
PARENT-TEACHER INVOLVEMENT:
A DEVELOPMENTAL PROCESS

Parents' active involvement in their child's growth experiences (both in the home and in the school) appears at the outset to be an elementary objective, one that should be easy to set in motion. The involvement process, however, is found to be a highly challenging system of human interactions with effective implementation dependent upon careful attention to a number of sensitive variables. It is, therefore, not surprising that school systems having successful experiences in the development and implementation of this concept are still a few in number.

This chapter focuses onthe concept of parent involvement from a developmental point of view. The first section examines the various "meanings" of parent involvement. The second section includes a discussion of points of beginning, questions to be considered by teachers and parents as they examine and analyze their feelings and attitudes about being a part of a dynamic parent-teacher relationship. The third section presents a developmental model for viewing the meaningful formation of parent-teacher relationships. The major theme in this chapter, then, is that parents and teachers must view their partnership as a developmental journey.

The Meaning of Parent Involvement

There are many preconceptions people have about the parent involvement process. Some of these ideas are incorrect and lead to conflicts between parents and teachers because of a lack of some common meaning about the process. For example, some teachers may feel comfortable with parents as classroom aides but are threatened as parents attempt to become involved in the decision making role of the school. Parents, in this regard, may see their role as limited to baking cookies for a PTA program but lack an understanding of the involvement role they perform at home in terms of educating the child. Citizens in the community may have similar problems in grasping a correct understanding of their role in supporting and actively pursuing quality educational programs for young children. An examination of some of the major misconceptions of parent involvement will help us to better understand parts of the meaning of this process.

One parent involvement myth is that parents must be physically active in school activities on a continuous basis. While the on-going physical involvement of parents is desirable it is only one dimension of the concept. The "involvement" process is developmental; beginning with the birth of the child and continuing throughout the life spans of child and parent. Parents who serve as volunteers in classroom situations are certainly doing a meaningful activity, but so are parents who work and support their children in other than school situations. The many possibilities for parent involvement should be studied by educators (and parents) as they formulate a view of their role in this process.

A second myth regarding the involvement of parents in the education of children is that many parents lack the motivation to carry out their role in this partnership. This may be the case if programs have been designed without regarding the needs and interests of all parents. Programs which cater to an elite group or are designed to meet only the needs of the school will obviously create little parental excitement. On the other hand, programs which are flexibly designed and contain things of value to parents will stimulate much interest among all members of the community. For example, when programs are diversified and organized around some common parent-teacher themes, the programs prove to be useful.

A third myth is that to be effective parent programs must be designed by specialists in education and/or child development. The fact is that when programs are designed by specialists who exclude parents from a significant role in the process such programs experience many failures. Effective programs must be designed by a team of people including parents, teachers, citizens and leaders in early childhood education. Education specialists (whatever their identity) should be facilitators of the entire process of parent involvement.

A fourth myth is that effective parent involvement programs have activities taking place all the time and are coordinated by some bureaucratic system. While it is certainly beneficial to have a systematic approach to program development, much of the work can be accomplished through an active parent-teacher leadership team. *The idea that productive programs have activities going on all the time is a misconception of the parent involvement process.* Well planned but properly sequenced activities are more desirable than having too many projects that have no meaning or logic. Program coordination, whether carried out by a parent coordinator or a team of people, can be effective if goals are clearly defined and those involved in the process are willing to share the responsibilities of implementing the program. (Colleta, 1977).

A fifth myth is the idea that to be effective parent involvement must happen at the school. Parent involvement programs are happening in many places besides the traditional environment of the school. Effective programs use church and civic groups as places to involve parents who otherwise might not participate. Utilization of community resources such as government agencies, universities and business groups can enhance the overall quality of the program. Indeed the most successful parent involvement programs have been community centered and multi-disciplinary in their approach. (Davies, 1975)

When the "myths" of parent involvement are understood, the meaning of this process emerges more clearly and, of course, is more functional for use in planning and carrying out programs. *Parent involvement is first a partnership between parents and teachers and their "helpers" in the community.* This partnership must be based on the premise that the partners understand their individual roles, how these roles relate to the partnership and how the process of relating individual roles and needs to the common good of the home-school-community relationship works. Further, there must be a mutual respect among parents and teachers for the roles they each perform and an understanding of how to best use their human talents in fostering quality programs for children and families.

Second, parent involvement is a developmental process that is built over a period of time through intentional planning and effort on the part of every team member. This developmental process begins through forming a trusting relationship among parents and teachers and is continuously extended and expanded through mutually supportive activities that improve both the educational environment and the home-school relationship.

Third, parent involvement is a process by which parents and teachers work, learn and participate in decision making experiences in a shared manner. As parents and teachers develop their cooperative relationship they should find opportunities to learn from each other. This may occur through parent education programs or in less formal ways such as in conferences or in other activities. In addition, as parents and teachers work together in planning programs such as teacher aide projects, family counseling programs, extended school day projects and/or parent-teacher association projects they will learn about the talents and skills of each other. Critical to this process of learning and working together is that parents and teachers value each others' contributions and focus on the positive facets of their partnership. In this way they can have a basis for making decisions regarding various aspects of their relationship in a constructive manner.

Parent Involvement: Points of Beginning

Once parents and teachers have established a framework of understanding some common meanings regarding parent involvement, they need to consider their readiness as related to proposed home-school involvement issues. *Three beginning reference points are : (1) philosophical basis of involvement, (2) understanding of the communication process, and (3) identification of some beginning points for developing the parent-teacher relationship.*

Teachers of young children who are about to enter into the arena of parent involvement efforts must consider their philosophy of teaching and learning in the largest context possible. For example, teachers who view the learning process as basically confined to the classroom need to re-examine their philosophical and knowledge base regarding how children learn. A similar assessment is due by teachers who see parents as primarily clerical helpers or other support roles in terms of involvement efforts. The philosophical view of teachers regarding the roles of parents, the learning process and the development and learning of the child are influential in terms of the kinds of activities eventually developed for parents and children. The following questions should be helpful to teachers in examining their philosophical status regarding parents and their role in the home-school relationship.

1. To who am I, as a teacher of young children personally and professionally responsible?

2. Who is the child's first and potentially most influential teacher?

3. How do I perceive the parents' role in the educational process?

4. What steps have I taken to involve parents in a meaningful way in home-school efforts?

5. Do I encourage parents to take an active interest in the school's program?

Parents face a similar task in confronting themselves with issues related to their various roles in activating parent involvement projects. Too often parents and teachers limit their view of the educational process to "immediate" concerns and neglect to place the process in a developmental context. For example, parents of preschoolers may not see the significance of their educational role as it will impact the child's school performance at a later developmental stage. Teachers may fail to recognize their connection to the home learning environment in spite of the evidence that the home is indeed the most influential learning setting. The following questions, when examined by parents in a sincere fashion, can provide initial points of departure for their meaningful involvement in home-school programs.

1. As a parent, what are my responsibilities both at home and at school in assuring the development of my child's learning skills?

2. Who was my child's first teacher? Was I an effective "teacher" during his early years?

3. What kind of community support for education exists? Is there an awareness by community leaders of the need for home-school-community teaming in making education a community concern?

116

Have school leaders initiated programs to involve citizens and community leaders in the process of educational planning?

4. Has a needs assessment of school programs and the status of families been conducted recently? If so, what priority needs emerged as the basis for some home-school planning? If not, how could this process be conducted so as to identify critical home-school needs?

5. Given a common set of needs and goals, what procedures could (or are) be used to establish a home-school planning team to develop a mechanism for meeting the identified needs?

Emerging from a study of these questions will be some "points of beginning" for the formation of a functional parent-teacher partnership. In order to capitalize on these beginning points two areas of attention by parents and teachers are: (1) communication skills, and (2) planning skills. While these skills are examined in other chapters of this book they deserve mentioning here in order to emphasize their significance in the positive initiation of parent-teacher programs.

School leaders can form a sound *communication base* by using various means to enhance parent and citizen awareness of the need for their involvement in educational efforts. Further, the use of on-going communication techniques can develop a framework for more extensive home-school planning. The development of *planning skills* can be accomplished through the involvement of parents and teachers in planned program development efforts. By utilizing leadership training workshops combined with experimental involvement of parents and teachers in actual programs the desired planning skills will emerge and, if continually refined, provide a basis for on-going efforts.

When parents and teachers examine their status regarding home-school involvement, they will identify some points of interest and areas of need they can jointly approach. In planning for the development of mutual efforts, parents and teachers need to take stock of their readiness to work together in a supportive and productive manner. This includes an honest assessment of where each is at in their own development and some planning on how to maximize each others' talents regarding the implementation of home-school programs. Thus, the following are questions parents and teachers need to study in a partnership manner with the ultimate goal being the formation of a beginning process for having an effective parent involvement program.

1. What kind of home-school efforts (including attitudes) have been implemented over the past five or ten years? For example, have parents and teachers had experiences in planning programs as a team? If so, how have these experiences influenced parent and teacher attitudes toward working with each other on such efforts?

2. Is there a "core" of parent-teacher leaders who can take the lead in initiating program development? If so, how can these "leaders" be facilitated in their efforts to activate program planning? If not, what kind of recruitment and leadership training would be most effective in developing this needed "core" of people?

3. To what extent have I designed the home to be an effective learning environment? How could I make the home more of a place where my child can develop his learning potential?

4. What has been my past involvement with the school? Have I developed a positive view of my children's teachers?

5. In what way can I foster a positive home-school relationship? Are there school support activities I could become a part of and thus initiate this home-school involvement process?

A Developmental Model For Viewing Parent-Teacher Relationships

Too often parent-teacher relationships are viewed in a simplistic and static manner. Yet, even the casual observer notices the dynamics of parent-teacher interaction reflect complex and ever changing life events and concommitant reactions. Four facets of the parent-teacher relationship are examined in this part of the chapter: (1) the meaning of the term "developmental" as applied to parent-teacher relationships; (2) the nature of "developmental stages" of parenting and teaching; (3) the substance of the "stages" of parent-teacher relationships; and (4) the use of developmental information on parent-teacher relationships as applied to organizing effective parent involvement programs.

The concept of "development" implies that human beings change and refine their selves as they interact with the environment. Our conceptions of learning are based on this premise: that individuals can use their experiences to improve themselves; altering behavior patterns where necessary and refining skills with information and perceptions acquired by reflecting on experiences in their lives. This concept can be applied to the study of various human relationships.

In the case of parent-teacher relationships this notion of development refers to the process by which each learns from the other and utilizes his experience base in enhancing the home-school relationship. This process includes the individual-developmental changes parents and teachers experience as well as the changes that occur in their relating to each other in various dynamic situations such as conferencing with regards to the child's learning, planning programs together and in general facilitating each other in carrying out their roles.

Inherent in the developmental view of parent-teacher relationships is the premise that parents and teachers can, through intentional efforts, build a relationship that is continuously growing, expanding and refining

118

itself regarding productive interactions with all members of the home-school team. This view, then, does not accept the notion that certain parents are unable to develop as full partners in home-school endeavors. Rather, this perspective sees each parent as an individual capable of growth — developing their skills in an interactive manner when the school climate and family support system are oriented toward maximizing parent and teacher potential.

Critical to the concept of a developmental parent-teacher relationship is that these individuals are the most powerful teachers children will ever encounter. Thus the "developing adult" (parent and teacher) can foster a setting where children can develop their potential to the maximum. Deficit oriented adults will have a negative influence on children; modeling passive and non-productive responses to various situations. It is this notion of modeling that Erickson (1982) refers to when he discusses how generative adults act pro-actively in the environment and thus guide children toward similar constructive behavior. Planners of parent involvement programs who fail to recognize the developmental nature of parent-teacher relationships will ultimately reach a point of stagnation.

Parents and teachers each experience a series of developmental levels by which they can strengthen their individual integrity which, in turn, will enable them to be more effective partners in home-school efforts. An understanding of these individual developmental experiences of parents and teachers is essential to utilizing their talents to the maximum.

Parents, beginning with their plans to become parents, are in a state of continuous becoming. Parents experience a cumulative growth in terms of becoming effective in their roles; otherwise they would atrophy and eventually fail in their attempts to nurture children. Parental development is a part of the individuals total adult development. There are several theoretical perspectives regarding the development of parents and families (Jaffe & Viertel, 1980; Elkund, 1980; Erickson, 1982; Duvall, 1977). A synthesis of these viewpoints provides us with the following framework of developmental stages of parenthood: (1) pre-parenting preparation, (2) initial parenting experiences, (3) organization of a parenting pattern, (4) refinement of parenting pattern; and (5) stabilization of parenting pattern. Just as the early development of the child weighs heavily on his later functioning so it is with the developmental nature of becoming a parent. Indeed, the failure of individuals to encounter these stages of parenthood successfully will often lead to pathological functioning on their part. Each stage of parental development is explained as follows.

Defined broadly, *pre-parenting preparation* includes all of the experiences an individual has integrated into his personality to the point in their life where they encounter parenthood. In a more functional sense it deals with the specific experiences an individual uses to prepare for becoming a parent. These "preparatory experiences" include formal courses in parenting and informal (but very significant) discussions regarding care of the infant, planning thenursery and related topics such as adjustments in work life. This is the stage of parenting which is devoted to *planning and preparing for a major life change.*

Initial parenting experiences include the actual parent involvement activities performed during the child's first year of life. This is an exploratory time where parents experiment with different approaches to handling child care tasks, work life patterns, new social activities, alterations of parent-parent relationships and many other events that occur during this time. During the second year of parenting, parents begin to form an *organizational pattern* for performing their many roles. Work routines are scheduled more effectively; child care processes are beginning to take on some routine and in general family dynamics are taking place in a more orderly fashion. As parents arrive at a scheme for conducting family activities they find a new level of confidence in responding to various situations and in activating (anticipating) available services for producing a positive climate for children and adults to develop.

As children enter the formal school years parents tend to *refine their performance of different roles and take on new roles* in regards to familial and extra-familial responsibilities. For example, parents may spend less time in direct contact with the child and more time in influencing social situations in the school and community where the child is now spending a significant part of his life. As the child matures parents can refine their interactions with the child; utilizing more mutually planned modes of guidance. With the development of a self reliant child *parents arrive at stabilizing their role* as parents and performing mostly as supportive and significant persons in the life of the emerging young adult. This stabilization process allows for more autonomy for both child and parent.

Not all parents engage in parenting in a developmental sequence. Some parents, for various reasons, become dysfunctional and fail to develop thus impacting children in negative ways. Other parents may form closure on their parenting orientation and thus function in a rigid manner — disavowing developmental opportunities and responding in a static manner to their child's development and their own development. Ideally, parents use developmental opportunities to learn productive modes of relating to children, teachers, and each other.

Teachers develop in their personal and professional interactions given a supportive environment in which they can experiment and learn from the situations they encounter. The initial stage of development for teachers takes place in the *pre-service education program.* Within a college or university setting (or a child care training program) teachers develop a knowledge base and practice some basic teaching skills. The depth of this developmental stage will vary depending on the situation each individual encounters. Having developed a set of pedagogical skills most teachers serve an *internship type experience* where they experiment with teaching practices and become familiar with the ecology of teaching. Ideally, this would be a time for interacting with master teachers and working on teaching practices in a positive, nurturing environment. Realistically, this is often a time when teachers are left to their "survival" skills and must grasp the environment in the best way possible (Katz, 1977).

If teachers experience success in their early efforts they will organize a set of workable teaching skills. In using these skills over a period of time they will find them incomplete — thus *sensing a need for renewal.* It is this "renewal process" that leads teachers on a journey toward developing into what Leland Jacobs (1978) calls the artistic teacher. During this developmental stage teachers formulate a philosophy of teaching which guides their continuous growth in the profession (Swick & Hanley, 1983). Once a philosophical base has been formulated *the process of stabilizing one's teaching approach* is a logical objective. During this part of teacher development the "master teacher" emerges — utilizing a series of experiences in teaching combined with serious study and thinking regarding the teaching-learning process. This stabilization process should not be confused with rigidification of teaching style. Rather, it is an integration of many skills and perceptions used in teaching to formulate a style of working with children and parents that incorporates the best knowledge we have regarding effective teaching. Indeed this "master teacher" will expend considerable energy in *refining* their teaching modes; keeping current regarding new ideas and new ways of using existing ones.

The developing teacher and parent are not simply passing through stages of human development; they are experiencing them in individually unique ways. The key to their development is in their intentional and throughful action regarding how they relate and react to the children and adults they teach. Adults who atrophy in their life perspectives are unable to teach or learn effectively because they have become disconnected from the developmental process. In order to be generative in human endeavors one must be actively engaged in the human development process (Erickson, 1982). *In order for parents and teachers to develop a meaningful relationship they must be considerate of each others development and ecological states.* The final section of this chapter focuses on some insights regarding the developmental nature of parent-teacher relationships.

The development of parent-teacher relationships takes shape in many different ways. In some cases no real relationship is ever established and in other situations a highly elaborate and supportive partnership is formed. The formation of a mutually supportive relationship between parents and teachers is an intentional effort that normally proceeds through five stages of development.

The *first stage of development* is a time in which *initial contacts* are made by parent and teacher. Ideally this would occur before the child enters school. It is a time for learning that parent and teacher are

121

in forming a partnership; sensing a common goal of helping the child and each other as the child's helpers in having the best human environment possible.

Once a mutual interest is determined the *exploration of some common basis for the partnership* can be initiated. This *is the second stage* of development. The substance of the basis for a partnership will vary according to the developmental stage of the parents and that of the teacher. For example, in preschool programs, parent-teacher efforts may be directed toward preventing problems with the healthy development of the child. During this stage parents may probe teachers on their views of child development and their teaching philosophy. Teachers may observe parent interaction with the child and inquire with regards to parental interest in the education of their child. In addition, parent and teacher will likely examine their orientation and confidence level regarding parent-teacher involvement. While most of this process may occur at a subtle level of interaction, teachers need to be sensitive to what is happening so they can maximize the potential for having a productive relationship with parents.

During the third stage of development parents and teachers formalize their relationship by establishing some mechanism for continuous involvement regarding the common goals that emerged in their early interactions. This may be accomplished through regular conferences or at a more informal level via phone calls or written notes. Usually a combination of communication modes are used to meet this need for having access to each other on a continuous basis. As parents and teachers accomplish some of their objectives their *relationship strengthens* with each person arriving at a new level of self confidence. *This is the fourth stage of the developmental process.* With increased confidence in each others abilities parents and teachers may initiate more advanced interactions such as solvingproblems together, developing programs to enrich the child's educational experience and organizing parent education programs for other parents and teachers.

The fifth stage of this model is a natural extension of the previous phase of development. It *is a time when parents and teachers have developed a sense of mutual interest and committment* to having quality programs for all children and families. The parent-teacher relationship is solidified and refined with a respect for each others' own developmental status. A mutuality is accomplished where parent supports teacher and teacher actively seeks out ways to enhance the parent in her attempts to function. *This mutuality is extended to include the needs of other parents and teachers.* Typically parents and teachers who mature to this phase of functioning are strong advocates for having quality educational and social support programs for all families.

These stages of development are symbolic of what can occur in the evolving parent-teacher relationship. In many cases parental involvement will not occur in these stages. Indeed the use of this model is in its' projection of how parent-teacher relations can be capitalized on in the most productive manner. For example, as a teacher, you may find only superficial parent-teacher relationships in your school. Through careful study of the ecology of the school and community and the application of a developmental perspective toward the formation of home-school relationships you can improve the influence of adults on young children and other adults. By viewing things developmentally and ecologically we can grasp "what could be" and initiate procedures to accomplish the best possible home-school learning environment.

Viewing parent-teacher relationships in this evolving context also provides us with an analytical tool for use in designing appropriate parent involvement experiences for parents and teachers who are, invariably, at different stages of development. This analytical tool can be used in a self-assessment mode by individual parents and teachers to determine their developmental status and thus for appropriate ways of building constructive relationships with others.

Educators planning parent involvement programs can utilize this approach to organize program objectives and activities to match the developmental position of parents and teachers who will be involved. The organization of effective parent involvement programs can be facilitated best when the individuals involved have insights into their own development and a perspective of how their relationship with others can be maximized.

CHAPTER THIRTEEN
STRATEGIES FOR ORGANIZING
PARENT INVOLVEMENT PROGRAMS

Parent involvement programs are organized by individuals who, through the process of development, are (or should be) continually refining and improving their modes to teaching and learning. The developmental process that influences the functioning of parents and teachers also impacts the development of parent involvement programs. Productive parent involvement efforts are based upon a developmental process. The gradual development of programs which include a sensitive study of the needs of the individuals involved as well as a perspective of the ecological nature of home-school-community situations will prove more effective than the organization of faddish projects which lack the needed substance for long range workability.

Poorly planned parent-teacher efforts result in many problems including the following: (1) conflicts on how to conduct the organizational process; (2) power struggles between individuals who want control of the group; (3) communication problems; (4) disagreement over the direction program efforts should take, and (5) confusion about various responsibilities within the membership. *These problems can be avoided or at least minimized when the process for developing programs includes the recognition of the developmental nature of parenting and teaching* as is explicated in the previous chapter.

Effective parent involvement programs are organized by parents and teachers who have developed a trusting relationship. This relationship is based upon the use of team planning skills and group communication skills. In carrying out the mechanics of organizing and implementing programs, parents and teachers focus on the following components: (1) needs assessment in relationship to home-school-community situations; (2) formulation of objectives that reflect the needs of the parent-teacher partnership; (3) selection of strategies to use in accomplishing program objectives; (4) implementation modes to facilitate program workability, and (5) program assessment and evaluation techniques (Swick, Duff, Hobson, 1981, p. 31).

Needs Assessment

Essential to the success of parent involvement programs is a clearly delineated plan of action. In developing this plan it is important to involve as many people as possible in the organizational process. While the needs assessment stage is a prime time for maximizing people's involvement, it is also critical that they be involved in training and development sessions as well as in all facets of the home-school program.

There are various ways of conducting the needs assessment process. The use of questionnaires, study groups, individual parent-teacher meetings, and school district evaluation studies are some commonly used assessment techniques. Regardless of the type of assessment used it is vital that information be gathered on how parents perceive their needs in relation to the school. As the data gathering process is being conducted the people involved need to be sure they are acquiring the views of a cross-section of people in the community. For example, one group of parents may desire support services such as tutoring for their children while other parents may want to have a more active role in the decision making process.

In assessing parental orientation and views regarding the role a parent-teacher program could play it should prove valuable to gather data on the past functioning of the home-school team. For example, what kinds of parent involvement activities were used in past years? How valuable were these activities judged to be by parents and teachers? What suggestions were made for improving program functioning that could be used by the current planning team?

An additional mode of acquiring parent input is the use of study sessions where people can clarify priority concerns they feel should be addressed by the planning group. These study sessions might focus on three main purposes: (1) the identification of critical needs as expressed by the parents; (2) the formation of objectives to be accomplished during the year, and (3) the identification of strategies that can be used to effectively carry out various program tasks (Swick & Taylor, 1983).

An important part of the needs assessment process is the examination of teacher views regarding the parent involvement process. For example, the school staff may want to examine their philosophical orientation regarding the involvement of parents in various facets of the educational program. In addition, teachers need to assess their knowledge base regarding the parent involvement process. Emerging from this part of the assessment will be varying areas of in-service education needs such as information on parent education, communication skills for working with parents, and organizational strategies for use in designing workable programs. School district leaders can lend support to this process by assessing their history of encouraging positive home-school-community relations. As a result of these analyses, teachers and school leaders can establish their objectives for meaningful involvement with parents and citizens (Swick & Duff, 1978).

Further needs assessment should be conducted on existing and desired resources for carrying out effective programs. Resource assessment can be accomplished by identifying needed resources in terms of: (1) finances; (2) personnel, and (3) materials. By matching needs with existing resources

126

areas of deficit can be articulated and plans made to acquire these resources. By utilizing a community based approach many resources can be obtained and the participation base broadened which should enhance the effectiveness of the program.

Formulation of Objectives

The data gathered during the needs assessment process can be used as the bases for developing a usable set of parent involvement program objectives. There are four essential stages in the systematic development of program objectives.

A first step is to organize the identified needs into clusters from which specific objectives can be formulated. For example, there may be a category of needs related to *family assistance* such as medical aid, social services, and child care needs. Another category of needs may relate to home-school and child care needs. Another category of needs may relate to home-school communications and could be grouped under the *family-school relations* heading. Additional clusters of objectives are parent-teacher *education* objectives, parent-teacher *participation* objectives, and parent-teacher *involvement* goals. By categorizing needs which were identified during the needs assessment process, more functional program objectives can be developed (Swick and Duff, 1978).

A second step in the process is to prioritize needs from highly important to desirable but less important. This step will require involvement of parents and educators in determining the most urgent needs. It is likely that as a result of parent-teacher discussions some long range needs will emerge as well as several needs of urgent concern. A useful way of prioritizing needs is to make a list of the identified needs and to use this list as a basis for discussion. The following list of needs is an example of how one parent-teacher group accomplished this task.

PARENT-TEACHER PROGRAM NEEDS

I. High Priority
    A. Establishment of better home-school communications.
    B. Involvement of community agencies in school programs.
    C. Formation of an after school program.
    D. Development of a child-care center.

II. Low Priority
    A. Formation of a summer school program.
    B. Organization of a parent-teacher council.
    C. Establishment of a school volunteer program.
    D. Acquisition of a bus for parent transportation.

After needs are prioritized, the development of program objectives becomes a process of specifying ways to meet the needs as identified. For example, a need identified in the above list was: to establish better home-school communication. Some ways to accomplish this objective are to develop regular times for parent-teacher conferences, for parent-teacher study groups, organize a monthly parent newsletter, and acquire parent feedback on various issues through questionnaires, inventories and informal parent contacts.

A third step in the process of developing objectives *is to establish a list of objectives of immediate concern.* This listing can be based upon the needs identified as priority concerns of the family-school team. For example, the need for extended school day programs may be an urgent need due to the parental work schedules. Thus an objective might be to develop an after school program. Items identified as important but not urgent can be incorporated into a long range plan. The formulation of long range goals is useful in that it helps parents and teachers focus upon an ideal arrangement they are desirous of attaining. Short range goals provide the sustenance that parents and teachers can use in their day to day efforts. These immediate tasks provide feedback to the teaching-learning partners on how they are doing in relation to accomplishing their ultimate goal (Swick, Duff, Flake-Hobson, 1981).

A fourth step involves the dissemination and use of the agreed upon program objectives. This process can be accomplished by developing a guidebook which explains the focus of the program and describes ways parents and teachers can help in carrying out the plan. This step could also be accomplished by incorporating the objectives into the school manual or through publication in the local newspaper or a newsletter. The finalized list of program objectives will become the basis for selecting and implementing appropriate strategies.

Selection of Strategies

As the parent involvement program is developed appropriate strategies should be selected to accomplish the desired functions. An important part of selecting useful strategies involves the matching of program objectives to family-school-community needs, then appropriate (and available) techniques can be chosen to accomplish the objectives.

There are many different strategies and techniques which parents and teachers can choose to use in their working partnership. Each strategy has a purpose and can usually be related to meeting specific needs and objectives. A systematic match between needs and selected strategies is essential for developing an effective program. The following list of needs and appropriate strategies exemplifies techniques as they are related to meeting individual family and/or school needs.

Family-School Needs	Stated Objectives	Suggested Strategies
Problem Solving Sharing Information Confidential Situation		Individual Parent- Teacher Conferences
Personal Support Common Concerns Parent Education Problem Solving		Group Conferences
Relating to Family Modeling for Children Personal Contacts Parent Education		Home Visits
Relating to School Learning Together Modeling for Children Parent Education		School Visits
Information Involvement Announcements		Newsletters
Assessing Needs Determining Interests Setting a Direction		Inventories and Questionnaires
Information Communication Awareness		Telephoning
Parent Education Citizen Involvement Awareness		Television
Group Information Parent Education Citizen Awareness		Radio, Newspaper, and Slide Presen- tation
Pupil Progress School Progress Home Progress		Anecdotal records, Test data, Program charts, and Work samples.

The appropriate match of strategies to objectives in implementing a home-school partnership is critical to making this joint venture successful. For example, if one of the program objectives is to bring about community awareness of early childhood programs, an appropriate tool might be television. If the objective is to foster closer working relations among parents and teachers, however, the use of home visits and conferences would be appropriate.

Program Implementation

In implementing a parent involvement program it is important to remember that this will be (in many cases) a new experience for the parents and in some cases for school personnel. It is critical that the initial program experience be of a positive and substantive nature so succeeding program years have a basis for further development of the family-school linkage. As strategies are selected and program events organized, these must relate to the needs and objectives identified during the planning sessions. As plans are finalized and implementation strategies designed the following questions can serve as guides in reviewing the feasibility of your plans.

1. Is the program well organized and reflective of the needs that parents and teachers identified as high priority concerns?

2. Have the mechanical aspects of the program been attended to by individuals given specific assignments? (It is very discouraging to attend a program where equipment does not function!)

3. Has the program been well advertised? Many people fail to attend programs simply because they are unaware of them.

4. If people are to be involved in some aspects of the program have they been notified and reminded of their assignments?

5. Has a method of implementing the program of activity been established? Is there an agenda or schedule to follow (if appropriate) in conducting the program? Systematically planned activities are more likely to succeed than poorly organized programs.

6. Have the goals that were set been realistic ones? Small increments in expectations are more likely to be met than large ones.

The development of a check list format for assuring that program details have been attended to is one way of insuring success. Setting a positive climate for human interaction and positive family-school contacts is yet another way of increasing the success level of such projects. Communication is a key element in preventing and eradicating problems.

The following example of a checklist is one method of increasing program effectiveness.

A PARENT INVOLVEMENT PROGRAM CHECKLIST

_____ Needs assessment of priority parent involvement concerns has been conducted.

_____ Parents have been involved in the needs assessment process.

_____ Needs identified have been sequenced in rank order indicating high priority, low priority, long range, and short range needs.

_____ Specific program objectives have been developed with input from all members of the learning team.

_____ Program objectives and corresponding activities have been advertised throughout the community.

_____ Appropriate implementation strategies have been selected to support the various components of the program.

_____ All individuals involved in implementing the program have been contacted, oriented to their tasks and provided resources to carry out their role.

_____ Facilities needed for program implementation have been readied and schedules for use with all responsible people notified.

_____ A process for evaluating and improving the program on a continuous basis has been designed.

As in the case with any system in which human beings work together, problems do arise and should be dealt with in a logical manner. The following are problems common to the introduction and implementation of home-school programs that involve people in facilitating the development and learning of families and schools:

— In some cases parent and teacher attitudes are not conducive to close working relationships. This may be caused by a lack of training or may result from previous times of isolation from each other (Honig, 1975).

— Due to the varying work schedules of parents and the very demanding job of teaching it is common for the scheduling of conferences and home visits to become a problem. Through planning in advance (in which the needs of parents and teachers are taken into consideration) can help to alleviate this problem (Swick and Duff, 1978).

— When people work together on a continuous basis, communication gaps and interpersonal disputes are a normal part of the process. Training sessions on how to effectively communicate with people can help to minimize this problem (Colleta, 1977).

— As new modes of family-school operations are introduced, problems of coordination, record keeping, and systems management are likely. It takes time to work out an effective system. The more thorough the pre-planning and the more cogent the definitions, the fewer the problems when the program is implemented (Gordon and Breivogel, 1976).

In order to alleviate problems that emerge during the implementation of program events some basic organizational process and structure is needed. The implementation system should serve as a procedural guide people can use to improve the program each year. Most school districts will find the following guidelines useful in forming an organizational structure for their parent involvement program.

1. Develop programs with local family and schools needs as the priority basis for decision making. While school districts may have a district wide program philosophy it is best to localize actual program planning at the school building level.

2. Involve a cross-section of parents, teachers, and citizens in the planning process. In order to have a meaningful planning process each school or program locale will want to develop a procedural guide for carrying out this process.

3. Organize program activities in conjunction with other community agencies. The use of community resources and cooperative school-community planning can strengthen individual parent involvement programs.

4. Plan experiences where leadership staff can acquire ideas on effective parent involvement efforts through visiting other programs and through forming study teams which concentrate on continuous assessment and refinement of program efforts.

5. Involve parents and teachers in the coordination of program activities. The use of parent-teacher cooperation teams can provide on-going experiences in leadership development thus assuring continuous availability of trained personnel in carrying out program operations.

Effective implementation of a parent involvement program is dependent upon the behaviors and skills of the program team. Staff members involved in planning and implementing this type of program should be skilled in human relations techniques and proficient in management and

132

administration of programs. Programs which are effectively planned and implemented will become the basis for successful continuation of family-school interaction in future years.

Program Evaluation

A parent-teacher partnership must be based on the idea that it can be improved. Through the use of constructive evaluation techniques (see the chapter in this book entitled: Assessing and Improving Programs) the leadership team can acquire feedback on the usefulness of various projects and activities. Future programs can be designed around some of the suggestions given by participants during this evaluation process (Berclay, 1977).

There are many ways to evaluate the effectiveness of parent involvement programs. Informal comments and brief narrative reports from participants provide information on their perceptions of the value of various programs components. Some program coordinators have found individualized activity reports from each participant to be helpful in ogranizing future activities. These reports may be simple check lists or narrative comments from the participants (Hanes, 1977).

Another evaluation technique involves the use of annual program assessment forms. Such a form identifies the parent-teacher activities conducted during the year and asks the participants to check those activities in which they participated and to evaluate them in terms of their usefulness to the home-school relationship. Additional modes of program evaluation include open forum discussions, formal assessment inventories and other data gathering techniques.

The basic purpose of any evaluation process is to ultimately improve the performance and effectiveness of the system being used to accomplish desired objectives. Those individuals involved in attempting to establish a workable home-school relationship certainly want some knowledge about the effectiveness of the program. Were the objectives accomplished? Were family-school relationships improved? What specific activities resulted from the program? As program leaders gain insights regarding these and other questions they can plan future programs with some basis for improvement.

An important part of the evaluation process is the assessmentof how personnel functioned in carrying out their tasks. Did the home-school coordinator provide effective leadership in developing a viable parent involvement program? Were parents and teachers active in participating in various program activities? Were citizens active in supporting the program? The answers to these questions can provide all members of the home-school team with ideas on how to improve personnel functioning in the program.

The following questions are intended as sample guidelines program leaders can use in conducting the evaluation process.

GUIDELINES TO USE IN THE EVALUATION PROCESS

— What was the original purpose for developing the program?

— Have program activities been designed to accomplish these goals?

— To what degree were the objectives of the program accomplished?

— If certain objectives were not accomplished, why not?

— Were the various program activities and projects judged successful by the participants?

— Do attendance records indicate the various events were well attended?

— Have the various program activities been supportive of the family and the school? Have they strengthened the home-school relationship? If so, how? If not, why not?

— Did the program, as it was implemented, reflect the input of a cross-section of parents and teachers from the community?

— Did program personnel such as the home-school coordinator function effectively?

— Were the financial resources, physical facilities, and administrative arrangements satisfactory in terms of achieving the objectives of the program?

— To what degree did the training and development sessions succeed in facilitating parents and teachers in accomplishing their tasks?

— Were teachers and parents able to acquire an understanding of how the program functioned and were they able to implement communications to make it work?

— What were some of the strengths and weaknesses of the program? What aspects of the program were highly successful? Where could the program be improved?

— What steps have been taken to assure continual evaluation and refinement of the program?

There are various modes of developing and implementing parent involvement programs. Many of the references listed at the end of this book include samples of programs used by early childhood centers and/or schools in various locations. The following sources should prove especially useful in acquiring ideas on the development of effective parent involvement programs.

134

1. S. Nedler and O. McAfee. *Working with Parents.* Belmont, CA: Wadsworth Publishing, 1979.

2. K. Swick and E. Duff. *The Parent-Teacher Bond: Relating, Responding, Rewarding.* Dubuque, Iowa: Kendall-Hunt, 1978.

3. I. Gordon and W. Brievogel. *Building Effective Home-School Relationships.* Boston: Allyn and Bacon, 1976.

4. G. Berclay. *Parent Involvement in the Schools.* Washington: National Education Association, 1977.

5. A. Honig. *Parent Involvement in Early Childhood Education.* Washington: National Association for the Education of Young Children, 1981 edition.

Parents and teachers can be effective teaching-learning partners when they establish a program of activities that enhances them and their children. Successful programs are based on advance planning and continuous refinement with each school year. Cooperative planning by parents and teachers and the shared responsibility of putting the plans to work is the key to forming stable and productive parent involvement programs.

CHAPTER FOURTEEN
WAYS TO INVOLVE PARENTS

There are many different ways to involve parents in classroom and school functions. Parents, through their voluntary efforts, can assist the teacher by helping with instructional activities, aid and entire school staff by doing clerical tasks or assist the entire school district through serving on any of a number of special need committees. In the same respect parents can be resource persons for the school staff. Utilization of parent power in the classroom, school or district can be categorized into two forms: assistance tasks and resource tasks.

Assistance Tasks

Teachers and related school personnel are heavily burdened with clerical requirements, classroom management tasks, as well as numerous other classroom-school related type jobs. Parents can and often want to assist school personnel in dealing with these many time consuming jobs. Examples of ways parents may assist and support the classroom teacher are as follows:

1. Parents can help with clerical tasks such as attendance records and monthly reports.

2. Parents can coordinate and organize home room activities.

3. Parents can organize parent-teacher communication activities by helping with the advertising of such events.

4. Parents can help in carrying out field trips and in assisting in class discussions about the trips in the instructional setting.

5. Parents, when properly trained, can work with small groups of children on various instructional activities.

6. Parents can assist teachers in handling individualized educational program records.

7. With proper guidance parents can assist in carrying out instruction in learning centers.

8. Parents make excellent tutors when they have a clear objective to accomplish and the needed training for the subject being taught.

9. Parents are helpful in reaching "difficult parents" and involving them in various home-school programs.

10. Some parents can make teaching aids for use in the classroom.

These are some of the many activities parents can help with at school. The organization and use of parents in school functions is critical to the educational success of children (Berclay, 1977).

In addition to utilizing parents in classroom functions the entire school staff can find many meaningful ways in which to involve parents. Most school personnel would agree that parents can be very helpful by assisting in the accomplishment of the following types of tasks.

1. Main office typing tasks.

2. Organizing and maintaining filing systems.

3. Assisting in organizing parent-teacher-organization events.

4. Managing teacher work rooms so that many clerical jobs are taken care of; releasing the teachers to do their job.

5. Assisting advisory committees in carrying out various school improvement projects.

6. Coordinating many school sponsored events such as picture taking, yearbooks, school dances or parties and many other such programs.

7. Leadership in initiating a school advisory group.

8. Coordinating the development of fund raising projects.

9. Assisting school librarians in managing the library.

10. Assisting in keeping the cafeteria a functional place where children can eat a nutritious meal (Rich, 1971).

Resource Tasks

In any given school the talents and skills of parents are varied and of essential value to the educational program. An examination of some of the parental talent in one school district is revealing of the vast pool of human resources available for use by teachers.

1. Mr. Edwards is a printer. He owns and operates a quick print shop in town. Each year he shows third grade children how to set type, run a simple printing press, and how small books are printed and bound. Each child is allowed to print one sentence and take the final product back to school with them.

2. Mrs. James is an accomplished pianist. For three years now she has voluntarily coordinated the early childhood music program. She spends one day a week working with young children and their music experiences.

3. Mr. Elson is a barber who also has a hobby of studying hair styles existent in American History. He combines his hair styling show

with a presentation on 'family trees' for the elementary school children.

4. Mr. Feltin is now retired. At one time he was a state legislator and has considerable knowledge of the history of the state. He is a resource person for the entire school on the historical and governmental aspects of the state.

5. Mrs. Ralstan is a newspaper editor. She has worked with the teachers in the district on how to use the newspaper as a teaching tool in the classroom. Currently she is working with parents on how to introduce young children to the newspaper at home.

Every community has talented parents that are willing to be resource people to the school. Organizing and involving parents in ways that relate to the school program is an important skill of the teacher. Too often we focus narrowly on a few community helpers only to leave untapped a reservoir of parent skills that can enrich the school experience for everyone (Swick, 1975).

Parent resource programs often emerge from the parent-teacher partnership. For example, one parent-teacher group focused their year long effort on developing such a program in the schools. In organizing a parent resource program the following techniques are suggested as ways of initating and developing a successful project.

1. Enjoin the efforts of parents and teachers who are supportive of the idea of utilizing parents as resource people. This group can serve as the coordinating committee.

2. Using various information gathering techniques find out what skills and talents parents in your community have to contribute to the school.

3. Provide leadership in stimulating parent interest in becoming involved in the school. Let them know they are needed and encourage their participation by rewarding those parents who do get involved.

4. Develop a resource file in which parent skills are included. This file can be up-dated each year and the skills of parents can be correlated with teaching areas and units being offeredn in the instructional program.

5. Provide teachers with periodic in-service educational programs on how to use parents effectively in this resource capacity.

All aspects of the school curriculum can be expanded by utilizing readily available human resources in the form of interested parents and citizens. The concept of parent volunteer programs is receiving renewed emphasis in all schools as economic conditions impinge upon the availability of funds for expansion of personnel. As the idea has gained in credence so the managerial problems of best utilizing parent volunteers have increased.

Organizing A Parent Volunteer Program

Ideally parent volunteer programs should be utilized to enhance the self perception of children, parents, and teachers. By working together these team members will learn the value of cooperation and should emerge as better human beings. The chief goal of parent volunteer programs is to make it possible for the professional educator to give greater attention to the personal and academic needs of the children.

Just as the effective use of parent volunteers can free the teacher to teach, the absence of the team concept on the part of the teacher in the classroom can cause serious problems for the volunteer. It should be remembered that parent-teacher programs are joint ventures and the needs of the parent volunteer must also be acknowledged. Continuous with this supportive relationship, educators should be sensitive to the time demands faced by parents. A one dimensional parent-teacher program will have difficulty becoming a strong and positive force in the school or home learning environment. *The key to success resides in a sensitive, cooperative attitude in both teacher and parent.*

Goals

Parent volunteer programs should be designed with several goals in mind: (1) the enhancement of the parent-teacher relationship, (2) the improvement of the learning environment in the classroom and school, (3) the cooperative, supportive involvement of parents and teachers in various educational tasks, (4) the promotion of positive self concepts in the children, and (5) the development of community understanding and support of the educational program (Feldman, 1975). Specific objectives for volunteer programs will vary according to localized educational needs. While one school may focus on parents as tutors, another school may have broader educational use of parents.

Identifying and Meeting Needs

When individual schools or entire school districts develop parent volunteer programs some form of organization is needed in order to make the program a positive force in the schools. A coordinating team of parents and teachers is needed to determine how parent volunteers will be used, what training is necessary, when and where parents can be most effectively deployed, and how the program is to be continuously assessed and improved.

Different teachers and different schools have varying needs. All schools can use parent volunteers in some capacity. How does a school or district determine how to use parent volunteers? The best way to answer such a question is for parent-teacher groups to examine the needs and resources of the schools.

Teachers are usually the best source of information on the needs facet of the school program. They can identify areas of need where parents can be utilized in the classroom as well as school-wide. Teachers often need help, for example, in managing small group or individualized instruction projects, monitoring the cafeteria, or in managing field trips.

Each school will have unique needs and thus use parent volunteers to meet those needs. In the same respects, the parents in each school will have special talents and skills they can use to meet the needs of their children and teachers. Matching existing 'needs' with available 'parent resources' is a vital part of developing and managing a successful program.

Some schools may find they are in need of personnel to handle assistance tasks such as record keeping, small group supervision, or support work for the school district office. Other schools may already have adequate staff to handle clerical work but desire parents to act as resource people to enhance the instructional climate of the school. In most cases teachers will find it valuable to utilize parents in both assistance and resource roles.

The Importance of Training

The training of parents volunteers to perform specified tasks in the classroom or school is an important component of the program. Parents who are going to be performing semi-instructional tasks need some training in how to conduct themselves in various group situations. They need to be appraised of the school's philosophy of discipline, appropriate ways to encourage and support children. Those parents who plan to assist in the library or media center should be involved in some in-service education sessions on how the library is arranged and how it is operated (Wallat & Goldman, 1979).

Practically all aspects of the educational process involves human relations. Parents and teachers will benefit from educational programs that help them to improve their ability to work with other people. By involving both parents and teachers in joint in-service educational projects their working relationship will have a secure basis upon which to develop.

Parent training programs will vary from simple information sessions to on-going programs of a substantive nature. Those who coordinate parent volunteer programs should examine how parents will be utilized and formulate their training sessions in accordance with the desired skills parents will perform in the school or center.

Some suggestions for conducting parent training sessions are explicated as follows:

1. Identify the various tasks parents are going to be involved with and design training sessions to meet those specific needs.

2. Involve parents in the planning of the training programs and conduct the sessions in places and at times they can attend.

3. Provide a comfortable atmosphere for parents who are involved in training. Select people to conduct the sessions who are able to work effectively with people.

4. Utilize simulated and/or real settings to conduct the training sessions. Time is of the essence in training people and reality based settings help people perceive situations they might otherwise overlook.

5. Provide some type of continuous in-service educational arrangement where parents and teachers can improve their skills and extend their understanding of each other (Kaplan, 1977).

The training and preparation of parents for specific volunteer activities will have much to do with how they may be used effectively in the classroom. For example, the volunteer who has requested to read stories to children in the kindergarten needs to be aware of some of the tecnniques important to make the experience satisfhing for the children. Additional factors to consider in effective use of parent volunteers include the interests of the parents, the needs existent in the school, the working styles of both parents and teachers, the capability of the children to work with paraprofessionals and volunteers, and community attitudes toward the involvement of parents in classroom and school functions (Gilmar & Nelson, 1975).

Assessment of Program Functioning

As with all aspects of the educational process the parent volunteer effort must be continuously assessed and improved. Many times parent volunteer programs tend not to be observed in an evaluative fashion because the professional staff fear that parent feelings will be offended. A parent who spends three days a week working with children on semi-instructional tasks wants to know if his or her efforts are contributing to an improved learning outcome.

Parent volunteer programs can be evaluated in various ways. Individual components of the program can be assessed to see if specified goals are being reached. For example, if volunteers have been assigned to assist with cafeteria supervision to increase the orderliness of behavior, has the behavior of the children improved? Parent volunteer perceptions of their success is important. Conduct some post assessments on how the volunteers saw the program and their involvement in it.

Here are some other examples of how to assess individual components of the parent volunteer program:

142

1. Several parents have been working with children who have reading problems. As a result of this individual work have the children made progress in the reading area?

2. Several parent volunteers have been helping teachers by running off ditto masters, filing student records and handling other tasks in the teacker workroom. Have these parent efforts helped the process of getting these tasks completed for the teacher? Have the teachers used this released time toward improving their instructional efforts?

3. If the school has been utilizing parents as special resource people what observations has the professional staff made of the program? In what ways can the resource program be improved?

4. If parents have been involved in managing the library or assisted in after school special types of programs, has such assistance improved these aspects of the curriculum?

5. Some schools use parents in the supervisory role to assist with field trips, bus travel and large group assembly programs. Have these efforts helped assist the children in these aspects of the program? (Berclay, 1977).

Parent volunteer programs can be a major force in improving the entire school-community setting. When parents and teachers work together in developing, implementing and evaluating a cooperative parent volunteer program they are establishing a relationship of trust necessary to ensure a successful situation for all involved.

CHAPTER FIFTEEN
INVOLVING PARENTS IN DECISION MAKING ROLES

Many educational problems and school procedural issues emerge from a context where decisions are made without parent input and/or support. In an attempt to be efficient school officials often make choices that impact families and fail to involve those constituents in the decision making process. Programs where parental involvement in all facets of the educational process exists report productive outcomes and a teaching-learning environment that influences children in positive modes (Sinclair, 1980). Professionals involved in aiding parents become as effective as possible are finding parental involvement in decision making is critical to long term gains in parent behavior and family well being (Schaefer, 1983).

The Process of Decision Making

Inherent in any learning experience is the "involvement" of the learner in the process of acquiring information and skills as well as internalizing the material learned. Parents are key learners in the child's education and development and thus must be engaged in the school decision making process. *The process of making decisions is continuous and is most effective when it is an intentional effort* — utilizing inputs from various sources and remaining open to change. The most desirable decision making strategies have a built in process for continually refining their efforts (Gardner, 1981). Parent-teacher efforts in the decision making process must be based on the use of intentional, reflective action that is in a state of continuous renewal.

Whether we recognize it or not parents and teachers are making decisions regarding the education of our children. For example, schools that isolate parents from involvement in the child's education are reducing the effectiveness of the instructional program. While individuals may shrink from making decisions, they are making a choice even in their passivity. Joint decisions arrived at through intentional planning efforts and then re-examined in light of new experiences or research are valuable means of improving the learning and development of children. Early childhood educators who use a parent-teacher decision making approach point with pride to gains made by children both academically and socially (Gordon, 1975).

The value of what each member of the human learning team can contribute to the educational process can only be realized when sincere efforts are made to involve everyone in the decision making process.

This "teaming" begins as early as in the birthing process. Many medical professionals are encouraging parents to take on a leadership role in birthing the child — thus establishing a productive parenting style at the outset. Quality daycare and child development centers base their efforts on joint decisions with parents and teachers communicating and working together (Swick, Brown, & Robinson, 1983).

Teaming among parents and teachers requires that individuals become sensitive to each others' perspectives on a variety of issues as well as skilled in basic communication and planning processes. While joint efforts among professionals and parents may lack the efficiency of a factory like management system, there is no better way of assuring that teaching and learning reflect the mutual concerns of members of the learning team (Swick & Duff, 1978).

Goals of Involving Parents in Decision Making

Why is it so important for parents to be involved in the decision making process? The research results on parental participation in educational decisions supports the following points of significance. A major reason for involving parents in this process is to give them more influence over educational policies that affect them and their children. In addition, decision making assures that schools are responsive to the needs of children and families (Nedler & McAfee, 1979).

Schaefer (1983) cites another benefit of parent involvement; namely an increase in internal focus of control over their own lives. This increase in self-management skills can be a powerful influence on the child's home learning. Finally, parents can assure the validity of school policy making in the sense that policies reflect the realities of family situations and concerns regarding the educaiton of children (Sinclair, 1980).

Roles of Parents and Teachers in Decision Making

Schaefer (1983) has explored role conflicts among professionals and parents as related to organizing and implementing effective partnerships. Role confusion and role conflict are synonymous in programs where the planning process has failed to articulate clear guidelines for what is to be accomplished and who is to perform specific foles. A major impediment to functional parent-teacher relationships is role confusion. An inevitable outcome of role confusion is communication problems which further inhibits the teaming process. Just as problem planners need to have clear goals to work toward they also need clear guidelines on how people can carry out the objectives.

Roles of parents and educators in decision making situations vary according to the structure and function each is assigned in this process (Sinclair & Ghory, 1980). There are different early childhood program models as related to parent-professional decision making. For example, the Head Start program requires collaborative decision making among all the teaching-learning partners. It accomplishes this through a policy making council which is comprised of professionals, parents and citizens. This policy council carries out decisions regarding funding, personnel and program operations. Other programs use parents and citizens in an advisory capacity with professionals making major decisions. Yet other programs may use a combination of advisory and policy making boards to carry out program goals. A philosophy of decision making undergirds these structural and functional divergencies. A strong belief in parent-professional collaboration requires that we engage as many individuals from all walks of life in making decisions that influence "our" teaching and learning system (Swick & Duff, 1978).

Encouraging Shared Decision Making

One of the most effective means of encouraging parents to become involved is to foster an atmosphere where their ideas are accepted as valid input into the educational process. School settings that welcome parents to visit and participate in school policy making are forging a major step toward improving the learning system. An inviting atmosphere is characterized by the following behaviors.

1. School adminisrators who actively involve parents in school policy formulation. This may occur through involving parents in establishing discipline guidelines, service on advisory groups or more informally by requesting parental opinions on school issues with periodic questionnaires.

2. Teachers who seek parent support and involvement in all aspects of the educational program. Examples of involvement strategies include those described in this book as well as in the materials developed by organizations such as the Responsive Education Institute, the National Association for the Education of Young Children and the Association for Childhood Education International.*

3. Schools and centers where parents and teachers communicate regularly regarding issues of common concern. See for example: Don Davies, *Schools Where Parents Make A Difference,* 1976.

Schools where parents and children feel a part of the program is their responsibility have successfully created an "inviting" atmosphere. Active

---

*Institute for Responsive Education, 701 Commonwealth Avenue, Boston, MA, 02215; National Association for the Education of Young Children, 1834 Connecticut Ave., N.W., Washington, D.C., 20009; Association for Childhood Education International, 3615 Wisconsin Avenue, N.W., Washington, D.C. 20016.

parent-teacher associations, student involvement in school beautification projects and parent-teacher initiated school improvement activities are some examples of what emerges from collaborative efforts of home and school.

Basic Assumptions of a Parent-Teacher Decision Making Model

Any parent-teacher decision making effort must be based on a set of assumptions that support the concept of human development and learning. More specifically, a firm belief that children (as well as parents and teachers) can alter their behavior for producing positive learning outcomes at home, in school and throughout the community. Sinclair and Ghory (1980) set forth the following as key assumptions for establishing a viable parent-teacher decision making partnership.

1. Academic and social competence of young children results from the successful completion of a broad range of activities both in families and in schools, particularly as these activities are reinforced through the interactions of the child with both parents and teachers.

2. As the persons who are closest to the learner, parents and teachers together should design and implement educational environments that will assist children in their cognitive, affective and physical development in the family and school.

3. The important variables in the family environment that affect academic competence can be altered to support the learning of children.

4. Teachers and administrators can provide leadership from inside the school to develop a curriculum that appropriately combine family and school environments.

Involving Parents In Curriculum Decisions

The education of young children, being a joint venture among parents and educators, needs the attention of every person involved. The concern for what children should learn and how they can be supported in their development is too important to be handled by a few individuals. While early childhood educators have a history which advocates parent involvement in all facets of the child's learning, it is seldom extended to the curriculum development process. Therefore, it is essential to develop curricula that reflect the common concerns of parents, teachers and citizens. Such a process, however, must be based on a thoroughly developed set of experiences in which every member of the team is knowledgeable and insightful about how children learn and how life experiences can be translated into a quality program.

148

Today's parents is more educated than in the past and is expected to exhibit more concern regarding their child's education. Teachers of young children constantly seek the involvement of parents in the schooling process. Thus it is no surprise that parents ask many questions regarding their children's school experiences. Typical questions that parents ask include: Why is there so much play time in the program? What do children learn from manipulating building blocks? Why do you have the children tell so many stories? This parental interest can be used as the stimulus for involving parents in a meaningful study of the center's curriculum.

The involvement of parents in curriculum development requires a recognition on the teacher's part that different parents will have different abilities — thus each parent will make a different sort of contribution to this process. Essential for all parents is a cursory knowledge of how early childhood curriculum is developed and the corresponding base of thinking regarding how children learn. This can be accomplished by involving parents in in-service education programs or through parent-teacher sponsored programs. Parents who elect to join study teams to examine curriculum in detailed ways will need more knowledge of early childhood education than parents who simply want some orientation to the program.

One school district used the theme "What Happens At School" as a starting point for involving as many parents as possible in studying the existing curriculum. A pictorial curriculum guide was developed to feature the main aspects of the school program. A series of articles were published in the local newspaper to complement such a guide. These articles focused on special topics such as "Your Child's Kindergarten," "It's Happening in Second Grade," and "Adults Can Learn Too." A further attempt was made to bring parents in touch with the existing curriculum by having a "Visit School Today and Learn With Your Children" project. Later in the school year, each school in the district held discussion groups where parents and teachers shared their insights, observations and concerns related to what they had learned about the school curriculum.

Based upon these experiences, several parents and teachers organized a curriculum study group. The members of the study team focused their attention on describing specific aspects of the curriculum and on formulating a process whereby other parents and teachers in the district could have input into improving the program. The study group invited teachers to "show and tell" their curriculum wares and to share with the participants ideas for improving the program. The study team then visited classrooms, acquired further input from teachers and set the stage for curriculum improvement.

There are many ways to examine what could be in terms of the educational process. One way is to visit other school districts that have acquired a positive reputation for their programs. One of the benefits of such a process is learning about the problems and prospects of school programs in other communities. Such experiences inevitably involve people in sharing and discussing their ideas about the way children can best learn and develop.

The use of consultants can be yet another mode of exploring the ideal curriculum. In selecting consultants, parent-teacher study groups should consider the experiences of the person, their philosophical orientation, how they plan to use them and how the information provided by the consultants can be recorded for future use. Consultants may be used most effectively when the users have specific objectives for them to accomplish.

Another source of expertise on curriculum development exists within the staff of each school district. These professionals should be utilized as internal consultants in their specialty area. Internal consultants are not only immediately available but are often aware of community situations as they relate to the school. Additional local resource people can be identified as various issues are examined by the study team.

As study teams examine various curriculum areas they should study the literature to see what is working in terms of the research. School leaders can make professional journals available to the team and acquire other materials as needed. The process of exploring an ideal curriculum for young children should always involve parent-teacher teams in asking themselves this question, What is best for the children? The transplanting of a curriculum from one district to another, without considering the unique needs of the local situation, can be disastrous. An ideal learning program never occurs at once. Rather, it evolves through the combined efforts of parents, teachers and children (Frazier, 1976).

Involving The Community Through Advisory Councils

Citizen participation in education is growing each school year. A prominent mode of facilitating citizen participation is the advisory council. Several states, local schools and federally sponsored education programs are utilizing such councils as one way of insuring community involvement (Swick, 1978).

Basic to the effective functioning of advisory councils is an understanding among citizens and educators of what participation is about and how it can be used to foster quality learning settings everywhere in the community. The concept of participatory decision making implies that individuals share and utilize each others' ideas and opinions in arriving at a conclusion to be tested in action situations. Unfortunately the concept of citizen participation is too often treated in a superficial manner by those involved. Suggestions made by parents and citizens need to be incorporated into the process of educational planning (Davies, 1976).

Objectives

A first task of school personnel and lay citizens is that of developing a setting wherein schools and the community can sense their power to shape the educational program (Greenwood, 1977). There is a critical need for specific tasks that councils can perform. Such tasks include development of local school program plans, curriculum evaluation and improvement projects, citizen awareness programs, and other projects that attempt to improve home-school relations.

Organizational Concerns

Councils, like other institutional groups, must be representative of their constituents and must be able to see the effect of their work in the improvement of school programs. Principals have the power and the mechanisms for developing functional advisory councils. As educational leaders, they must be certain that council members are chosen democratically and that they represent all the people in the community. If part of a council membership is appointed, such appointements must be made with the best interests of the community in mind.

Once formed, a council can benefit from an orientation and planning session in which its members can acquire specific information regarding the tasks to be accomplished, meeting times, and the procedures that can be used to make its efforts most productive. Principals can plan these orientation sessions with assistance from school-community co-ordinators and/or local and state school personnel.

Implementation Issues

An advisory council will function most effectively where there are a confortable and centrally-located place for its meetings, an agreed-upon meeting time, planned agenda, and established procedures for the conduct of its meetings. There should be the sincere belief that the council is an important part of the school's operation, or it should not exist. If it is given specific and useful tasks to perform, generally it will perform in an effective manner. Nevertheless, educators must remain aware of problems that have been encountered in the past by school systems. One of these has been the failure of some council members to attend meetings. Mandatory attendance as a requirement for membership has been helpful in increasing participation and action on the part of some councils. In some areas, alternate members have been named to attend meetings when regular members are absent.

Assessment

Every group needs to know how effective its planning and action have been. Therefore, school personnel should understand what has happened in the school or community as a result of the work of a council. The most effective evaluation often is that made by the council. In that process, the use of annual reports can be helpful in identifying specifically what the council has accomplished. For example, the council members may wish to compare the data found in a report with their original objectives.

Councils, when developed and supported in positive ways by principals and other school personnel, provide excellent opportunities for the improvement of school programs. They can be part of curriculum improvement, facilities development, library improvement, and various other school-community tasks related to the development of effective programs for young children.

CHAPTER SIXTEEN
ASSESSING AND IMPROVING PROGRAMS

All aspects of education are open to and benefit from continuous assessment. Parent involvement programs need continual feedback from participants on their relevance to parental needs as well as assessment of program activities. The basic purpose of evaluating a parent involvement program should be to improve the program as effective as possible. Successful parent involvement programs have used various forms of evaluation to continually strengthen themselves. Parent involvement is a significant part of effective educational programs and thus needs continual refinement (Sinclair, 1980).

Various Functions Evaluation Serves

In the past decade, a variety of parent involvement programs and approaches have been proposed as a means of improving the educational system. Unfortunately, many of these initiatives have failed for lack of proper planning, poor use of local resources, and inadequate evaluation procedures. Evaluation and assessment are key elements in forming and later refining programs designed to involve parents in the educational process. At the outset, successful programs must be based on the actual needs of the participants. *Preassessment* of parental perceptions of critical needs is one way of determining a framework for program development. Similar preassessments should be conducted with teachers, citizens and others who will be involved in the program. If preassessment is carried out thoroughly, the program will have a viable basis for development (Berclay, 1977).

Another function of the evaluation process is to *take stock of existing resources* in terms of goals and objectives. For example, if the implementation of parent education seminars is a desired goal, then existing resources can be organized to accomplish this task. Some common questions program planners should ask related to this facet of the assessment process include the following.

1. Do the program objectives reflect the needs identified by parent and teachers during the preassessment?

2. Have parents and teachers examined their "readiness" for participating in collaborative efforts that are an inherent part of parent-teacher partnerships?

3. Have training experiences been designed to facilitate teachers and parents in acquiring the skills, attitudes, and knowledge necessary for meaningful involvement in home-school programs?

4. In designing program activities has care been taken to integrate cultural, social and other community attributes?

5. Have the program activities been organized and scheduled at times and in places convenient for the intended audience?

6. In selecting resource people for programs has care been taken to use people not only skilled in their area of expertise but who are also able to communicate their knowledge to groups who have diverse interests? Additionally, have resource people been prepared for their role in the program.

7. Have parents been consulted on the planned sequence of activities and then informed of each event in advance? Have individual activities been planned to accomodate the needs of parents who have diverse work and family schedules?

8. Has a team approach been used in the program development process? Have local resources been used to enrich the program and to foster closer school-community relations?

By using these planning questions many problems can be avoided. Unfortunately, many programs are planned without some examination of these issues and consequently face difficult problems that could have been dealt with in advance (Sinclair, 1980).

The most often used evaluation function is that of *determining if program activities were effective in meeting the original goals.* For example, many parent involvement programs use an end-of-year evaluation form. These forms usually ask the participants to assess the value of individual events they participated in and to assess the general effectiveness of the program. Such use of evaluation is (or can be) very helpful in determining the success of the program and in planning the program for future years. To be most effective, however, continuous evaluation should be conducted. At the completion of each activity, some form of assessment is necessary to see how the program was received. This can be in the form of a narrative report by the participants or handled on a more informal level using one of the assessment instruments discussed in this chapter. Continuous assessment provides an immediate method for detecting and solving problems which otherwise can impede the program (Swick & Duff, 1978).

Another function of evaluating parent involvement programs is to maintain a quantitative record of the various activities carried out in the program. Keeping records of attendance, for example, provides substantive information on the number of people who participated, tells who they were, describes their interests, and can include information on where they can be reached for later involvement. Quantitative measures of the reactions of participants to the substance of workshops attended and about other home-school interests can be assessed through inventory items. Various inventory forms are discussed and presented in this chapter. This form of evaluation is helpful to those planning future programs and to school personnel who may have need for contacting parents for volunteer efforts or for other school functions. Additionally, the data can be used to inform the public of the kinds of home-school programs available in the community (Swick, Duff, & Hobson, 1981).

An emerging function of evaluating parent involvement programs relates to the effects of such programs on a variety of factors of significance to home and school. For example, various studies have examined the effects of parental involvement on children's school achievement, intellectual quotient, readiness for school, and attendance at school. Those involved in implementing parent education programs have evaluated the programs in terms of effects on the behavior of parents. While still other studies have attempted to find out if there are any effects on the community's attitudes toward the school. Basically what researchers are attempting to do in these evaluation studies is to find out if parent involvement programs are working and what specific effects are impinging on the home-school-community relationship (Sinclair, 1980).

Evaluating Parent Education Programs

Parent education programs are designed to facilitate parental acquisition of skills, knowledges, attitudes and behaviors relative to improving the parenting process. In reviewing parent training efforts, Hanes (1983) identified three areas of focus: knowledge, attitudes and skills. In assessing parent acquisiton of skills observation is an often used assessment tool. Can the parents perform the desired skill? In assessing attitude changes in parents as a result of their involvement in parent education sessions the use of questionnaires, interview forms or anecdotal records are functional assessment modes. While parent gains in information are difficult to assess some parent educators use sociodrama, role playing scenes and group discussions to determine the degree to which participants have acquired a working knowledge of the material presented. The broad implications of parent education are recorded in the social system by specific parent behaviors and citizen sensitivity to the care and nurturing of children and young adults. While these "macro system" effects are not easily assessed, Bronfenbrenner (1979) puts forth an ecological framework for viewing the dynamics of human behavior. For example, increases in child abuse cases would indicate some parents are in need of more support services and increments in maladaptive behavior in children indicate the issue of parenting needs extensive study. Further, as the nature of society changes,

155

parents need information and guidance on how to deal with these social forces.

Parent educators can utilize various procedures to assess program development. Beginning with the major goals of the program and identifying personnel tasks used to accomplish these goals a check list can be devised to focus on program components. For example, are resources adequate to carrying out the program objectives? Is staff training pertinent to enabling people to accomplish their roles in a productive manner? Additional program assessment modes include the use of self study teams, external consultants, and staff brain storming sessions. The major point here is that continual assessment and renewal is essential to having quality parent education programs (Hanes, 1977).

Evaluating Parent-Teacher Decision Making Efforts

The most critical involvement parents and educators undertake is their effort to collaborate on various issues and procedures related to the development of home-school programs. Unfortunately, this joint decision making role is often viewed as a low priority by parents and teachers alike (Schaefer, 1983). The following are some examples of parent-teacher decision making activities: (1) consultation on the child's status in learning and development, (2) joing school improvement efforts, (3) collaborating in resolving home-school conflicts, and (4) continuous communication practices focusing on deepening parent-teacher-child understandings of their roles in the educational process (Schaefer, 1983).

In assesing parent involvement practices as related to parent-teacher success in decision making efforts the following ideas are suggested.

1. Do the program objectives reflect joint planning on the part of parents and teachers?

2. Does the staff want parents involved in joint decision making efforts?

3. Do parents see themselves as significant decision makers in the educational process?

4. What specific program activities are designed to involve parents and teachers in collaborative efforts?

5. Are parent suggestions used to improve the program?

In answering the above questions parent involvement leaders will acquire some insights regarding the focus of their program. Programs where parents are part of the decision making process have a positive influence on how the school program is implemented (Sinclair, 1980).

156

Central to our functioning in learning environments is the continuous validation we receive from those around us. Parents and teachers who sense their value to what happens in home and school learning settings perform at higher success levels than their peers who function without this psychological and physical support (Bronfenbrenner, 1979; Goodlad, 1983). A major goal of parent involvement programs is to develop mutually supportive relationships among parents and teachers. Assessment of program functioning needs to include an examination of parent-teacher support systems.

Parental attitudes and behaviors toward the educational staff have been related to the effectiveness of various educational ecologies. For example: Are parents involved in assisting teachers with school tasks? Do parents see the complex job teachers have and act to support teachers in their efforts? In taking inventory of the school environment do you see evidence of parent support through parent volunteers, parent tutors, and parental initiation of school improvement projects.

Teachers of young children are most effective when they extend their efforts to supporting a total family learning and development approach. Teachers need to assess their involvement with the family learning team. For example: Are teachers sensitive to family schedules in planning conferences and activities where parental attendance is desired? Do teachers invite parents to participate in the school's educational planning efforts? Are school programs designed to support total family learning and development?

Parent-teacher support modes evolve from a relationship in which the needs of each other and the talents each person brings to the endeavor are respected and recognized as vital to the home-school program.

Methods of Evaluating Parent Involvement Programs

There are various methods to use in assessing the effectiveness of parent involvement programs. Evaluation methods should be selected to correspond with the objectives to be assessed and with the functions dealt with in the program. It is important to avoid using one-dimensional evaluation modes. By utilizing a combination of assessment techniques a better view of how the program is functioning can be developed. The following are some examples of methods currently used to evaluate various aspects of parent involvement programs.

Preassessment Inventories

The preassessment inventory is used to gather information from parents and teachers regarding interests and issues they would like to have incorporated in the program. The following are sample items often included in such inventories.

157

1. List in priority the ranking issues and/or topics you see as important for inclusion in our parenting program this year.

_____

_____

_____

2. Please identify times and days of the week which would be most convenient for you to attend the programs offered this year.

Days: _____

_____

Times: _____

_____

3. Do you need child care assistance in order to attend the programs:

Yes _____   No _____

4. Do you have a means of transportation for getting to the programs?

Yes _____   No _____

If yes, would you be willing to drive someone else to the program?

_____

5. How long do you think each program should last?

_____ 1 hour

_____ 1½ hours

_____ 2 hours

6. Would you be willing to call others to let them know of the programs and to encourage them to attend?

Yes _____   No _____

Information gathered from the above inventory items will be useful to the planners in developing an effective program that will have parent support.

158

Feedback Forms

Feedback is essential in determining how effective program events were so that problems can be corrected and future projects improved. One method of doing this assessment is to use a feedback form after each program activity. The following is a sample of such a form.

HAYWOOD PTO FEEDBACK FORM

1. Tonight's meeting was _____

    _____

    _____

2. Our speaker this evening was: a. Excellent
                                   b. Good
                                   c. Average
                                   d. Poor

3. Tonight I learned _____

    _____

    _____

4. In planning the next meeting I would suggest the following:

    a. _____

    b. _____

    c. _____

Through the use of this form the Parent-Teacher-Organization of Haywood School District can plan better meetings and find out how parents reacted to the activities conducted that evening. Some organizations use the feedback time to enlist talent from the parent body. By adding some questions to the form, talented parents and teachers can be enlisted for future programs.

End-of-year-questionnaire

At the end of each school year the parents and teachers should evaluate the entire parent involvement program. The content of the questionnaire should reflect the types of activities which comprised the program and be correlated to the original program goals. The following are sample items from such a questionnaire.

1. The parent involvement activities held this school year were:

    a. very helpful to me as a parent.
    b. somewhat helpful to me as a parent.
    c. not helpful to me as a parent.

2. The parent-teacher conferences held during this school year were:

    a. very helpful
    b. somewhat helpful
    c. not helpful

3. In future years I think the school should have the following kinds of parent involvement activities:

    a. _____

    b. _____

    c. _____

Volunteer Attendance and Assessment Record

Keeping a record of parents and citizens who provide volunteer assistance in the classroom (and in school related activities) provides the basis for assessing how and where parents are being utilized in the school. In addition, teachers can keep track of their reactions to the value each volunteer contributed to the program. A profile of parent involvement activity in the school can be developed from such material. The following is an example of such a record keeping system.

PARENT VOLUNTEER RECORD

Volunteer	*Date*	*Contribution to Program*
Mr. John Shook	3-12-83	Shared fishing hobby. Very useful and enjoyable.
Mrs. Ellen Fitt	3-16-83	Talked with the students about her work at the chemical plant. Informative, but next time I need to ask her to use simple terms.
Ms. Georgia Walk	3-19-83	Allowed us to visit her and the new baby at home. Very good activity.

Home Visitor Rating Form

Home visitor rating forms will vary depending upon the basic function of the program and the specific purpose of the visits. The main purpose of assessing home visits is to provide the parent educator and the parents with some feedback on the usefulness of the activity. Elaborate forms are available for use in this type of assessment (Morrison, 1978). Reality, however, usually dictates the need for an efficient and short form that can provide essential feedback without impinging on the work schedule of the visitor.

HOME VISIT FORM

Person Visited	*Date*	*Purpose and Value*
Tom Wick Family	1-16-83	Discuss John's behavior at school. Parents were defensive and very uneasy during the entire visit.
Sue Frank	1-28-83	Share child development materials that can be used at home. Went very well and Mrs. Frank is highly motivated to use the materials.

Anecdotal Records of Group Seminars

Many parent education programs are utilizing small study groups to discuss various parenting skills, trends and issues. One method of assessing the value of such group meetings is by having a recorder keep notes on the contents of the meetings. Later, the notes can be synthesized into a document that keys on the major topics discussed. This will provide continuity to the meetings and provide the leaders with insights into the major concerns of the parents. Emerging from these study groups can be more formalized parent education/training sessions on the actual needs of the parents.

Conference Evaluation Form

Parent-teacher conferences have become one of the most commonly used forms of communication in early childhood programs. The following is one form used to assess such conferences.

PARENT-TEACHER CONFERENCE EVALUATION

1. Purpose:

2. Parents attending the conference:

3. Date:

4. Topics Discussed:

5. Proposed Follow-up:

6. Comments and suggestions:

Lending Library Usage Record

One of the more promising practices in early childhood education is the use of home lending libraries. Assessment of the value of these center-based practices has been positive. The following usage form is one way of determining whether the lending library is of value to parents and children.

BELTON CENTER LENDING LIBRARY
Usage Record

Person	Item Borrowed	Return Date
1. Edward's Family	Picture Kit	3-12-84
2.		
3.		
4.		

In addition to keeping track of usage, many centers conduct an assessment of the value of the items in their library and request parents to suggest new items for inclusion in next years' edition (Nedler and McAfee, 1979).

Home Support Inventory

The involvement of parents with their children at home has been shown to be positively related to children's school achievement (Swick, Brown, & Watson 1983). The *Home Support Inventory,* originally developed by Paul (1975), contains items which relate to parental involvement within the home setting. It asks parents to respond to questions regarding their direct and active involvement with their children. Data from the inventory can be used to determine the level of support a child has within the home learning environment. The inventory can be used to assess the effects of parent involvement programs on parent behaviors with their children at home and in school.

Neighborhood Support Inventory

A recent research finding that parents who live in highly supportive neighborhoods are more effective at parenting than parents who lack such a support system has lead many educators to look beyond the home and school for success indicators (Sinclair, 1980). The *Neighborhood Support Inventory* (Brown, 1978), aims to provide information on how parents perceive their surroundings. For example, do parents feel comfortable in asking their neighbors for help? Do they interact with their neighbors in social and work settings. Inactive and nonsupportive neighborhoods are likely to negatively influence parent-teacher involvement efforts. Information generated from the inventory can help schools and families better understand their community situations and lay the foundation for solving problems that are beyond their immediate relationship. An active parent involvement program may lead the way toward revitalizing neighborhood support.

Assessing Program Effects on Children

What are the effects of parental involvement on the children? This is a question being asked by early childhood educators, parents, and citizens. One objective of most programs is to improve the school performance of children. There have been various studies showing a relationship does exist between parent involvement and school success (Lazar, 1976; Swick, 1979; Sinclair, 1980). Methods used to accomplish this type of assessment include standardized tests, readiness tests, developmental assessment instruments and observation techniques. Usually the performance of children is assessed and then related to some facet of parent involvement. Through this process it is possible to determine how

163

effective such programs are in accomplishing this function. In addition, the findings of such studies can be used to show parents the significance of their role and to encourage school personnel to pursue the development of quality educational programs with the family as the foundation.

Guidelines For Evaluating Parent Involvement Programs

A parent involvement program can be improved through continuous assessment. Through the use of positive evaluation approaches, feedback can be acquired relative to the effectiveness of the different program components. Future parent-teacher programs can be developed more effectively when people have voiced their ideas on what was useful and what needs to be improved (Berclay, 1977).

People who have worked diligently and on a voluntary basis are eager for some reward in the form of program results. Thus evaluation should be conducted in a positive manner and based upon the assumption that mistakes are part of the human makeup. Programs that are based on productive relationships are usually improved by first pointing to the accomplishments and then identifying areas that can be improved during the next school year (Swick & Duff, 1978).

An important consideration in conducting the evaluation process is to constantly examine the original goals and objectives of the program. Evaluative sessions that focus on gossip and personal feuds are of no value and have no place in any aspect of the parent-teacher relationship. The major reason for having activities that bring parents and teachers together is to create a trusting relationship that is used to enhance the lives of the children in that community.

Program coordinators can assess the overall effectiveness of their efforts by asking and discussing questions such as the following.

1. What was the original purpose of the program? Have the program activities focused on attaining these goals?

2. Have the various programs, activities and projects been successful? How many people have participated in the programs? What were the reactions to the activities presented?

3. Have the various activities been supportive of the family and the school?

4. Did the program, as it was implemented, reflect the input of parents and teachers in the community?

5. Was there a good mixture of the kinds of people and activities offered?

These and other questions, as examined and discussed by parent involvement leaders, can provide an excellent means of self-study (Hanes, 1977). Program improvements result when people use a variety of evaluation techniques in a constructive manner.

CHAPTER SEVENTEEN
A SUPPORT SYSTEM DESIGN FOR
PARENTS OF LEARNING DISABLED CHILDREN

The involvement of parents in the educational process has been advocated by most educators as a major way to improve the entire educational process. (Swick & Duff, 1978). Research has validated the significance of parent participation in the child's educational endeavor. A series of investigations (Gordon, 1975; Lazar, 1976; Watson, Brown, & Swick, 1983) have shown that parents, teachers, and children benefit from the active participation of parents and citizens in the educational process. Further, it has been hypothesized that parents who have a supportive environment in which to parent, perform more effectively than parents who perceive their support level as low or nonexistent. (Bronfenbrenner, 1979; White, 1979) While all parents can benefit from high support settings, parents who have unique situations seem to benefit the most — probably because they have the greatest need. (Heatherington, 1979) Parents of learning disabled children confront a special parenting situation and can benefit from a supportive stance by school personnel. (Zigler & Muenchow, 1979)

The purpose of this chapter, then is to provide educators working with parents of learning disabled children with a process for organizing and implementing a support system/involvement program for parents. Specific attention is given to the sources of the objectives for such a program; including some methods of assessing parental needs and designing program components that will address those needs. Additional sections of the design focus on strategies for implementation of the program such as how to conduct group sessions and the role of home visits in supporting parental efforts. Finally, attention is given to formal and informal modes of assessing the program's effectiveness in terms of being a support system to the parents. While the material presented focuses on needs of parents of LD children, many of the planning processes and support system components can be integrated into programs for meeting the needs of parents of all special needs children.

Sources of Objectives

The objectives for having a support program for parents of learning disabled children are derived from the needs which prompt its initiation. Most parents of LD children experience needs in the four areas of: information relative to learning disabilities in general and specifics as related to

167

their child; skills for dealing with the LD child in a positive manner; a support system in which they can function effectively; and the involvement of an informed citizenry in making the community a functional place for LD children.

Need Information Relation To Learning Disabled Children. Many parents of LD children lack information regarding proper expectations of their children's behavior. For example, a common misnomer is that LD children are slow learners. While LD children learn in different modes and process information differently, they are no slower than other children in terms of acquiring concepts and information. A major objective of parent support programs must be to educate parents of LD children about characteristics of various learning disabilities with specific data regarding their child's problem. In formulating parent education programs, for example, you will want to assess two types of information need: general awareness needs regarding accurate information relative to characteristics of learning disabled children, and information regarding specific disabilities as revealed through parent feedback on an assessment form.

Need Skills For Providing Child With Education And Guidance. Parents of LD children, like other parents, need information on how to carry out the parenting role. Additionally, parents of LD children need information regarding how to receive and then manage various child behaviors that are implicit in his disability. For example, in the case of the normal child the parent can simply carry out their educational role with minor adjustments in the ecology. However, in the case of the LD child, parents will need to make various intervention efforts (depending upon the actual disability) regarding learning materials and processes. A clear objective of a program that hopes to assist parents in coping with their LD child must be to provide them with needed skills for educating and guiding that child. Generic parent education skills sessions might focus on child development, communication skills, basic nutrition and family management techniques. Specialized skills in working with children on perceptual deficits, motor compartments, visual and/or hearing skills and a variety of other specific tasks will become parent education content as parental needs are assessed.

Need Support System For Carrying Out Parental Role Effectively. In addition to handling the normal family operations, parents of LD children face unique situations which extend their efforts beyond the normal daily routine. Guilt over the child's disability as well as frustrations confronted in trying to help the child are just two examples of issues parents have to confront. The need for support systems of parents is critical to enabling them to carry out their role. By providing a flexible and responsive school environment that involves parents in all parts of the child's educational and social development we can meet the significant goal of supporting parents in their efforts to establish a viable relationship with the LD child. Such support will strengthen the microsystem of the family and establish a workable relationship in the mesosystem of the home and school. (Bronfenbrenner, 1979) Support needs will range from simply needing a source of information to requests for family counseling services. As parents are expected to perform an ever infreasing number of tasks, the burnout rate among parents (especially among parents of special needs children) is on the increase. Attention to "parent needs" in terms of providing them with supportive programs can go a long way toward increasing their effectiveness — qualitatively and quantitatively.

Need An Informed And Active Citizenry To Assist In Educating The Child. Misinformation and a lack of knowledge regarding the learning disabilities syndrome plagues our citizenty in general. Parents need the support of every citizen to do the job of helping children maximize their potential in communities that are accepting of varying learning modes and styles. A focal point of support programs for parents of LD children would be the involvement of the community at large toward receiving and responding to the needs of such families. A team approach (home-school-community) is critical to having successful LD children. The cultivation of positive expectations on the part of all citizens can result in a very desirable manifestation of the self-fulfilling prophecy. (Rosenthal & Jacobsen, 1968)

A vital part of this design to formulate a supportive process for parents is the involvement of these parents in articulating the goals and objectives of the support program. Clearly, through parental participation is the decision-making arena, specific objectives regarding their needs will emerge to give each program a unique focus. Finally, as these objectives evolve the parents will form new mesosystem relationships (with neighbors, helping professionals and relatives) as a part of a life style to deal effectively with the challenges of raising an LD child.

Strategies For Implementing The Support Program

Various parent involvement and support strategies have been used to activate home-school ties that in turn have a positive effect on the child's learning and development. (Swick & Duff, 1978) Selecting strategies is critical to the success of the program. Given the nature of our objectives (information, support and awareness) and the need to meet both group and individual needs of the parents, the following process is proposed as most likely to correspond with the intent of this design. Naturally, you will want to adapt these strategies to the unique capacities of the parents you are working with.

Group Strategies. The initial part of the support process will focus on awareness level activities necessarily designed (but not confined) to reach the entire population. A steering committee (comprised of teachers, parents and hopefully citizens) will accomplish two tasks: (1) conduct some form of needs assessment to gather general information on those parents interested in participating in the program, and (2) carry out an awareness campaign designed to inform people of the general nature of learning disabilities and to advertise the formation of a program aimed to support families of LD children. Local media resources and individual contacts through schools, churches and civic groups can be used to assure that massive coverage of the community is accomplished.

Large group meetings at each school in the community will follow the awareness effort. By confining these initial meetings to local schools, hopefully parents and citizens will feel "invited" to attend and participate. The objectives of these meetings will be to inform people of the nature of learning disabilities, a desire to organize a support system to enhance the child's chances of being a success in school and life, and to organize a "core group" of people to extend the design to meet identified needs of parents who elect to participate. The following is an example of how such a group meeting could be carried out.

The steering committee will welcome participants and make introductions of appropriate people. The functions of this initial meeting will be explained. Then an appropriate LD staff member will give a brief presentation focusing upon clarification of the concept of LD and the unique ways in which the syndromes operate in the individual child. Stressed will be the possibilities for success with the learning disabled and the ways parents and teachers can colloborate to provide maximum benefit to students with various learning disabilities. Following the presentation parents will be encouraged to ask questions about unique aspects of their own child and how these might be better comprehended. Hopefully, this discussion will give parents some immediate feedback on their concerns and thus motivate further participation in the program on their part. Following this presentation/discussion, a representative of the steering committee will explain other facets of the support program such as home visits, parent education programs, and individualized parent-teacher contacts. Toward the end of this initial session, each steering committee member will work with "small groups" of parents to answer their questions and to lay the groundwork for further extension of the program design. Names of definitely-interested parents will be recorded and a date set for a membership meeting at which the group would become more self-governing; utilizing the LD staff as consultants having some directive influence until organization processes are stabilized.

A natural extension of the above meeting is the use of small group meetings for participant designed parent education programs and for purposes of helping parents strengthen mesosystem linkages (parent-to-parent support activities) which will, in turn, strengthen their microsystem relationshps. Assessment of parent desired educational sessions can be accomplished through the use of a simple questionnaire. Parent-support needs can be identified in small, confidential group discussions. These "support group discussions" usually emerge as the parents feel secure in their feelings about each other and accepted within the framework of the program intent. LD staff acceptance, nurturance, and implementation of parental involvement is the key to making this effort successful. Each group meeting should have a defined purpose, method for functioning, and a moderator who established a friendly but task orientation in the group's deliberations.

Individualized Strategies. While group sessions can be an efficient way of meeting common needs of parents, individualized approaches enable helping professionals to identify and resolve specific concerns unique to a particular family. Parent-teacher conferences are an integral part of this support design. These conferences should be designed to accomplish the following: (1) establish a working relationship between parent and teacher/support staff; (2) develop an individualized educational plan (required under Public Law 91-142) with the parents continual involvement and feedback; (3) provide a forum for privately discussing all problems a particular family faces and offer strategies peculiar to each situation; and (4) encourage and — where appropriate — provide direction from parents in the development of a continuous and viable support system.

The home visitation process is another mode of individualizing parent-teacher contacts. Home visits can be used to contact parents unable to attend conferences at school or used to extend the relationship formed during the school-based conference. In extending contacts to the home some natural advantages emerge to help strengthen the parents' role in educating and guiding their learning disabled child. For example, a home visit provides LD teachers with a chance to share with parents how they (the parents) can use the home as a learning situation. Specific learning activities can be demonstrated using home items as materials or home situations as examples. Parents, of course, have an opportunity to share feelings in their context and have access to concrete examples to show or describe to teachers. Finally, and of critical value, is the mutual sharing between parent and teacher that can best occur in the informal setting of the home.

Individualization of parental involvement is necessary for having a truly effective design. Given the unique work schedules of parents, their varying needs and personalities, as well as variance in their motivation for being involved, the use of individual contacts is paramount for having a meaningful program. Additional modes of involving parents in individual activities are identified as follows:

1. Classroom visitations by parents thus giving them a view of strategies being used to help their child.

2. Involvement of parents in tutoring programs where they can assist their child or other children in learning situations.

3. Referral of parents to appropriate counseling sources for special problems they may be having in the family. Follow up to see that some constructive resolution of the problem has taken place is necessary on the part of the teacher.

4. Involvement of parents in the LD organizational structure so they can extend and share their concerns and skills with others.

5. Encouraging interested parents to further their knowledge of learning disabilities through parent education or where appropriate through university courses on selected topics.

Finally, parent-teacher contracts — if used within a positive framework — can enable both teacher and parent to direct their efforts toward specific tasks of obvious concern to home and school. Such contracts help to formalize our involvement and increase the likelihood of our following through on desired objectives. Contracts have been used to assure parental time is allocated to helping the child and for purposes of guiding parents in the type of involvement they have with the child.

Potential For Further Development of This Support System Design

The development of support systems is a continuous process which reaches the potential of the people involved. The sensitivity of the participants to their needs and to finding out how the human potential of their children can be maximized along with acquiring needed supports to accomplish this process are critical to the success of this design. The tendency to be enveloped in the status quo of surrounding systems can impede the realization of any support program. While dealing with existing needs is certainly a starting point for the organization, an attempt to reach beyond the current status of the situation must be a part of the program. Unfortunately, this growth potential is often left untapped and a settling for the immediate needs filling process is accepted.

Some strategies for extending this support system design include: (1) involving parents with macrosystem groups (i.e.: national professional associations dealing with learning disabilities) to increase their awareness of problems and potential solutions to LD issues; (2) extending your parent group to contacts with other such groups for purposes of information exchange and the development of community wide support activities; (3) incorporating a developmental view of the parent-child relationship in terms of shaping program content to meet their changing needs; and (4) expanding the design to training parent-members to become leaders in the community regarding issues related to LD children.

Involving Parents in Macrosystem Groups. Bronfenbrenner (1979) describes the macrosystem as the place where policy is made affecting human functioning at every level of the society. In many cases people deal only with local issues and needs. Utilizing local potential to influence

172

policy making at the national and international levels is critical to creating a truly effective support system for parents of LD children. This might be initiated through the involvement of parents in national LD associations and then extended to their active participation in congressional hearings and service on state advisory groups. As parents build confidence at the local leadership level, they can and should be nurtured toward more global participation. Once this has been actualized a continual flow of ideas is assured between micro, meso, and macro systems. This will increase the positive influence of society on dealing with LD children and their families.

Extending Support System To Include Other Groups. The tendency toward closure must be avoided if support group functioning is to be fully actualized. Groups that fail to build bridges to other community groups usually deteriorate and rarely accomplish their objectives. The formation of partnerships with other LD parent groups assures some contact with others who have similar needs and usually prompts a sharing of resources and the development of new support contacts for members of both groups. Other external group contacts can occur through liaisons being appointed to PTA's, civic groups, teacher associations, and local church federations. This involvement will certainly increase the LD group's impact on meeting their needs through acquisition of more support resources. Additionally, these external relationships will serve to educate others regarding the needs of LD children.

Incorporating A Developmental View of Human Relations In The Design. The needs which dictate the substance of parent support programs change as the family grows and develops and as parent-child relationships enter new developmental stages. For example, with young children, parents may need more helping type supports such as day care or homemaker services, while in dealing with adolescents they may need more counseling type services. As parents master initial skills in helping their LD child deal with his disability, they are ready, then, to advance to learning about enriching their relationship with the child. Ecological influences such as the child's teacher or changing community attitudes toward LD children influence parental need-shifts and alter their stance toward life. The spiral of human development as influenced by events in the social ecology of the family must be integrated into planning useful support activities. (Erikson, 1982)

Training Parents To Become LD Leaders In Their Communities. The ultimate success of any support design is the development of group leaders in which some parents become the community organizers and cultural change agents. Ira Gordon (1975) used this concept in training parents to train other parents in basic parenting skills. As parents of LD children acquire competence in becoming self-managers of their environment, they usually have reached a point where they can foster similar competencies in others. Effective support systems depend on a cycle of capable people continually emerging to handle the tasks of leadership. This approach to the continual renewal of support programs for parents has a positive effect on everyone. Parents acquire a new view of themselves and the community benefits from having a talent pool to use in its' development as a social system.

Assessing The Effectiveness Of Parent Support Programs

The improvement of the *quality* of human functioning is the ultimate purpose of parent support program and should serve as the guide in determining the outcome of your design. For example, have parents of learning disabled children increased their knowledge of the child's learning situation? Have the parents developed skills for receiving and then guiding various behaviors elicited by the child? Has the home-school-community system improved its ability to function as a support network for LD children? These and similar questions will elicit responses pertinent to making judgments about program functioning. Data relative to answering these questions can be gathered in various ways; use of questionnaires, interviews, and parent feedback forms to name a few. Observation of how LD children are functioning and using their talents is the best assessment made available because it is the observable changes in the quality of human relationships that determine the impact of the design.

CHAPTER EIGHTEEN
THE PARENT-TEACHER COMMUNICATION PROCESS

The key to developing an effective parent-teacher relationship revolves around the communication process. Parents and teachers must communicate with each other about various mutual concerns regarding the child. The communications process is built upon the premise that people want to convey their ideas and feelings and are capable of listening to the ideas of people. Parents and teachers should be the most effective communicators in our society. Communications is a process by which people formulate their plans for either acting in concert toward common goals, achieving individual aspirations or attempting to modify the behaviors of other people (Coletta, 1977).

Communication is the Key

There are people we point to as good communicators. "Mrs. Speltry is able to get us together, she has that talent!" It is Mrs. Speltry's entire style of relating to people that enables her to communicate with them. She makes herself available to people by being there whenever the need arises. When she is with people they sense her concern and know she will listen and then act in the best interests of everyone. People know they can trust Mrs. Speltry as she does not betray people by breaking their confidential relationship with her. She is known as a person who looks for the positive aspect of any situation no matter how serious it may be. How did people come to believe in Mrs. Speltry? They saw their children grow and learn under her guidance. "She treats each child in a special way," says one parent. "I used to feel uncomfortable around teachers until I met Mrs. Speltry," says another parent.

Very few people reach the stage of maturity and growth that Mrs. Speltry has reached. Yet every person (teacher and parent) can attempt to use positive modes of communicating with others. Every teacher can search out the best in the children and parents they work with. Forming effective parent-teacher relationships takes time and much effort in terms of on-going contracts and sincere responsiveness on the part of both parties. Communication is the key in this relationship forming process. Effective communicators understand that initial parent contacts provide a chance for "getting to know each other" and continuous contacts help strengthen this partnership effort. While any communication with parents seems worthy, planned and meaningful contacts are of most value. Continuous parent-teacher communication enables us to orient parents to new programs, learn from parents their perceptions of children, solve (or prevent) problems together and to discuss the child's progress and to organize strategies for use in improving the classroom setting.

The lack of positive and productive parent-teacher relationships is a major cause of parent-child-teacher related problems. For example, studies of exemplary early childhood programs indicates that children of involved parents (parents who are in constant touch with the center staff) performed better during their early years and internalized these successful habits throughout their school experience (Lazar, 1976). School practitioners also report that "parent involvement" increases the effectiveness level of the child in school and has been positively correlated with regular school attendance, completion of homework assignments, and overall high quality performance of children in school (Sinclair, 1980). The lack of parental linkages to their children's teacher has been related to truancy, delinquency and academic failure.

Some Communication Guidelines

Early childhood educators spend a majority of their working time communicating with people. A series of guidelines are presented here for use in making teacher communications with parents, children, peers and others the most fruitful venture possible.

Effective communication begins with each of us as we attempt to relate to others. Begin your preparation by answering the following questions.

1. Do I express myself clearly and in a nonthreatening manner?

2. When communicating with others do I allow time for others to express their concerns?

3. Am I a good listener? Do I actively respond to inquiries of others or am I closed to new ideas?

4. In communicating with me do others feel comfortable with me?

5. Do I prepare myself for intentional communication with others or do I take a reactive, passive stance most of the time?

6. When communicating with others do I focus on strengths and deal with weaknesses in a positive fashion?

7. Am I "personal" in my contacts with others such as using their name and relating to their personal concerns?

8. When critiquing another's behavior or work do I offer suggestions on how he can improve?

9. Do I avoid stereotyping people and deal with them in individual modes?

10. Have I refined my communication skills by examining materials on the topic and/or attending inservice sessions related to communicating effectively with parents (Swick, Hobson, and Duff, 1981, pp. 72–74).

While each of us must recognize our weaknesses the above questions should serve to help us focus on how we can be more effective in working with parents and children. As "we communicate with each other we need to recognize that our environment also influences our interactions. Generally speaking a pleasant and inviting setting promotes productive parent-teacher communication. For example, a classroom with children's work on display invites parent questions and clearly communicates to the parents the sincerity of the teacher. Further, our non-verbal behavior (gestures, eye contact, etc.) gives us away. Extreme distance of visually focusing on activity beyond the "communication lines" discourages parents from becoming involved in the process. Effective communicators discipline themselves to self-study these guidelines and use them as steps to continually reach for better relationships with parents.

Key Behaviors for Effective Communication

What happens between parents and teachers (or does not happen) that so often causes parent-teacher relationships to deteriorate or worse dissolve? An examination of some parent-teacher contacts will help us to identify some of the problems.

Telephone Conversation.

Mrs. Edwards: "Mrs. Juniper I really don't understand why you are having Bobby color a lot of circles. He already knows his colors."

Mrs. Juniper: "Mrs. Edwards I use the district kindergarten guide and that is what I'm supposed to teach. You should talk with the Director of Curriculum. I'm doing my job."

A Conference.

Mr. Hall teaches first grade and has his desk organized today for conferences with the parents. He has his desk situated so he is behind it and a chair in front of it for parents to sit on during the conferences. Mrs. Palmer has just arrived. Each conference is scheduled on a ten minute interval time pattern.

Mr. Hall: "Mrs. Palmer just sit here! Sorry that you are late. As you know we must keep right on time. Now let

>me tell you that James is not doing well at all. He falls asleep a great deal and never completes his work on time. Now he's not a bad boy, he is just not getting on with it. His reading and math scores are poor. He just doesn't seem to be ready for first grade. Or maybe something is wrong at home! (with an intense look at Mrs. Palmer) Is there something at home, Mrs. Palmer?"

Mrs. Palmer: "Yes, Jimmy's father and I just recently separated."

Mr. Hall: "Oh! I see, well I suggest you work more with Jimmy, he needs it. Any questions that you have Mrs. Palmer?"

Mrs. Palmer: "No."

These two parent-teacher communication situations happen more often than any of us would like to think. Not all teachers or childcare professionals behave in such a manner. Yet, no helping professional should ever behave this way. When a parent such as Mrs. Edwards initiates contact with teachers about some aspect of the early childhood program we should welcome her interest and concern. When you conduct a conference be more personable then Mr. Hall was with Mrs. Palmer. Never "hide" behind a desk but provide an open space where you allow the parent some accessibility to you. There are four basic communication behaviors that neither Mrs. Juniper nor Mr. Hall practiced. These communication behaviors are: *approachability, sensitivity, flexibility,* and *dependability.* Applying these four behaviors to the parent-teacher communications process is the key to making such interchanges successful for parents and teachers (Swick and Duff, 1978).

The approachable person is an individual with whom people feel comfortable. Mr. Hall could have been approachable in his behavior by setting the stage so Mrs. Palmer could feel she was with a teacher that cared and was genuine in his concern for her child. For example, Mr. Hall could have done the following:

Mr. Hall: "Hi, Mrs. Palmer!" How are you today? I really appreciate your taking time to visit with me today. Would you like a cup of coffee?"

Mrs. Palmer: "Yes, thank you. The classroom looks so nice. Oh, may I have a doughnut, too?"

Mr. Hall: "Yes, please have one and I want to show you the bulletin board that Jimmy helped to make."

Mrs. Palmer: "The children made this? It is really nice!"

In this way Mr. Hall could have set the stage by allowing Mrs. Palmer to relax, interact and observe the surroundings in which the conference was to take place. By having some refreshments available and some work the children have developed on display Mr. Hall could have exhibited a genuine and positive concern for Jimmy — which should be the focus of the conference. An inviting setting — where parent and teacher are able to perceive themselves as wanted — is the basis for then developing communications essential for helping each other in efforts to assist the child in development and learning (Purkey and Novak, 1984).

Sensitivity is necessary for making parent-teacher relationships meaningful. The sensitive person communicates a desire to understand the other person in positive ways in both their verbal and non-verbal behaviors. Mr. Hall, instead of talking at Mrs. Palmer about her home life could have shown more of a positive concern for her life by approaching the situation in a way such as the following:

Mr. Hall: "Mrs. Palmer I want to tell you how delighted I an to have Jimmy in the classroom. He gets along well with the other children and is a very well behaved child."

Mrs. Palmer: "That is so good to know as I have been concerned about Jimmy. He hasn't been sleeping well at night. How is he doing in his school work?"

Mr. Hall: "Well there is nothing to be alarmed about but he is having some difficulty in reading and math but has done very well in social studies. I must say I have been concerned that Jimmy seems very withdrawn lately and doesn't seem to care about school as he did earlier in the year. Is it something I might have done? Sometimes I get very busy Mrs. Palmer and may have done some little thing to hurt Jim."

Mrs. Palmer: "No, I don't think it is you at all Mr. Hall. In fact Jimmy really likes you. I should tell you that Mr. Palmer and I recently separated and it has been difficult for all of us."

This approach to the conference by Mr. Hall indicates he is concerned about Jimmy and the family in a constructive fashion. The fact that Mr. Hall points out positive aspects of Jimmy's behavior and is willing to entertain the possibility that he (Mr. Hall) may be a source of the problem

179

indicates to Mrs. Palmer that she is dealing with a sensitive person. The emergent portrayal of the family situation is freely given by Mrs. Palmer because Mr. Hall has shown that he truly would like to see Jimmy doing better in his school work. Mr. Hall, in this scenario, portrays the "active listener" that is essential to gaining the confidence of a parent such as Mrs. Palmer. With a communication network established he can now offer suggestions that may help advance the entire family's situation.

Flexibility is like a security valve in the communications process. Parents and teachers, like all human beings, want to have options so they can find room to grow, change and direct their motivations toward constructive outcomes. Parents and teachers need to develop flexible attitudes and behaviors as they communicate with each other. Teachers, as skilled childcare workers, will have to take the lead in helping this component of the parent-teacher communications process. For example, when Mrs. Edwards called Mrs. Juniper about the reason why she was teaching Bob the color scheme she (Mrs. Juniper) could have responded as follows:

Mrs. Juniper: "Mrs. Edwards I'm sorry to hear you're upset. I went through the colors at the beginning of the year and none of the children knew them. But I must admit the children were still getting used to school and maybe many of them did know their colors. I'm glad you called! Why don't you stop by some afternoon or I'll be happy to visit you as I really do want to make sure I am doing my best for Bob and the rest of the children."

Mrs. Edwards: "Why thank you, I certainly will visit and I didn't mean to sound so upset. I was just, well a little concerned about Bob."

The response by Mrs. Juniper to Mrs. Edwards inquiry indicated a desire on Mrs. Juniper's part to look at the situation, consider alternatives and find a meaningful solution to the problem. She was open to looking at the situation and thus Mrs. Edwards was too.

Dependability is the bridge between parents and teachers as they develop long term, trusting relationships. Teachers who develop an image inthe community that they can be counted on usually have productive relationships with parents. Mr. Welton who has taught for eight years in Ridgeville community schools is such a teacher. Recently one of the children's fathers called Mr. Welton and expressed concern that his son in the seventh grade was behaving funny, like he was on a sedative or something. Would Mr. Welton keep an eye on his son?

Mr. Welton: "Sure Mr. Ralston. It may be that your son is just going through one of the valleys of pre-adolescence but I'll keep an eye on the situation. I'll get back in touch with you."

Mr. Welton followed through on his promise and a week or so later called Mr. Ralston to tell him there was no problem. "Ed seems to be fine and I've got him involved in a new science project which he seems to really enjoy." Following through on a promise (as Mr. Welton did) is one of the most powerful communication skills we have for building continuous and substantive relationships with parents. It is a non-verbal, active-listening role that says to parents that we are reliable, sincere and secure people (Swick, Hobson, and Duff, 1979).

Mr. Welton has done this type of active communication with parents and children over years. He has been active in starting youth programs, served as a member of the child abuse council, and also has been active in helping delinquent children with their problems. He has been a steady, approachable, and dependable person and the parents trust his word.

In all aspects of parent involvement *communication is the key to bringing about a positive home-school relationship.* Sensitive, flexible, approachable and dependable teachers are usually effective with parents because they are open to the parental perspective, desire parent involvement and want to work wtih parents to improve the educational process.

Non-Verbal Communication is Important

Daniel Stern (1977) notes that initial mother-infant communications are non-verbal. Yet it is during this period of "relationship forming" that both mother an infant form the basis for later verbal interactions. The mother is the primary organizer of the environment in which she and the infant learn and develop a relationship. Of course, the mother's behavior is influenced by those significant to her (husband, relatives, friends, etc.). Given a basically secure setting mother and infant (and in many cases the father) develops a "silent rhythmiticity" to their lives and mutual interactions (Stern, 1977). In other cases, however, mother and infant fail to thrive and develop silent but powerful attachments to each other. The non-verbal communication is usually highly stressful in such cases.

A similar process seems to occur in parent-teacher communication. The "silent world" of the teacher (or the parent) may tell more than her spoken messages. The non-verbal or silent communication aspect of relationship building has been largely neglected in the education of human services professionals. Yet, research indicates teacher expectations of others are formed as a result of many interactive forces – of which a large number are non-verbal (Hall, 1959). For example, we tend to value those people we see as capable and sincere while we interact less with those we view as deficient in human capacities. Our awareness of non-verbal communication skill can improve our ability to use the "silent world of interaction" as a force for strengthening not destroying relationships with parents and children.

There are several non-verbal components to our communication world. Consider, for example the impact of the *physical environment* on parent-teacher communication. A cluttered and/or dismal room tends to inhibit the free flow of communication among people. Overcrowding influences human behavior in negative ways and disorder seems to interfere with normal communications. A pleasant, well organized and physically attractive environment provides a setting where parent-teacher communication can take place in a positive manner. Displaying children's work, sharing class projects and having a neat and orderly classroom are essential to establishing an "inviting climate" for conducting conferences or other parent-teacher activities (Sunderlin, 1976).

The teacher's physical appearance is another "silent" factor that influences our communication effectiveness. An unkempt teacher gives signals of disorder and may cause the parent to focus on their personal appearance more than what is said during their communications. Proper dress and appearance are usually equated with "personal effectiveness" on the part of most people. The physical and psychological environment of the classroom and the physical appearance of the teacher establish the basis for positive or negative communications with parents. The teacher sets the stage for effective communication by using positive verbal and non-verbal modes of interacting with parents (Vantil, 1977).

A significant part of our interaction with parents is conducted through our eyes and physical gestures. Our eyes, says, William Purkey (1978), give us away. Sincerity, interest and "human contact" are conveyed through the eyes. I can be speaking and yet doing so rather mechanically but my lack of interest will show through my visual expression. Eye contact is essential for conveying your spoken message as well as eliciting a response from the person you're attempting to communicate with. Pleasantness, empathy and many other "tones of communication" can be generated through eye contact. Facial expression also influences the rhythm of communication. For example, an expression of disgust by the teacher (conveyed totally through facial expression) may impede the normal flow of verbal interaction between parent and teacher. On the other hand, an expression of empathy can be a way of eliciting trust in the parent for the teacher's viewpoint. Gesturing can be used to strengthen a point of importance during discussion. Open arms, for example, usually indicate an openess to the other person's ideas. A clenched fist may be used to express firmness, anger or other emotional states. Teacher control of gestures and other non-verbal communication techniques is critical to their establishing an effective framework for working with parents (Hall, 1959).

The physical space and distance between people signals what type of communication will be taking place. For example, the use of distance by leaders of governments in communicating with each other is mostly for formal purposes; however, some leaders like John Kennedy, would use close, intimate space and thus minimize the need for formal lines of communication. Teachers who use objects like the desk to keep parents at a distance will notice they end up doing most of the talking. Only when the physical environment is designed to open up lines of communication do parents offer ideas and share concerns with teachers that are vital to having meaningful home-school relationships. The use of a small, circular table with coffee or tea on it helps parents and teachers to become comfortable and thus focus on the communication process (Gordon, 1976).

Ultimately the effective communicator follows through on the task to be accomplished. Just as our behavior speaks louder than words to children — so it is in our contacts with parents. By taking action on parent concerns and providing them with feedback on issues they've discussed with you, a sense of trust is developed between parent and teacher. Positive guidance, constructive suggestions and proper handling of parent inquiries are non-verbal modes of communication that impact parent-teacher relations far more than any verbal interactions we may have with parents (Swick and Duff, 1978).

The physical setting of the classroom, teacher attitude toward parents and teacher performance regarding many home-school issues influence the kind of relationships that are developed between home and school.

Communication is a Learning Process

The various parent-teacher communication modes are carried out by people. People, especially parents and teachers, are human; they make mistakes, get angry, sometimes over-react to situations but above all are desirous of growing as individuals who are valued by others. There is no perfect parent-teacher communication technique. Thus it is necessary to be aware of some of the things that can go wrong when parents and teachers are communicating and relating to each other. At the same time parents and teachers should be reminded that nothing can be accomplished without their attempted efforts.

The Explosive Conference. Because parents and teachers are human and often labor under intense pressures they can become irrational. "Mr. Ryan, my child is not a discipline problem. Your just not a good teacher!" Furthermore, "I don't have to listen to this anymore — goodbye!" Such emotional outbursts by a parent or teacher do happen. Usually the person who behaves in such a manner has been building up to the emotional explosion. They may have had similar problems with the child and felt helpless in the predicament. When a parent or teacher explodes in this way it is best to let them release their feelings and try to end the conference on a solution oriented basis. A phone call or a home visit at a later time may help in restoring the situation to a more rational status. Remember: All human beings have their irrational moments!

The Open House No One Attended. When teachers find it necesssary to take unusual actions to awaken the community to their situation there are, at least on some events, negative consequences. For example, the parents and teachers of District 122 have spent two months preparing for a "visit your school day". However, the local teacher union found it necessary to call a city wide strike. The teachers, as part of the strike, refused to conduct the open house program. Some parents, obviously disappointed, went ahead with the open house activity. Many other parents and citizens, upset about the strike, walked with signs "TEACHERS SHOULD TEACH" in front of the school the day the program was to have taken place. The program never materialized and even when the strike was over a frustrating and tense relationship existed. Such situations need not occur when continuous parent-teacher communications exist. But they do happen! What do you do? Preventive measures are the most effective. Keep your parents informed and be honest with them. When it does happen be willing to reach out and explain why it happened. Be the first to attempt to restore positive communications with the parents. Continuous and honest communications with parents should prevent most problems and should provide a sound basis for dealing with problems when they do occur.

The Overly Involved Parent. There are parents, who through their eagerness to help, become too involved in school situations or improperly involved in certain parts of the school program. Mrs. Benton is such a parent. She is at the school everyday and constantly finding something wrong with the way things are managed. She is very helpful in what she does for the school but very damaging in what she says about the school staff. Some of the teachers are very angry and have complained to the prinvipal. How do you tell someone they are overly involved? The best approach is to praise the individual and re-direct their involvement toward more constructive activities. If this fails it will be necessary to have a clear and pointed discussion about the problem with the individual. Whatever approach is used try to be positive as usually this type of person is a meaningful ally to the school; albeit misdirected in their efforts.

A Disastrous Group Conference. "I guess it can happen to any group but it was sure disappointing to see it happen in our school." Mr. Dent, Principal of Elmwood School, had helped the parent-teacher group organize a discussion on "Children and Discipline". It was a well organized group conference with every detail attended to. No one even imagined the possibility that a parent would use the group meeting as a chance to chastise everyone for being permissive parents and teachers. Mrs. Reynolds angered the group by her long, oratorical message on how everyone was too liberal and not disciplining their children. Several parents tried to react but she continued her emotional speech. Several parents left the meeting and others began arguing with Mrs. Reynolds. Finally, Mr. Dent closed the meeting amidst a very emotional atmosphere. "It was a real disaster," Mr. Dent explained. "I called every parent the next day and apologized for what happened and most of them were very understanding of the situation." This type of experience can happen to anyone. Mr. Dent handled it well and aided the parents by putting it into a learning perspective. In organizing future programs he will be alert to the possibility of the sermonette parent.

Repairing the Damage. The most effective way to avoid parent involvement tragedies is to utilize sound planning and communication procedures. Even when all the details have been attended to, however, problems can and do happen. When a problem does occur the best way to deal with it is in an honest and open manner. Find out what is at the basis of the problem. Involve those concerned in working out a solution to the problem. If the mistake was your fault admit it and communicate your apology to the appropriate individuals. A sign of an effective communicator is the ability to correct their behavior based upon experiences they have been party to. If the problem was the fault of no one individual let people know that and formulate plans to have a better conference or open house program next time.

A sense of humor is a needed characteristic for people who wish to get involved inparent-teacher activities. The best planned event can end in disaster. Most parents and teachers understand this and are willing to live with it. Do not allow one tragedy to destroy our parent-teacher involvement program! Be the type of individual who is there to repair the damage and help others re-new their confidence in themselves and in the process of growing and learning together. The following are some suggestions you can use in dealing with parent-teacher communication problems.

1. The best way to avoid a problem is to prevent it from happening. Through planning and careful consideration of the needs of the participants can help you avoid many problems.

2. When a problem does occur handle it in a positive way. Avoid over-reacting to a problem situation and encourage others to put the situation in a balanced perspective.

3. When communication problems arise between parents and teachers it is not unusual for someone's feelings to be hurt. If you are at fault apologize and make every effort to develop positive relations with the person(s). If you are the one offended accept the apology to be more sensitive to the needs of others in the future.

4. If the problem was caused by mechanical equipment failure or ineffective lighting be sure to correct this situation for the next

185

meeting. It is a good practice to have extra bulbs on hand when utilizing film projectors or overhead projectors. Double check all the equipment and other arrangements and you will find that many technical problems can be avoided.

5. Sometimes there will be a parent or group of parents and/or teachers who attempt to dominate the group. Try to avoid such situations of the preaching parent or teacher. If it does happen let the dominator know that they must change their behavior and be sensitive to the needs of others during group discussions.

Effective parent-teacher communication is based on the development of mutual trust among all involved persons. The use of effective communication behaviors and the organization of an "inviting" environment can enhance parents and teachers in their efforts to build quality educational programs for young children.

CHAPTER NINETEEN
COMMUNICATING STYLES FOR
PARENTS AND TEACHERS

In a recent workshop which was held to help parents and teachers develop communication skills, parents were asked "What do you think and feel when your child's teacher calls you for a conference?" The parents responded with comments like the following: "I feel worried." "I feel guilty that I haven't done enough to help my child in school." "I feel nervous, I think that Roddy has done something wrong." "I think Dorene is not doing her work." Then teachers were asked to respond to a similar question. They gave similar answers: "I feel nervous." "I feel a little scared." "I think that I have done something to make the parent angry." "I think there must be some problem." These reactions are centered around worry, concern, and problems. Not one parent or teacher out of the entire group of people reported that they had positive feelings or thoughts when they were called and asked for a meeting. These negative feelings and thoughts are commonplace and shared by parents and teachers alike. These mutual emotional states set the stage for many communication problems among parents and teachers (Swick & Duff, 1978).

A first step in overcoming communication difficulties is to develop an understanding of the basic communication styles. Four basic styles of communication have been identified (Miller, Nunally & Wackman, 1975). The effective use of these four styles is a requisite for meaningful parent-teacher interaction. The following are brief portrayals of the four styles of communication.

STYLES OF COMMUNICATION

STYLE I (Superficial)

"Ms. Shabazz, I love your new hair-cut!"

"The weather has been bad all week, hasn't it? It's too bad when the children can't play outside."

STYLE II (Command)

"You must let James get by with murder at home. He has misbehaved in school all year."

"Don't you ever give Corrine a bath?"

"Why do you let Timmy watch so much television?" "He should be getting more sleep at night."

STYLE III (Intellectual)

"It is important that we consider all the alternatives before we make a recommendation for Ron's placement for next year."

"In a course I am taking, I learned that too much television can cause children to become passive."

"Sex-role development is dependent on conditioning and modeling."

STYLE IV (Caring)

"I am concerned about Timmy. Sometimes he seems so tired in school. I am worried that he isn't getting enough sleep."

"I have some concerns about James' behavior in school. I have heard that too many sweets in a child's diet may affect behavior. I am wondering if you have noticed that he begins to behave aggressively after eating sweets at home?"

An examination of the communication styles reveals that each style serves a distinct purpose. For example, Style I is an informal style. It is the type of talking that is done at an open house or when people are just visiting. It is not very useful for solving problems. The second style is a command style. People often use this style when they are angry or are trying to defend themselves or to persuade others to see things their way.

This style often hurts people or causes them to feel angry or defensive. The third style is a factual-information style. It is usually helpful in solving problems but sometimes people may become intimidated if they are given information they cannot understand. When the intellectual style is used with the caring style, they are very effective in problem solving. Style IV is a caring, open, and authentic style. When people use this style, they state feelings and personal information and they ask others to share their feelings and concerns. Styles three and four used together are a good combination for effective communication.

People have been communicating with others for years. Everyone has developed some effective communication skills and others that are not so effective. Most people know how to use Style I because they have practiced it frequently in social encounters. And this is an important style. Someone who cannot "make small talk" will be exceedingly uncomfortable on many of the social occasions of our society. The important thing is to know when to use this style and when another style would be more appropriate. Style I is a very "low-risk" style, very little information is shared while using this style, it is rather superficial. Therefore, Style I is not a good problem-solving style, but it is an excellent style to be used as an ice-breaker when people are first meeting. In parent-teacher communications, Style I would best be used during casual encounters, at an open house, or at the beginning of a conference.

Style II is another style that many people can use effectively. It is a command style, but sometimes this is a good style to use. For example, if you have a lot of information on a topic and I want to learn it from you, you might just give me a fifteen minute lecture. This would be an effective use of Style II. On the other hand, the command style can be used in trying to force change. Used ineffectively, Style II can precipitate defensive reactions among parents and teachers. Thus Style II is a "high risk" style and should be used with caution.

Style III is an intellectual mode of communication. A person may use Style III in gathering information for problem solving. Although Style III has the advantage of objectifying a predicament, it also can be used to avoid personalizing a difficult situation. When used to an extreme degree, ths style can become a factor in dehumanizing the parent-teacher relationship. This style can be a "high risk" style when people utilize it to dehumanize themselves or others. It can also be damaging to a relationship when people use it to justify their position without regard to the ideas of others.

Style IV is a caring, open, and authentic style. This style is one which many people have not practiced and therefore cannot use effectively. This caring style when used in combination with the facts and information gathered in the intellectual style is essential for solving problems which involve parents, teachers, and children and their relationships. Style IV is a risky style in that people using it open themselves up and report personal feelings, throughts, and intentions. However, it is such a powerful tool of communication that the risks are worth taking.

A caring style requires four sets of skills: (1) listening, (2) self-disclosure, (3) shared meaning, and (4) combining the above skills with a commitment to build and maintain self-other esteem. Listening skills involve attending to the ideas of another person. Planning what you will say next while another is talking is not listening. An important clue to watch for while listening is body language. Good listeners usually give themselves away by their body language; they maintain eye contact and orienttheir bodies toward the person to whom they are listening.

Skills of self-disclosure include being aware of self-information and being willing and able to share that self-information with others. There are five kinds of personal information that can be shared with a good listener. Sensory data is the first. This includes what is seen, heard, tasted, touched, or smelled. Next is interpretation or thought data. For example, "I saw Timmy fall asleep in class every day last week. I interpreted that to mean he was staying up late watching television." If you shared this self-information with a parent, the parent might say, "I am glad you told me that Timmy was falling asleep but he actually has not been watching television, instead his father is sick and I have been leaving him with a baby sitter who cannot seem to get him to go to bed on time." Contrast this approach with the teacher who says only "You are letting Timmy watch too much television." A quite different reaction would be forthcoming from the parent. After sharing sensory information and interpretation, the next step in sharing self-information is to share feelings. Feelings are emotions and usually involve gut-level reactions. Sadness, anger, fear, joy, and happiness are some words for feelings. The teacher mentioned before could report feelings like this. "Timmy fell asleep in school every day last week. I interpreted this to mean that he was watching television late at night. I am worried about his school work. I am afraid that he will fail in many of his studies." An additional type of personal information is intentions. In this area, I tell you what I plan to do and then the last step is to actually implement my plan.

A caring style also requires shared meaning. The skill to be acquired in this area is to receive the actual message sent by the other person. This of course requires careful listening on the part of the receiver and accurate self-disclosure on the part of the sender. In practicing shared meaning the sender sends an important message to the receiver. For example, a parent may say "Delores told me that all she does in school is play." The teacher's immediate reaction might be to get defensive. Instead the teacher could say, "I understand that Delores said we play all day in school. I interpret your concern to be that you don't think children should play in school . Is that right?" Only through additional questions and answers and establishing shared meaning can the teacher and parent realize that the teacher sees play as a child's work. What Delores has described as play may involve many learning experiences for her.

Finally, the use of Style IV requires people to integrate the skills of listening, self-disclosure, shared meaning, and a caring attitude toward people as the communication process is actualized. Unfortunately, many people have habituated the use of a command or intellectual or superficial style in defense of self rather than to share their ideas and feelings in an open fashion. Inherent in the use of Style IV is a requirement that people "risk" themselves in interactive situations with others.

Communication: The Vital Link

Translating the human goal to communicate effectively with other people into a system for accomplishing that goal requires the development and use of appropriate communication styles. Each communication style described in this chapter can be used to enhance parent-teacher-child relationships. Just as sensitive teachers use Style I informal comments about a child's dress or summer activities to open up communications, so they can use this style to get to know parents. As parents and teachers get to know each other they will hopefully develop a Style IV caring style of communication in which they genuinely show respect and share with each other their knowledges and skills about children.

Communication, as experienced human service professionals know, is not always a smooth process. In home situations a Style II commanding style is required in order to raise our consciousness about a problem and in most problem situations some Style III intellectualization is required to sort out the issues and arrive at a conclusion. The development and implementation of parent and/or teacher education workshops in which communication techniques are practiced and various styles simulated can be helpful in terms of 'readying' people for relating to each other in productive ways. As parents and teachers search for ways to help children, they will find their own styles of relating the link to improving conditions for children's learning.

CHAPTER TWENTY
PARENT-TEACHER COMMUNICATION TECHNIQUES

The use of a variety of communication techniques is essential in meeting the diverse needs and situations of today's parents. Conferences, group meetings, school guidebooks, newsletters, open house programs and many other strategies are used by parents and teachers in maintaining workable relationships. Some of these techniques are examined in this chapter.

The Individual Conference

The successful conference is the end result of teacher and support team planning. Those involved in conducting such conferences should be versed and experienced in using both communication skills and organizational-management skills. Parent-teacher conferences, have a distinct purpose: to develop the best possible educational plan for each child. In order for this to occur, educators must be able to organize a section for involving parents and professionals in meaningful communications essential to formulating an individualized educational program.

Communication Skills

A basic understanding of the ways in which people communicate is vital to successful conferences. See the previous chapter for a discussion regarding the use of different communication styles. In addition, re-examine chapter eighteen for further insights regarding effective communication behaviors teachers and parents can use to develop quality relationships.

As teachers and support staff set up conferences, they should find the following questions helpful in sharpening their responsiveness to parents.

1. Have I left time for parents to express their concerns?

2. Have I expressed my major points clearly and in a nonthreatening manner?

3. Have I established an environment conducive to having "productive parent-teacher exchanges" at the conference? For example, many conferences may appear threatening to parents who feel outnumbered by professional persons.

4. Have I laid any groundwork with parents on ways they can better communicate during the conference? Advance workshops where

parents and teachers get together to explore ways of making conferences successful can be of help to everyone.

5. Have I refined my communication skills by examining materials on this topic and/or attending inservice sessions related to communicating with parents? (Rotter & Robinson, 1982)

Remember, conferences are conducted by people. People make mistakes, get angry and sometimes overreact to situations, but above all want to grow as individuals who are valued by others. The parent-teacher-specialist relationship can produce the most meaningful results when those involved use good communication skills.

Organizational-Management Skills

The most effective way to insure successful conferences is to use sound planning and organizational practices. In terms of organization, the conference can be viewed as three dimensional: preconference planning, the actual conference, and post-conference follow-up activities (Swick & Duff, 1978).

For the best conference, plan well in advance. Formulate the objectives to be accomplished. As you examine the objectives, decide whether or not to include the child in the conference. Establish a time, date and place in which the conference is to take place. Be sure to consider the parents' work schedule in organizing the conference. Allow an adequate amount of time for conducting the conference.

The purpose of the conference dictates the kinds of materials needed for use in the actual conference. The specifics will vary, as the idea is to develop an individualized educational program. As you ready required materials, make copies for the parents if possible. Additionally, teachers have found it helpful to have samples of the child's work, anecdotal records, and progress reports on hand to share with parents. Whatever materials are used, make sure they are understandable by parents. Remember: Parents who take the time to come to the conference expect to leave knowing more about their child's progress in school than they did before the conference.

More than once parents have missed a conference because their child lost the note advising them of the conference details. If you have any doubt about the parents' knowledge of the conference, follow up with a telephone call. Be considerate of different family needs and provide flexible conference times to meet these needs. Communicate with parents on all aspects of the conference.

The most productive conferences are conducted in physical settings that invite discussion and exchange of ideas between parent and teacher. Avoid creating physical barriers of authority between you and the parent.

194

Organize a setting that is comfortable, open to movement, and equipped to deal with the requirements of the conference.

Some attitudinal preparation for the conference can be most helpful to teachers in approaching it with a positive viewpoint. Here are three formulas to use throughout your conference.

1. Always begin and end the conference on a positive note.

2. Never criticize, condemn, or complain unless it can be done constructively.

3. Always show sincere appreciation, make the parent feel wanted and important, listen carefully, indicate an interest in the parent's ideas, and give genuine responses (Satir, 1972).

The actual conference provides an excellent opportunity by parents and teachers to share their resources in developing the best quality education program for the child. In conducting the conference, set a positive tone by first focusing on how the child has progressed and then offer constructive ideas on how the child can improve. Allow time for parents to share their concerns with you. Be respectful of such concerns by being a good listener. Be cordial and relaxed as well as confident in your competence in working with young children. Above all, be supportive of parents by considering their values and ideas as important, Begin the conference on time, and end it in a similar way with a positive tone (Swick & Duff, 1978).

As the conference comes to a close, assure the parents that their continued involvement is vital to the child's school success. You might give parents a "home learning packet" that includes activities they can do with their child, resources in the community they can contact and where you can be reached if they need further assistance.

One of your first postconference activities will be the finalization of an individual plan for the child. As you develop it, recall some of the major concerns expressed by parents during the conference. In addition, include a parent feedback form to be used at home and then forwarded to you or brought to the next conference. When you send the plan to the parents, include a personal note of thanks for their participation in the conference. Keep in mind that the initial conference between parent and teacher can establish a basis for continuous communication throughout the year (Berclay, 1977).

When educators take time to plan and implement individual conferences, they are modeling the kind of behavior they desire for parents to use in relating to their children. When teachers use positive communication skills and effective management behaviors in conducting conferences with parents, they are certain to enhance the home-school relationship.

The Group Conference

There are various times when a group of parents and teachers need to get together to share and discuss information of common concern. Group conferences whould not include the discussion of any event or activity of a confidential nature. Parent-teacher groups may be held at the classroom or school levels.

Valid Reasons for Having Group Conferences

The main reason for having group conferences is to provide parents with information or deal with problems a team of parents are interested in studying. Many times there is information the teacher can most effectively share with parents in a group situation. For example, when a program director wishes to describe and discuss the learning program it may be useful to hold a group conference. When changes are being made in the school day, curriculum plan or in the student behavior code, a group meeting is in order. Too often such matters are handled by sending home mimeographed sheets on the subject. It is best to at least provide parents with a chance to discuss such issues. Meet with parents in a group and gather their ideas and make them a part of the decision-making process (Swick & Duff, 1978).

Other reasons for conducting group conferences include the education of parents about child care techniques, the dissemination of information on school policies, the solving of problems that relate to all the parents in the school and related issues that can best be handled in a group setting. In addition, the group meeting can be of value in bringing parents and teachers together to develop materials for the classroom, make needed school improvements and to clarify their understanding of how the home and school can work together on sensitive issues.

Conducting Successful Group Conferences

The key to successful group meetings is to conduct them in accordance with the original plans. For example, if a conference was organized to provide parents with an opportunity to discuss their concerns about the school program then let them do so. It is very disconcerting to parents who come to a group-discussion expecting a chance to express their views and end up listening to someone lecture on the virtues of a good education.

Remember a group conference usually includes a heterogeneous set of people who have special interests and individual reasons for attending the program. Develop and maintain an accepting atmosphere where everyone feels confident about expressing their ideas during the conference. The conference leader or group coordinator is the individual who is responsible for promoting a setting where members of the group feel at ease in stating

196

their ideas about the topic under study. Warm, accepting and task oriented persons make the best group leaders as they create a setting where people can express themselves and yet focus on their discussion on the topic.

Additional suggestions for conducting successful group conferences are listed as follows:

1. Begin and end the conference on time.

2. A group conference should last no longer than two hours. If more time is needed hold additional meetings.

3. Plan the meeting so participants have a chance to take a break from the action of the meeting.

4. Establish an agenda for the participants to use in accomplishing the objectives.

5. Summarize the results of the meeting by keeping a list of major items discussed on a chalkboard or worksheet (Swick & Duff, 1978).

Individual and group conferences provide parents, teachers and children an opportunity to confer with each other about the status of an individual child or to discuss various aspects of the shcool program. The main purpose of these conferences must be to promote positive and facilitative relationships among all members of the teaching-learning team (VanTil, 1977).

Newsletters, Surveys, Inventories

In developing effective home-school relations teachers of young children must use many different types of communication skills. Periodic conferences and home visits provide for the face to face meetings parents and teachers need but are too cumbersome to be held everytime information is disseminated to parents. The written communication tools such as newsletters, survey devices, or inventory forms are examples of techniques teachers can use to communicate with parents on a regular basis.

Newsletters

Classroom, school or district-wide newsletters can, if developed and used properly, provide parents and teachers with a means of continuous information sharing. Whatever the content of a newsletter, its primary purpose is to facilitate the home-school relationship. Newsletters also provide an efficient means of keeping school staff and students informed of policies and events that are to be implemented during the school year. Some school districts have refined this idea by developing and disseminating school calendars to everyone in the community.

Whether constructing a newsletter for use at the classroom level or for use in the entire district there are some useful guidelines to follow (Swick & Duff, 1978, p. 83).

1. Keep the newsletter brief in content and small in size.

2. Regardless of the format make sure the newsletter is personable, attractive and readable.

3. Be sure the newsletter is meeting the objectives for which it was designed.

4. Provide a place in the newsletter where parents can offer you feedback on issues or concerns they see as important.

5. In developing the newsletter involve parents and children in the process so the final product is pertinent to their needs.

Inventories

The parent inventory usually serves the purpose of involving parents in the process of taking stock of some aspect of the school program such as the curriculum. An inventory can be used to determine the talents various parents have and thus could contribute to a parent resource program. In addition, some personnel may want to inventory parents regarding topics for meetings or to acquire information on the parent-teacher-association. An inventory should only be used to gather specific information from parents in the school and not to sample parents on topics such as the passage of a local school bond issue. The survey technique is the proper device to use when sampling of parent opinions is desired.

The parent inventory is most effective, as a communication device, when designed and used at the school or classroom level. It is virtually impossible (except in small school districts) to inventory parental views on controversial topics such as the adoption of a sex education program. Group conferences are the appropriate device to use when "controversial" issues need to be studied. It is important to acquire feedback from all parents when using the inventory process.

Surveys

The basic purpose of the parent-citizen survey is to acquire a sampling of their opinions with regard to either a specific issue or a series of issues. The survey technique, if used properly, can be a constructive mechanism for continuous parent-teacher communication.

Unfortunately the survey technique is too often used only to acquire information on topics of a crisis nature. Remember, the survey technique, like all other forms of communication should be used to facilitate the home-school partnership. If the school district staff have never initiated communicative procedures with parents and then suddenly employ a survey to gain the confidence of the public for a new school tax the results (as many educators know by experience) are likely to be disastrous.

As a survey is used to gather the opinions of people it should only be used after the public has been provided needed facts upon which they can make rational choices on the issues under study. For example, if the intent of the survey is to find out how parents and citizens feel about the possibility of having additional courses of study added to the curriculum the school staff should first provide people with information such as the following:

1. What is the substance of the proposed courses of study?

2. Of what value will these courses be to the children?

3. What will these additions cost in terms of money?

4. Are there adequate facilities to house these new courses?

5. Why are these courses needed?

Only after parents have information on the above questions can they intelligently respond by completing the survey form. A note of caution: parent surveys should be used judiciously to meet important needs. Over-use of this communication vehicle can irritate parents to a point where they will not cooperate in completing the forms.

Telecommunications

In order to accomodate the various parenting styles and unique family situations educators must use a variety of parent involvement techniques. The entire composite of telecommunications provide parents and teachers with a medium by which they can relate and respond with each other in an instantaneous manner. This method of communication enables teachers to reach busy parents who for a plethora of reasons are unable to participate in the traditional parent-teacher communication sessions.

If used effectively the telephone can be one way of involving parents in the educational program. The teacher can use the telephone to converse with parents about the child's progress at school. At a more sophisticated level some schools are using taped phone messages as a means of keeping parents informed of the daily activities of students and teachers. For example, one classroom teacher taped the homework assignments for that day and summarized what happened in the classroom that day. Parents could call anytime each day except between 3:30–4:00 when the new tape was being made.

Other audio and visual communication modes are available for use in improving parent-teacher interactions. Radio and television have been used to bring special events into the home of parents and citizens. Some large school districts have televised their school board meetings; a few such districts have used telethons where people can call in while the board is meeting and ask questions regarding some of the important issues.

A more recent use of the television involves the development of video-cassettes for parent education programs. These tapes are made available for individual viewing in the school and, in some cases, are aired on instructional television for the entire community. The advancements in computer technology and in the field of telecommunications provide teachers with a new arena for involving parents in educational and support activities.

The Open House

Too often open house programs are used because of tradition. There are many valid reasons for conducting open house programs. It can provide a chance for parents and teachers to meet each other, an opportunity for community awareness, and a time for displaying student and teacher accomplishments (Berclay, 1977).

The open house program should not be used to solve individual parent or child problems. Conferences with parents is a more appropriate way of handling such problems. On the other hand, the open house can be used as a way of handling on-going relationships with parents. For example, some schools initiate parent-citizen talent files during open house programs by having a table set up where people can volunteer to use their skills in the school. The open house is one way of furthering the home-school partnership in a positive direction. The following are some suggestions for planning functional open house programs.

1. Form a planning team inclusive of parents who are willing to help with the program.

2. Decide upon a specific purpose for the open house.

3. Settle upon a time, place and date for the program.

4. Inform and involve appropriate school staff in all phases of the planning.

5. Communicate with parents and citizens about the program.

Parent Visitations to the Classroom

There are two primary reasons for conducting parent visitations to the classroom: to provide parents with information on the learning process and to share with parents the nature of the classroom. Parents, through

200

their visitations, acquire direct experience with the way their children, other children and the teacher carry on the learning process. In addition, through such visitations, the parent can gain empathy toward the teacher and the problems and prospects he faces in the classroom.

Above all else the parent visitation must facilitate the development and learning of the children. The productive parent visitation period enhances the self image of the children and fosters improved understandings between parents and teachers. Successful programs depend upon planning. Consider the following as some methods of planning for a productive visitation program.

1. Prepare the children for the visitation. Let them know a visitor is coming to the classroom to participate in some activity or event.

2. Prepare the parents for their experience in the classroom. Inform the parents of how the daily activities are scheduled and of any issues they should be aware of during their visit.

3. Prepare the classroom so the visit can be a productive one. The physical environment needs to be flexibly arranged so parental involvement can be integrated into the regular program.

4. Prepare yourself for relating to parents in a classroom situation.

5. Limit the number of parents to two or three per visit. Too many parents visiting at once can create chaos.

Student Progress Report Forms

An effective method of keeping parents informed about the performance of their children is the progress report form. It is an efficient mode of communicating with parents between personal conferences and other face to face contacts (Swick & Lamb, 1975). There are various types of progress report forms. The grade card is probably the oldest report form used. This card usually contains the letter grade assigned by the teacher to students in terms of their performance in different academic subjects. Some types of grade cards include a place where the teacher can make narrative comments about various student behaviors. A major problem with this type of report form was and is the issue of interpretation. What does a grade of A mean in terms of what the student actually knows about the subject?

As a result of criticism by parents and teachers that the traditional report card is inadequate, other progress report forms have been developed. More recent forms have been based on the idea of giving parents and students specific information about the performance of the students. For example, the individual instructional program which has gained credence in recent years uses charts, graphs and student performance sheets as a means of reporting pupil progress. Other modifications of the report form include the use of narrative reports, product descriptions and other means of showing parents the actual results of student performance. In designing a method of reporting student progress to parents the following are some guidelines.

1. Make the form brief but specific in content.

2. Emphasis should be focused on the progress the student has made since the last report.

3. Make the form personal by having some place on the form where you and the parent can enter anecdotal or informal comments.

4. Where possible attach student work samples to the report form so parents can see what kinds of activities their children are doing at school.

5. In noting problem areas of student performance, provide specific suggestions on how parents can help and offer to meet with parents to discuss serious issues further.

Informal Modes of Parent Involvement

In the contemporary social setting many parents find themselves with little time to attend formal school functions. These parents are interested in being involved in the education of their children but due to various reasons are unable to attend conferences and other events. There are ways to involve parents who are unable to attend the formal aspects of the parent involvement program. Informal activities and projects such as the following are some modes of involving parents who are constantly "on the run".

1. In some educational settings parents bring their children to school and/or pick them up after the completion of the school day. The informal 'drop-off' and 'pick-up' times can be used by the teacher to make contact with the parents. Having a coffee corner where parents can get a quick cup of coffee and chat with the school or center staff for a few minutes can be very useful for involving otherwise uninvolved parents.

2. The utilization of parent-child lending libraries is another informal method of involving parents and children in the learning process. These lending libraries can be small or large and usually contain materials useful to both parents and children. They should be appealing in design and placed where parents have easy access to them. Parents should be informed of the existence of the lending library and encouraged to use it.

3. Many parents would like to be helpful to the school but are unable to do so on a regularly scheduled basis. Too often the talents of these parents go unused. Develop a *Parent Room* in the school. Some schools may not have the space available to set aside an entire room but can develop some 'parent space' within the physical setting of the school. The parent room can be a place where parents can come when they can and leave when they must. It can be a place for parent socialization, parent education and parent participation in school events. A work table can be placed in the room with school projects parents can work on at their pace and on their schedule. Most important the parent room should belong to the parents; a part of the school that is theirs.

4. Informal parent-teacher social events are valuable modes of bringing together the members of the learning team. Father-son breakfasts, family-school picnics and other informal events provide an avenue for involveing parents and teachers in mutually enriching experiences.

5. Parent to parent contacts can provide a springboard for informing informal parent education and discussion groups. These parent education and discussion groups can be used as informal modes of involving parents who will respond to a friend but fear the formality of the school. The concept of parent-to-parent contacts and support efforts is gaining credence in all of the helping professions (Gilmar & Nelson, 1975).

CHAPTER TWENTY-ONE
SUPPORTING FAMILIES AS LEARNING SYSTEMS

Researchers who have expanded their focus to include the home as a part of the student's learning have found it is a significant part of the support system that enables young children to learn. Basic skills should be learned in a continuous fashion throughout life. This suggests that any decline (or rise) in test scores or student achievement is a result of what happens in the family as well as in the classroom (Russell, 1979). Thus it is clear that any discussion of learning must include both home and school settings.

In projects and research work with parents and other family members, the values of family-assisted-learning has been substantiated. Examples of some of these findings are discussed as follows.

1. Parents who are trained to relate with their infants in an organized manner effected improvements in the child's performance on cognitive skills as well as other areas of development (Gordon, 1977).

2. An assessment of the long term effects of preschool programs on children's later school performance found that programs in which a parent component existed were more positively rated than programs that lacked parent involvement (Lazar, 1977).

3. Research on home support (the quantity of parental support of children's home learning) indicated the more the home support behaviors elicited by parents the greater achievement gains made by children (Swick, 1979).

In addition, program reports based upon parent and teacher comments indicate the home and school form a closer relationship when a family learning component exists. Parents report improved methods of assisting their children, better modes of family management, clearer understanding of school situations, and more involvement with their children and school staff. Teachers point out that children improve in most all facets of school performance and that parents are more supportive of their teaching efforts (Swick & Duff, 1978).

Although many social agencies have instituted family assistance projects, little has been accomplished in helping the family function better in a learning capacity. As researchers in medicine, education and social sciences have identified critical parenting behaviors, the need for a

205

family-assisted-learning process is evident. These parenting behaviors include modeling, guiding, problem solving, and nurturing (Bronfenbrenner, 1979).

Conceptual Aspects of Family Assisted Learning

The concept of assisting families in becoming more effective has existed for years. Usually such assistance has focused on meeting needs of a peripheral nature. Social problems, medical assistance, and even school sponsored family involvement projects have been more general than specific in nature. The concept of working directly with the family in shaping a learning pattern is unique in the field of education. With the exception of family therapy and rehabilitation (often used in families where child abuse is a problem) most attempts to help families have been very generic in substance (Kempe & Kempe, 1978).

In the field of education, some efforts have been made to implement family-assisted-learning. For example, Gordon (1977) piloted a program to train low-income mothers in strategies for assisting their infants in developing cognitive and social skills. The subjects were also trained to then help others learn these skills. Findings of studies conducted on the project indicate infants improved in all facets of development and parents reported improved self concepts.

Family-assisted-learning is not restricted to any single approach. For example, pediatricians are utilizing individual and group sessions to educate parents in basic child development. Many hospitals are sponsoring programs for expectant mothers related to the birthing process and/or the parenting process. Schools are becoming involved in sponsoring parent education programs that focus on helping parents become aware of how they can assist their children in the learning process. Although many programs have lacked specific structure, their existence has heightened parental interest in their children's learning and development (Swick & Duff, 1979).

The Family and the Learning Process

As our society has become more complex, the functioning of the family has changed. Historically, families have always been the primary educational and socialization agent of the community. It is only recently that other social institutions, such as the school, have taken on more and more responsiblity for the educational and social development of the child. With industrialization, changing social mores and resulting pressures on the family, the roles of parents and children have changed. In contrast to the family unit where the parents taught children through the use of the Bible, other moral documents, and involving them in daily jobs, today's family setting is more fragmented. For example, children spend more time in day care, school, watching television and outside recreational

206

interests than with their parents. Parents and children spend more time in activities out of the home, thus reducing time available for family inter- action. Yet what happens (or does not happen) in the home is still a most influential part of the child's life (Bronfenbrenner, 1979).

It is within the family unit that the child is introduced to a style of behavior and thinking (Coleman, 1979). Regardless of the style or com- position of the family, the learning process exists. The infant should be nurtured and gradually introduced to the world. Through verbal and non- verbal contacts with parents, the child learns to grasp, make sounds, simple, and be responsive to the environment. Later, the child learns initial language skills, internalizes social behaviors existent in the home, and in general forms a view of how things happen. If family influences are strong enough and positive in nature, the child will develop prosocial behaviors (Swick & Duff, 1979).

Family-Assisted-Learning As A Process

All families can benefit from some type of assistance which enhances their ability to learn. The concept of family-assisted-learning applies to parents and children from all backgrounds. For example, the same devel- opmental lag found in many deprived children is often found in the more affluent because both groups suffer from a lack of parental support. The kinds of learning and format followed vary greatly from one family to another. For example, some families may spend time in directed activity; others may use more individualized activities. Obviously each family will need a different type of assistance.

Family-assisted-learning is, when utilized properly, a process by which families can improve their position as a force in helping each other be- come better persons. An ultimate outcome of this process is a positive change in the behaviors of parents and children. Thus an intrinsic part of any family program is that parents and children have a desire to improve their life.

The idea that the family is a learning unit is an accepted anthro- pological fact (Mead, 1970). When families had fewer social choices to make, this process could occur in a spontaneous manner. Even in more simplistic times assistance from the extended family and community was accepted in supporting the efforts of parents and children. As the tasks and situations confronting families are becoming more complex, the concept of family-assisted-learning has taken on a broader meaning. For example, the once predominant extended family no longer exists thus creating a vacuum in the way parents and children function. The use of community learning sources by families can help to fill this void (Swick & Miller, 1979).

With continued increases in knowledge about how children learn and develop, many schools and child development centers have instituted family-assisted-learning programs. The content may vary from home learning activities and family management to parent-child relations and academic learning at home. Although the content and structure may vary, a common element to all programs is the intent of assisting the family.

Inherent in any learning situation is the processing and utilization of information in changing behavior. Thus family members can utilize new information to change, refine or adapt behaviors within their settings. In conjunction with family-assisted-learning is an acceptance of the family as a changing and flexible social unit. The basis of this process must be a desire to improve the behavior and quality of life for everyone involved.

Goals And Objectives of Family-Assisted-Learning

Schools that sponsor family-assisted-learning programs should attempt to focus on three major goal areas: improving the family as a learning system, improving the school as a learning system, and improving the family-school arrangement as a learning system. The family-school arrangement as a learning system will determine success or failure of any program.

The Family As A Learning System

Some form of a learning system exists in all families. A goal of family-assisted-learning should be to help parents and children define, improve, or enhance their system of functioning. As parents are the primary leaders in the family, their position as teachers must be strengthened. Those in charge of implementing family-assisted-learning might ask the question: What can we do to strengthen the parents' situation as leaders in the family? A most important consideration deals with the parent-child relationship. Do parents and children talk with each other, plan things together, and help each other in the learning process? The needs of parents and children and their system of communicating must be a part of family-assisted learning goal development.

The School As A Learning System

Family-assisted-learning will only be effective when the school environment includes parents and children in the designing of the curriculum. Educators must be trained in working with families and knowledgeable about planning and implementing projects that include the community. Those working with such programs must also consider the child's performance in school. How can we expect children who are failing in school to suddenly succeed in family designed curricula? Teacher and child must have a positive experience in the classroom in order to build a home-school relationship necessary for having an effective program. Thus a

208

prerequisite goal must be to enhance the attitude toward school as a place where children and parents can learn in positive, accepting ways.

The Family-School Learning System

Provided positive attitudes exist within the family and the school, attention can be given to developing a cooperative learning system. A major goal area should focus on providing ways for families and schools to work together in designing a curriculum. Is there an administrative system for activating a family-assisted-learning curriculum? What kind of communications between family and school exist for making such a program workable? How should parents and teachers participate in this cooperative effort? Some type of system for implementation is necessary if parents and teachers are to be effective in making the program work.

Examples of Family-Assisted-Learning

As agencies and other human service workers recognize the needs of today's family, an increase in family-assisted-learning projects is taking place. The diversity of programs and approaches is evidenced in their increasing numbers. The utilization of family-assisted-learning, as indicated in the following examples, will increase the effectiveness of helping professionals in improving the quality of family and community life.

Non-Education Agency Sponsored Programs

The medical profession provides several examples of family-assisted-learning being used to promote a more rational approach to health care. Educational programs on childbirth, infant development, patient response to surgery, preventive health care, and child abuse treatment are now being successfully implemented. The basic premise underlying these programs is that families provided with information related to their health and well being, will be more effective in handling their own health care (Keniston, 1977).

Social workers are also utilizing similar approaches to increase the family's ability to become self-directed. Home visits by aides have been used to help parents improve their management skills, child care techniques, and related home care behaviors. Ministers and other religious workers are finding family counseling, religious education, and family enrichment projects as valuable methods of helping parents and children.

With the advent of a more knowledgeable public, industrial groups are using educational methods to promote more effective use of their products. Public utilities are developing educational packets on conserving energy. Oil companies are providing instructions on how products are made and can be used more effectively.

209

A prime example of how effective family-assisted-learning can be exists within the dental profession. The use of educational campaigns through newspapers, public schools, television spots, and public affairs pamphlets have made people aware of the importance of preventive dental care. Follow-up instruction is then conducted by individual dentists with their patients. When this family education model is followed, the incidence of dental health problems decrease.

The focus of these efforts is on helping families acquire new knowledge and skills to improve their physical, social, and emotional well being. Similar procedures are being used in schools to promote improved family-school relationships.

Education Agency Sponsored Programs

The concept of family-assisted-learning procedures is deeply engrained in our educational history (Gordon, 1977). At the turn of the present century, many public schools used adult education offerings to instruct immigrants in language skills. Since that time, professional associations and organizations, like the Parent-Teacher-Association, have sponsored conferences and publications dealing with parent education, parent involvement, and home-school relations. Currently there are a variety of professional papers directed toward the area of family-assisted-learning (National PTA, 1978).

Early childhood professionals have used family-assisted-learning to reach parents and children to develop positive learning behaviors. Home based programs have been used to instruct parents in methods of nurturing infants and establishing home learning settings (Russell, 1979). In addition, programs have been developed to familiarize parents with child development and the teaching-learning process. The establishment of toy lending libraries, home visits, conferences, and other activities are further evidence of continued efforts in family assistance by public and private schools.

Efforts such as forming advisory councils, curriculum study groups, and committees have been effective in stimulating a closer examination into the needs of families. Efforts are now being undertaken to refine family-assisted-learning to the point where school tasks are more closely linked to home activities. This "match" of school and home learning tasks has the potential to make learning more effective for children and parents.

Organization, Implementation, And Evaluation

The organization and implementation of family-assisted-learning curriculum should follow accepted practices, such as the formation of a planning team, the establishment of objectives, implementation of a design, and use of an evaluation procedure.

The first step is the establishment of a planning team, advisory council, or some group composed of parents and teachers. A primary activity for the planning team is to build attitudes that are supportive of a family-school learning approach. Attitudes are built by showing a willingness to involve parents in school decisions and by demonstrating the benefits of such activities. It has been suggested that in-service education for faculty, discussion groups involving parents, and other home-school involvement techniques can be effective in establishing needed attitudes.

The next step is to establish goals for the family-school curriculum. Any specified set of objectives will depend on the unique needs of a particular school and community. Every facet of the community should be involved in the goal setting process.

The third step is the determination of where the school and home are in relationship to the desired objectives. Determining the existing situation may reveal some of the goals have already been achieved whereas others require more emphasis. A planning team may find it advantageous to select certain goals as priorities that reflect the most crucial needs and existing resources.

The fourth step is the selection of strategies to reach the desired goals. Examining parent involvement projects can provide a plethora of ideas that have been found effective and from which a planning team may select. The modification of a successful project or of new strategies may be necessary in order to provide the most effective means of carrying out the project.

The final step in the process is the evaluation. The data collected, whether through discussion groups, questionnaries, or more formal means can be used in refining strategies for future program development. The evaluation process will also reveal which goals have been attained and provide feedback for changing goals or adding new ones to the original plan. The evaluation process is most useful viewed as an on-going activity for improving program development and the family-school decision making process.

Family-assisted-learning has been part of the educational scene since colonial times. The process of helping families become more effective has been refined in recent years and is beginning to take on a more structured format. Research in areas such as child abuse, surgical education for patients, and home-school relationships indicate that all members of the community benefit from family-assisted-learning programs. Future attempts to strengthen the family as a societal unit will certainly include more widespread use of this concept in all the helping professions.

CHAPTER TWENTY-TWO
THE WORK PLACE:
SUPPORTING FAMILIES AND SCHOOLS

The meaning of the term community is found in words and phrases such as togetherness, unity, interdependence, forming a union, and linking needs and services. Ecological studies such as those reviewed by Bronfenbrenner (1979) indicate that the more communities function in synergistic modes the more positively they are perceived by their members — thus creating a cycle of successful individual/group relationships.

Unfortunately, in the present cultural setting, human learning and development are perceived as happening in separate (and isolated) places. While many educators acknowledge that learning and development are contiguous and occur simultaneously in all parts of the community, this premise still lacks complete support of the citizenry. Separation of the learning and development process continues to happen when we assign roles to institutions (such as learning for school or social development for home) and fail to form linkages among schools, businesses and civic agencies.

Children function in a community sense: they are influenced by each component of the environment. For example, a positive family setting, inviting school, supportive neighborhood, and productive and humane work places would go a long way toward creating a cycle of success among children and adults. Communities with inadequate schools, high crime and unemployment, and other social problems provide unlikely settings for children and adults to develop and learn in productive ways.

Research reveals that productive child/family/school relations result when communities place high priority on participatory/supportive living. A recent study by Brown and Swick (1981) indicates that performance of children and adults is positively influenced in neighborhoods where social exchanges, supportiveness, child/child play interactions and concern for others are valued.

While major emphasis has been on family and school environments as primary socialization factors in the child's development, Urie Bronfenbrenner (1979) purports that the quality of life in the next generation will be determined in two places outside the home: the neighborhood and the workplace. In Bronfenbrenner's view, parents' workplaces affect their perceptions of life and the way they interact with family members. In this sense parents' job perceptions and family relationships are transactional in nature. Swick and Rotter (1981) state: "The interface between

213

family and living and job performance can be a productive endeavor. By utilizing the good of socitey as the basis of family life and work life everyone would benefit." The same premise can be applied to the relationship between business and industry and the total community.

Business and industry can play an integral role in shaping a quality environment for children and adults. By supporting recreational, educational, health, safety, family-living, youth-employment and senior-citizen programs, business/industrial groups can influence the present and future in yet untouched or untried ways.

Practices Business/Industry Can Use
To Promote Quality Communities

Business and industrial firms have successfully used many practices in making life more meaningful for employees, families and schools. In general, people are most productive when they feel secure in their situation: have a purpose for what they are doing and are involved in shaping their own lives as well as the lives of the next generation (Swick and Rotter, 1981). Some of the more promising practices that exemplary business/industrial groups have used are shared here.

Practices Supportive of Families

Business/industry practices supportive of quality family life also serve to enhance school and community life. This is especially true during the formative years of family development. The prevailing attitude in society that places responsibility for child nurturing totally in the hands of parents and then teachers is self-destructive. Parents and teachers need a supportive setting with resources and "helping hands" to meet the challenge of caring for and educating the next generation. Consider the following as some positive business/industry practices that facilitate development of quality families:

One of the most promising techniques for enabling family members to meet the dual needs of family and career living involves flexible scheduling of work hours and places. First used in Germany in 1956, this practice is now in use in Japan, Europe and to a lesser degree in the United States. (Scott Paper and Sun Oil are two U.S. companies that offer flexible scheduling.) Most parents use the options made possible by "flexitime" to meet family needs (Hengstler, 1975). A combination of flexitime with company-sponsored parent and adult education programs can be used to the benefit of everyone in the community.

Also benefitting both families and business is the practice of part-time work on a full-time basis. The McDonald's restaurant chain, for example, hires people on a full-time basis for a "20-hour" week. Many small business firms utilizing this arrangement find it mutually beneficial to employer/employee relationships. The practice also benefits the family that needs additional income yet desires adequate time for meeting family and personal needs.

The birth of a child — the initial formation of family life — is a critical time. Adequate maternity/paternity leave practices not only enable parents to begin or expand their families without pressure to return to work immediately after childbirth but stimulate job productivity as well. Moreover, children of parents who have time to form a stable family life tend to be healthier and lead more productive lives. This, in turn, exerts a positive influence on the quality and quantity of industrial output. For an example of a maternity/paternity leave policy, see Swick and Rotter (1981).

Additional family support practices of the business/industrial community might include:

1. Utilization of reentry practices for parents who, out of need or desire, decide to seek employment beyond the home.

2. Development of a "work hour bank" for parents to use in emergencies or for becoming involved in school or community improvement projects. Parents would bank hours during overtime, later using them to tend a sick child or become involved in a school activity.

3. Organization and implementation of industry-sponsored and/or supported child care.

4. Formation of "work transfer" policies that would make it possible for parents to be promoted within their immediate community, or when necessary, assist mobile families in making the move in a positive manner.

5. Development of family advisory councils that would provide business and industrial groups with perspective on how their operations affect family life in the community.

Finally, since most people spend a great deal of their waking hours on the job, the workplace should house centers for counseling and health services, parent education programs and related family/community services. Cooperative planning by private and public agencies could bring about a major improvement in the delivery of human services to families and other citizens (Palme, 1972).

Practices Supportive of Schools and Communities

The school, like other community agencies, must have linkages to the various "socialization" facets of the child's environment. The adult world is, in a very real sense, the school of reality for children. Unfortunately, this reality is distorted toward an isolationist, segmented culture in which children and young people find it difficult to forge any meaningful roles (Swick, 1979). Many of our young people are missing out on essential social and emotional facets of healthy development. Coleman (1979, p. 491) states:

> We can identify missing socialization tasks by reflecting on what used to be done by the institutions we have said are vanishing. These tasks include learning to take responsibility for others, learning to lead and to follow, learning how to make decisions and take action when necessary, and a host of other things that are ordinarily summed up in the words, "becoming adult"

The school alone is unable to accomplish the large task of enabling children and young people to become functional adults. Business/industry can play a major role in making the community an effective educational and social tool for linking generation to generation, thus enhancing adult/child relationships.

Support roles of business/industry might include: fostering school and related educational/recreational/work projects; providing specific schools with materials, financial aid, human resources and professional support (e.g., business-sponsored "adopt a school" programs); serving on school advisory councils, school boards and other decision-making groups that affect schools; offering schools the use of business/industrial settings for job placements and/or field sites for work programs; and supporting community and adult education programs that focus on linking education to community improvement (Burt and Lessinger, 1970).

Business/industrial practices that support worker involvement in the schools may be one of the most effective means of introducing children to the adult world. For example, many businesses could provide parents with leave time for taking part in parent/teacher conferences, visiting their child's classroom as a resource person, helping with special events such as field trips, and handling emergencies that might arise at school. The visible and participating adult signals to the child that school is a place where everyone is involved.

Some business/industrial groups have sponsored child care centers within their workplace, co-sponsored community child care centers, and/or provided parents with the needed resources to have child care available while at work (Angle, 1980). For parents of children in elementary and middle school, some business groups have supported (mostly through cooperative financing) extended school day programs that offer children varied social, recreational and academic activities. This enables parents to complete the work day without worrying about their children's after-school situation (Keniston, 1978). Bronfenbrenner (1979) says family support programs and school assistant projects produce a viable system in which all community members can learn and contribute in humane ways.

216

Additional support modes have been identified as ways business and industry can bridge the school/community gap. Burt and Lessinger (1970) provide three categories of support activities:

I. *Administrative and Operations Support*

   1. Membership on school boards

   2. Membership on administrative advisory committees

   3. Fund-raising on special school projects and assistance in passing bond issues

   4. Assisting school districts in budgeting and accounting operations

   5. Providing schools with help in working out transportation problems and in developing safety/fire protection plans

II. *Teacher Improvement Support*

   1. Sponsoring professional improvement programs such as conferences, workshops, and graduate study.

   2. Providing research and work experiences for teachers through business related centers

   3. Sponsoring special travel programs where teachers can visit sites related to their teaching expertise

   4. Developing economic education programs

III. *Instructional Services Support*

   1. Offering use of industrial facilities for student field trips

   2. Sponsoring student clubs and work experience programs

   3. Helping in vocational training, counseling and guidance programs

   4. Co-sponsoring (with schools and community agencies) work-study programs and student field-research projects

In addition, business/industry can collaborate with schools in many direct volunteer activities. The use of manpower from the corporate community can enhance the total operations of many schools. For example, specialists from a computer technology company could be placed on loan to a middle school to teach a unit or interest course on basic computer language. Agricultural and dairy businesses could (and some do) provide early childhood educators with resource people and materials in the area of food production and processing.

Other types of volunteer involvement include: conducting workshops on job-seeking skills for students; assisting in curriculum revision such as redesigning a high school drafting course; providing equipment and materials realted to vocational skills and job needs of the local community, such as the "school-job match" developed under the South Carolina Technical Education Plan; sharing of employee time in conducting school/business-sponsored tutoring programs; taking part in school assessment projects; and sponsoring school appreciation days (Burt and Lessinger, 1970).

As business, industry, schools and families develop linkages between childhood and adulthood, a more cohesive, meaningful and productive society results. Commenting on the need for this kind of cooperation within every community, Havighurst (1977, p. 405) states:

> In brief, we need to inject into the experience of youth a generous service-and-work-oriented program that will enable young people to experience adult society first-hand even though some of them may have to wait until their early twenties to find a proper place in the work force.

Some examples of cooperative business/school efforts are described below:

Philadelphia's Edison Project Dropout Prevention Center

At Edison High School in Philadelphia, a dropout prevention program has been established through the use of school and local business resources. The focus is on career education. Half of each school day is devoted to helping students improve their basic skills, with instruction individualized through the use of teacher-developed curriculum packets. The rest of the day is spent in some facet of career education. Three components of the "career orientation" are a work-stipend program (includes up to ten hours of work a week); work exploration in-school; community-based experiences that introduce students to the working world through lessons on available careers and application procedures, and visits to job sites (Staples, 1977).

Cooperative Science Education Project

Providing a cooperative career orientation to the medical profession, the CSEP program is operated by the New York University School of Medicine and the New York City Board of Education. The main thrust of the program, designed to motivate disadvantaged minority youth toward academic and career achievement, is described:

> Four days a week a different class or approximately 30 eight-and ninth-graders travels from Joan of Arc Junior High School

218

to the Medical Center. The students divide into two groups upon arriving; half go to work with their preceptors (professionals and paraprofessionalswho act as supervisors and role models); the other half go to a fifth-floor laboratory where, with their science teacher, they have the opportunity to investigate and solve scientific problems in a professional environment. After lunch there is an hour lecture period. Following this, students reverse the morning preceptorship and lab sessions until it is time to return to school (Schine and Harrington, 1982 pp. 25–26).

Emeryville Junior Docents Program

Since 1971 the University of California's Botanical Gardens and Lawrence Hall of Science have been centers of learnig for third- to eightgraders in Emeryville, California. At the Botanical Gardens students learn about many aspects of botanical and environmental studies; at the Hall of Science they focus their efforts on the arts and sciences. While some students construct simple motors, others work on more advanced topics such as entomology. Upon completing a semester of once-a-week study with professional employees on the job site, students select an area of interest and begin to conduct tours for visiting elementary school groups. The program enables young people to learn about the world of work and about themselves (Schine and Harrington, 1982, pp. 26–27).

Project Math Company

In Wascasset (Maine) Middle School, students learn about mathematics through exploring the world of careers. These students have developed a new kind of math textbook for their peers. A summary of this school/community project is described:

> The project had two goals: to expand the students' awareness of career opportunities and to highlight the relevance and importance of math in those careers studied. Forty-five eighthgraders participated in the project on a voluntary basis. They selected and researched careers of interest, interviewed professionals in the community, transacted and summarized the interviews, and worked with the professionals they interviewed to develop work problems typical of each career. They also made decisions about layout of the book, met with printers, proofread the book, and held a press conference (Schine and Harrington, 1982, p. 27).

The previous examples illustrate that business/school partnerships and other school/community programs can provide children and youth with a sensible transition from school to work.

219

Tomorrow's Workers are Today's Children

Our economic future depends not only upon the productivity of those now in the work force but the habits, perceptions and behaviors of today's children and youth. Throughout civilization a united and basically harmonious family/community life has been the cornerstone of social and economic wellbeing (Palme, 1972). When the following questions are examined, they provide some insight into the critical nature of family/school/community relationships — especially as these forces influence children's vision of the future.

1. How much quality time do parents, teachers and citizens (such as business/industrial leaders) spend together?

2. What arrangements exist for the "quality care" of children and youth in the community? What programs and family/school practices exist as a result of business/community agency initiatives?

3. In what way has business/industry altered scheduling patterns to enable parents to deal with unique family situations such as illness or school-involvement activities?

4. Is there a mutually productive relationship among families, schools and business/industry? That is, do business practices support family integrity and school/community partnerships?

5. Are children involved in the work- and family-life aspects of their parents' lives? In what way do schools and the business community involve children and youth in learning about their roles in making family life and work life meaningful experiences?

Answers to these questions are not very pleasing to those who work with families and schools on a continuing basis. In too many cases parents and children are spending less and less quality time in family, school or community endeavors. The need and potential for developing more family/school/industry relationships is apparent in the social context of today's youth. Let us never forget that in all successful cultures, children and youth learn most of their skills in family/school/community arrangements where intergenerational lifestyles are practiced.

Family-School-Business Bridges

Fundamental to the success of the practices described here is a major attitudinal change among people toward relationships among family, school and the world of work. The substance of this change is described by Swick and Rotter (1981, p. 11).

What good will it do our society to have a large Gross National Product if future generations have no identity, little human vision to carry on the gains made and even less vision of their role in the continuous process of humanizing the world? Likewise, the quality gains made in the lives of children will have little meaning if, as adults, they confront a deteriorating economic system.

The following attitudinal and perceptual changes are needed if families, schools and business are to re-establish a viable relationship.

1. Parents, educators and citizens must begin to perceive business/ industrial settings as more than "places to work" and "places to consume". They must begin to see them as integral parts of the quality of life.

2. Business/industrial leaders need to see their roles in the community as more than simply economic. A more comprehensive view of how business affects the lives of families and schools is needed, as well as a view of the laborer that includes his/her personal and familial context.

3. The concept that profits alone are the determining factor in defining the success of a business venture must be modified. While profits are essential to any business enterprise, the qualitative relationship between business and community needs to be incorporated into the success concepts of business practices.

Children and young people need to understand the interdependence of work life and family life. They need to become a significant part of industrial living and members of positive families, schools and communities. Only through a concerted effort by parents, educators and business leaders can we produce a future work force of contributing and effective people (Wirth, 1982).

CHAPTER TWENTY-THREE
THE NEIGHBORHOOD AS A
FAMILY SUPPORT SYSTEM

An accepted fact regarding families throughout the world is their urgent need to function in supportive environments. Research findings related to factors that seem to have a negative effect on family life continuously lead scholars in the direction that supportive behaviors among all members of the community are a requisite to positive parent-child relations (Bronfenbrenner, 1979). For example, recent research related to parental abuse of young children indicates that negative parenting behaviors are performed by people who lack support of others, find themselves in powerless situations, and have few intimate relationships with other adults (Kempe & Kempe, 1978). Families that have adequate support systems in which to function, perform more effectively in all aspects of work and family life. Recent research by White (1979) indicates that the more positive the support system surrounding parents, the more effective they are in being productive parents.

Supportive environments for families are a requisite to any future social development of children and adults alike. Today's family will function as well as people want it to and no better! Current social and economic practices are hindering the development of healthy families. Currently it is more appealing to many fathers and mothers to spend their leisure time away from their children because societal values glorify non-family activities. These types of social values must be changed if young adults are to grasp the proper significance of parenting.

Supportive Environments Take A Variety of Forms

Far too often we view family assistance as some task performed by formalized social agencies such as food stamps or aid to dependent children. Yet the most significant forms of family support relate to people around us and the individuals we work with — in effect — the human setting in which our lives are enacted. Each setting is embedded in others, which suggests an inter-relatedness, so that events happening in one setting can also have an impact on the individual as he moves to a new setting. Settings which have the potential for becoming family support environments inlcude at least the following: (1) school, (2) place of work, (3) church and religious groups, (4) social service agencies, (5) the neighbor hood, and (6) extended family. Each of these environments either promotes the positive development of the family or inhibits such development. For example, when the single parent is penalized in wages for missing a day of work to attend to the needs of a sick child, that particular industrial setting is having a negative influence on the family. A supportive work setting would have flexible scheduling of work hours, thus providing parents a non-penalizing form of meeting both work and family needs (Swick, 1982).

A similar situation can be found in school environments. The teacher who produces (or increases) negative attitudes toward the shool is likely to have negatively effected parental attitudes in the same direction. Teachers who are highly supportive of students are probably producing positive parent support of the learners' and schools' objectives. Schools that have active home-school programs are expanding the possible learning experiences children can have by recognizing the transactional relationship which exists in parent-child-school settings (Swick & Duff, 1978).

The neighborhood is yet another setting which can produce either positive or negative responses among parents and children as well as among others who live there.

The Neighborhood: Supporting Families

The development of supportive behaviors which enhance the lives of parents and children is more likely to occur when people feel their immediate surroundings are a positive part of their lives. In ecological terms, positive experiences in one setting can have a carry-over effect on individuals as they move into related settings and roles (Bronfenbrenner, 1979). The supportive neighborhood is a place of immediate access of individuals to each other. It is a network of human relationships in which families have helped to create a supportive environment which promotes growth and development. Or, as it is in too many instances, the neighborhood can become a dysfunctional setting where people find little help, are unable to identify with their surroundings, and perhaps even experience destructive relationships. When this latter process takes place, parents and children tend to withdraw from the neighborhood and to form a network of human relations with people beyond their immediate surroundings − at school, in church activities or in other community settings (Powell, 1979). The family in crisis is frequently one which has severed or damaged all ties to the outside relying totally on themselves. Healthy families seem to have the best of both worlds, a supportive network of relationships in the neighborhood and extending on into the larger community.

Characteristics of Supportive Neighborhoods

Neighborhoods are social networks that have the potential of providing the following support for families: (1) social/recreational, (2) emotional, (3) exchange of goods and services, (4) information sharing, and (5) developmental processes in children and adults. Neighborhood settings that are active networks of social development may provide families with all of these supports (Brown & Swick, 1981).

A requisite characteristic of supportive neighborhoods is that they provide social and recreational contact with others. The need for social contact with other adults is often cited by parents of infants and toddlers. Working adults have ample opportunity to interact with other adults whereas home-caregivers to infants and toddlers find themselves isolated from the adult world. Social networks, such as neighborhoods, provide a context where social activities such as picnics, porch setting, card playing, and other recreational pursuits take place. These and other social contacts provide the setting in which the other characteristics can occur. Emotional support, information sharing, exchange of goods and services, and the developmental processes all require contact with other people and the social network of the neighborhood provides for these contacts. Another benefit of these social contacts is that they provide a third party support system in which it becomes not only valid to help each other, but expected. This social/recreational contact expands that process to include other people or third party contacts. For example, in many neighborhoods the informal socialization that goes on while mowing the grass leads to other helping relationships, such as watching each other's children, or car pooling, or sympathy over a work related problem. When families have access to this "third force" support system they usually function bettern than when they are isolated from such support (Heatherington, Cox & Cox, 1978).

One of the primary characteristics of healthy neighborhoods is that individuals and families perceive the neighborhood as emotionally supportive. In order for this perception to exist, individuals must have contact with others whom they respect, care about, and like. Neighbors thus play a major role in family development by being emotionally supportive. This can happen in several ways. It may occur when people confirm that another parent or child is valuable and worthwhile by recognizing some special trait they have. It also can occur when neighbors empathize with each other about common situations such as a new baby waking up during the night, excessive food costs, or a problem at work. Another example of this emotional support can be found in the sympathy which neighbors share over the loss of a loved one. This emotional support can provide a haven from the daily stress and tension of living and is a stabilizing factor in a crisis situation. The positive reinforcement received from such an environment builds confidence and enhances the likelihood of consistent behaviors which lead to stability of individual relationships and the network in general. This secure stable atmosphere in which families and individuals carry out their lives greatly enhances the probability of positive outcomes to all involved. Such support is vital to the effective functioning of families (Powell, 1979).

Another characteristic of supportive neighborhoods is the exchange of goods and services. Social networks (such as neighborhoods) in which goods and services are exchanged formally or informally provide a support system which enables families to carry out many tasks. Simple child care exchange arrangements, sharing of equipment such as lawn mowers, co-op agreements on tools, food sharing, and sharing of finances to cover needed neighborhood protection are some examples of how this support factor works. Where this kind of support exists, families have another resource to draw upon. The pooling of resources make many goods and services available to all. The exchange of goods/services provides an excellent example of the inter-relatedness of the supportive neighborhood characteristics. No one wishes to place their child in the care of another individual unless they have confidence their child will receive good care. This confidence comes only through the building of solid relationships, which require social contact in a supportive environment (Swick, Brown, Watson, 1980).

Information sharing is often taken for granted, yet, parents of young children know how valuable this support activity is to their functioning. For example, finding a pediatrician, child rearing information, cooking ideas, budgeting suggestions, and knowing about sales, all are topics about which neighbors can share information. Knowing that all the other children in the neighborhood have had the same illness your child now has, and that the pediatrician recommended asprin, liquids, and rest can save the cost of a trip to a medical center and provide reassurance that the illness is minor and quickly recovered from, will reduce stress. Information sharing is important to all members of the neighborhood whether they have young children or not. Job seeking information, choosing a church, problem solving strategies, and knowing about a clothing sale can be of help to any one. In isolation, such activities might appear over-simplified in terms of their value to families, however, when they are combined they have considerable impact on how parents and children function. Parents who are able to find a pediatrician to suit their needs are more likely to carry out the health care of their children effectively. Information sharing is made possible by having social contacts, trusting those who provide the information, and being willing to share information in return (Cochran & Brossard, 1979).

Finally, the interactive nature of neighborhoods can be a positive force in nurturing the developmental growth and learning of children and adults. Knowing that others are available is as important as actually utilizing their talents in providing a sense of security. Young children and parents of young children seem to need this security most because they face new situations each day. Living in a neighborhood which has regular interaction between neighbors provides a psychologically and physically secure setting for developmental processes to occur. Adults and children feel free to walk the streets, spend time out of their homes which enhances the probability of additional social contacts and opportunities for the developmental processes to occur. The more opportunities an individual has to interact with diverse people in a variety of settings, the more that individual will learn about themselves and life in general. A supportive neighborhood can provide greater opportunities for cognitive development such as multiple attachments, independent behaviors, different social roles, different child rearing attitudes and behaviors, and a broader conceptualization of self. Adults can acquire many new learnings of the same type as children, but on a more sophisticated level.

Supportive or Non-supportive Neighborhoods

It is the combination of factors within the neighborhoods that make it either a supportive social network or non-supportive system. A key factor is how the family perceives itself and the outer world! For example, does the family see itself as a positive part of life? Or, do family members perceive themselves individually and in totality as negative participants in life? The perception of self and the wold is a culmination of the total life experiences of the individual and family. Neighborhoods can only be as supportive as individual families make them. The desire to participate in and to create a supportive social netwoek is dependent on the families' perception of the world. Where neighbors view each other as less than positive forces in each other's lives a supportive social system is unlikely. Where neighbors perceive others as threatening the neighborhood, social networks can actually become destructive to the family processes (Swick & Taylor, 1982).

A second factor in determining whether a neighborhood will be supportive or not is how the family perceives its needs, the needs of others in the neighborhood, and how these needs can be met. For example, does the family see its needs such as emotional support or exchange of goods and services as potentially being met within the immediate neighborhood. In some instances, it may be a simple case of identifying existing resources or organizing them for usage. Another possibility is that people do not recognize each other as human resources and thus fail to utilize the greatest resources they have: themselves. If not, they are likely to look elsewhere such as the church, a community agency, or contacts from the working environment. Conversely, families who do not view themselves as being able to meet others' needs are unlikely to offer help. The use of human relations skills by people in neighborhoods is essential to making their interactions productive and their accessibility to others visible and apparent to everyone. The ability to clarify one's needs and to explicate one's concern for others are integral parts of creating a social network that has continuity and meaning (Swick & Taylor, 1982).

Family stress is a third factor related to the development of effective neighborhoods. This factor becomes especially critical when a majority of

227

neighbors are under some form of stress. Stress can come from a variety of settings. Divorce, drugs and alcohol, sexual promiscuity, and loss of a job are all classical examples of stress producing situations within the family. Stress from external sources can come in the form of neighborhoods being re-zoned for business, a major employer closing, natural disasters, or rampant destruction by juvenile delinquents. Unhealthy levels of stress tend to inhibit family functioning and lessen the family effectiveness in relating to the world. On the other hand, some stressful situations may provide neighbors with a common goal to organize around, providing a reason for social contact and an opportunity for a positive social network to develop. Some neighborhoods find that social networks developed to combat a particular situation are maintained even when the problem is solved.

The demography of a specific neighborhood can effect that neighborhood's ability to develop a support network. The preliminary results of the author's ongoing research into demographic characteristics of supportive neighborhoods suggests that space for children and adults to safely congregate for play and to carry out meaningful social encounters is an important factor. The number of children in the neighborhood can be an influential factor because children tend to create conflicts between families. The length of time families have lived in the neighborhoods and the frequency families entering and leaving the neighborhood effects how supportive the neighborhood can be. High rates of mobility in neighborhoods restrict the amount of time available for the development of supportive networks and families who know they are in a neighborhood for a short time and do not want to establish relationships that will soon be broken. Home ownership, educational level, income levels, and the number of people in each family who work may all effect the development of supportive networks, particularly if these factors vary within a given neighborhood (Brown & Swick, 1981).

When neighborhoods have some combination of positive factors that give meaning to people's lives, they have the basis for organizing a family support system with the neighborhood.

Organizing Neighborhoods into Family Support Systems

People organize into social groups for a variety of reasons. Some reasons why neighborhood groups are formed include: (1) to protest proposed zoning laws, (2) to protect people from crime, (3) to form a good buying cooperative, (4) to organize a cooperative child care program, (5) to revitalize an old neighborhood, (6) to share skills and services, (7) to assist fellow neighbors in trouble and for many other reasons.

An essential part of neighborhood organization is the emergence of a leader. Leadership provides the basis for identifying the type of involvement desired and the level or degree of involvement that is to occur.

The consensus on the type and degree of involvement can be either a formal decision made at a meeting or simply an understanding that evolves as relationships develop. For example, the formation of a neighborhood child care cooperative will take more organizational planning than less involved undertakings, such as social gatherings. It should be noted that informal neighborhood interactions may be just as valuable to families as more formalized programs. More formal programs appear to have the advantage of involving more people. The disadvantage in a formal organization is the lack of flexibility to easily evolve as the needs of the neighborhood change. However, whatever program is organized, it must be focused on being supportive of families if it is to fall within the rubric of family support system criteria.

As neighborhood social networks develop, they will be attempting to fulfill a purpose. While the basic purpose will or should be to provide families and others with a support system in which they can live effectively, more specific objectives will emerge — depending upon the neighborhood — to be used as guidelines for accomplishing the task of providing people with supportive environments.

Communication is the primary vehicle by which people carry out social functions. Neighborhood communications is essential to having effective human support systems. Frequent contacts among neighbors will enhance their capability to meet common needs. For edample, criminologists have substantiated that in neighborhoods where citizen patrols are used on a continuous basis, the crime rate is reduced. Neighbors who know and communicate with each other are usually very supportive of each other's well being. And, this is the primary function of any civilized social network.

Neighborhood Support Systems: Vital to Productive Families

While research efforts have provided much insight into parent-child relationships, more recent research (Bronfenbrenner, 1979) indicates that social systems surrounding this relationship play a major role in making them effective. The following are some examples of this emerging research on helping relationships within human ecological systems.

1. Single parents who have another adult to share their concerns with have a more meaningful experience as parents and their children tend to be less troubled in adjusting to the loss of a parent (Heatherington & Cox, 1978).

2. Research related to child abuse indicates clearly that abusing parents change their behavior for the better when a supportive environment exists (Kempe & Kempe, 1978).

3. Research related to the effectiveness of early intervention programs designed to improve children's academic performance indicates the supportive relationship between parent and teacher is one of the critical success components (Lazar, 1977).

CHAPTER TWENTY-FOUR
SCHOOLS AS FAMILY SUPPORT SYSTEMS

Recent events have increased the public's interest in advancing closer home-school relations. Declining test scores, an increase in school and community behavior problems, and increased expectations for parents and teachers regarding their guiding and teaching young children have influenced many educators to see the family-school relationship in a new, more dynamic way. Other professionals who work with children and families have developed similar perspectives regarding the interactions that occur in the family and between the family and social support systems in the community. A significant part of this emerging role of home and school as co-planners of the child's education is the activation of various projects by parents (Swick, Hobson, & Duff, 1981).

More cognizant than ever of the importance of education, parents have become vociferous in establishing themselves as major influencers of many school improvement programs. Parents have established school support centers during funding drives; raised money for library acquisitions and computer centers as well as lobbying legislators for funds to educate special needs children. A natural part of this emerging home-school partnership is the development of some tensions between home and school (Swick & Duff, 1978). If handled properly, these conflicts can become springboards for action to develop better schools and homes.

One example of how home-school conflicts can be organized into productive ventures exists in the Head Start literature. The policy making process used in Head Start was heavily oriented toward parental and citizen involvement. Yet many teachers in Head Start were not trained in this shared decision making strategy. In many cases it took time and training to aid the personnel and the parents in learning how to make joint decisions. When the process was internalized, program leaders pointed with pride to their accomplishments (McCarthy, 1968; MIDCO, 1972). An important lesson was learned in that early childhood educators realized the need to focus on the entire family as a learning system. An analysis of recent research and developments on family support programs indicate the need for more and earlier involvement of parents and citizens in the education of young children (Breedlove, C., & Schweinhart, 1983).

For example, the involvement of parents in educating infants and toddlers has been shown to have a direct effect on the child's language development as well as the social and cognitive competence of young children (White, 1979). A recent study in New York State (1979) showed a direct correlation between the amount of parental involvement and children's performance in school. In addition, a longitudinal study of effective preschool programs found that where parents were involved in program activities the success level of children was higher than it was in programs where little or no parent involvement existed (Lazar, 1978). Narrative reports of successful schools consistently describe the school staff as supportive of family life and as actively engaging the parents as their allies (Davies, 1976). In essence, research and scholarly studies indicate that a family-school approach to education benefits everyone in the community.

Examples of Schools as Family Support Systems

Recently some school systems have initiated a variety of efforts toward facilitating the child's first learning environment — the home. While many of these efforts were initially viewed as experimental projects, more and more they are being identified as means of preventing learning problems and ways of establishing positive family-school relations. Throughout much of this century educators focused their attention on developing public school kindergartens. Now the focus is rightfully turning toward the entire birth through early childhood range of development and is emphasizing a family centered approach (Hymes, 1981).

Some of the reasons for the increased interest in family centered, early childhood education programs are discussed as follows. The research on early learning indicates we learn more during this period of development than at any other time of life (Bloom, 1981). Not only are we rapid learners during the early childhood years, but we can develop many problems if they are not diagnosed and treated. Family centered practices have proven effective in preventing many learning and development problems in young children (White, 1980). A support system perspective toward the family is essential if we desire to influence the long range development of children (Bronfenbrenner, 1979).

Traditionally, schools served the function of helping children acquire skills, knowledges and attitudes for use in society. Until recent times this was a process begun at home and expanded at school. The teaching of basic skills was and remains a central function of schools. However, the dynamics of our changing society have made the task of teaching these skills more complex. With the advent of a theoretical learning base in early childhood education, many schools have initiated programs which encourage a home-school approach to the development and learning of young children. For example, as noted previously, children who have stimulating home learning environments perform more effectively throughout their school years (Watson, Brown, & Swick, 1983). This brings us to one of the most critical services of early childhood educators

232

perform: that of establishing productive communication links with parents of young children (Swick & Duff, 1979).

While the traditional approach has been to commuٓncate with parents about the performance of children in school; this post-facto arrangement is of little value in preventing learning and behavior problems. Thus the development of programs which encourage parent-teacher communication during the preschool years has been a major step toward establishing workable home-school linkages. The basic premise of most early pre-vention of school failure programs has been that of relating to the family context as early in the life of the child as is possible. The use of a team approach, as is the case with programs like Saturday School, has been a successful way of assisting the family in developing into a functional social unit (Williamson, 1977).

The development of educational programs for 3 and 4 year old children is a fine example of family oriented thinking among educators. The per-centage of families where both parents work out of the home on a full time basis is reaching sixty percent. Thus schools can act as a part of the "extended family" by providing social, educational, medical and related child development supports (Miller, 1975). Related to this concept is the practice of providing extended school day activities for chiildren in the elementary and middle grades. This activity provides children with super-vised experiences after the normal school day is completed — until their parents can pick them up from school (Galinksy & Hook, 1977).

The use of the school as a community education center has always been a part of American education. The recent resurgence of this practice has prompted many educators to develop some innovative curricula experiences. Parent education sessions, for example, are used to assist parents of preschoolers as well as focusing on the needs of middle school students. The State Office of Education in South Carolina, for example, has developed a state-wide program for parents of young children which contains information on language acquisition, child development, nutri-tion and many other topics.*

Family Support Practices

Supportiveness can be shown in various modes to families. Beyond some of the formal methods are the daily behavioral patterns existent in the school. Most parents relish a school climate that is inviting and sincere. Far too often we focus on the negatives and/or the rigid aspects of the school environment. By telling parents of the achievements of their children and by reinforcing their involvement with children, schools are

---

*South Carolina Parent-Oriented Education Program, Columbia, South Carolina: State Department of Education.

showing a supportive attitude toward home-school relationships. Consider the following as examples of family support practices schools can carry out in productive ways.

1. Use of informal drop-in events such as open house programs, social activities and classroom visitation days to strengthen parent-teacher-child bonds.

2. Conferences and telephone contacts where parents and teachers keep each other informed of family or school concerns of mutual interest.

3. Home visits by teachers in which the educational and developmental facets of the entire family are the focus of concern.

4. Provide new parents with learning materials and suggested resources they can use to make the home environment stimulating and safe for the infant. These "gifts" can be accompanied by workshops for parents on topics such as parent-infant relationships.

5. Coordination of available school and community resources that parents can use in carrying out family functions. This type of service is especially helpful for parents who have moved into the community and need assistance in establishing their family in a new setting.

6. The development of school and community services (cooperatively sponsored) such as family counseling, adult education, career development and placement centers, social service activities and other mechanisms for the development of strong families.

Examples of Family Support Programs

Parent support programs are being implemented in various school-community situations. Program designs usually reflect a local need that was identified by a planning group and then formulated to resolve the issue in a workable manner. For example, the "Exploring Childhood" program in Owensboro, Kentucky focuses on educating high school students about the parenting process through various experiences with children and families. Students have the opportunity to learn about child development as it is related to the practical aspects of being a parent. Similar types of parenthood education programs are being implemented in high schools throughout the nation (Kirkland, 1975).

The "Parent-Child Early Education" project in Ferguson, Missouri, is an example of programs that reach families of infants and small children. Objectives include diagnosing and treating any learning problems before the child reaches kindergarten, helping children master readiness skills related to school success, and increasing parents' awareness and effectiveness as their children's teachers. Home visits, parent programs, and "Saturday School" are a few of the techniques used in this program.

234

Project reports, materials, and videotape samples of program activities have been developed and are available for purchase from the school district (Williamson, 1977).

Other school districts are utilizing a broader approach. They combine parent education and home-school devices in a single program. The Des Moines Family Learning Centers, for example, provide a central place for children and adults to relate their needs and interests to the entire educational process. Through the use of family-learning specialists and educators from local public schools, parents and other citizens can utilize resources, counseling, and programs to enhance their skills or improve their understanding of the learning process (Miller, 1975).

The parenting process and the home-school relationship must be the concern of every citizen in the community. Community agencies have been a vital force in the development and implementation of parent education and family-assistance programs. The parent-child program in Leitchfield, Kentucky, is one example of a community-based program. The primary purpose of the program is to educate proverty-level parents to teach their children. A combination of classroom instruction and home visitation is used to accomplish the goal of improving parenting (Swick, 1979).

Guidelines for Developing Schools That are Family Oriented

The development of a school that is supportive of the family must be a priority of the entire staff if it is to be successful. The initial focus must be on building a positive attitude toward family-school relations as mutually beneficial to everyone involved in the teaching-learning process.

The formation of positive family-school linkages occurs when people are communicating with each other regarding common concerns that form a basis for having a helping relationship. Thus, a first question to examine is: Are we communicating with parents regarding their needs, the school's needs and the needs of the children? As this question is seriously studied by school leaders various answers will emerge which can give direction to initiating or refining the family-school communication system.

Communicating with families in an intentional manner is one way of forming a supportive relationship. As with any process, forming a communication arrangement with parents takes time, planning and continued efforts to understand the situations that arise in home-school programs. A random approach will not serve the purpose of such relationships which is to address family and school issues on a regular basis.

Planning for family-school communications may take many different forms. For example, initial efforts may take place in group settings or through contacts with parents. The following are some strategies schools and child development centers have used to establish productive arrangements with families.

1. Prior to school opening telethons where families are contacted regarding plans for the school year.

2. Send each family a letter welcoming them to the school and providing them with an overview of school events.

3. Involve staff members in visiting families of the children they teach. Making these visits prior to the opening of school can be helpful in establishing a positive framework for having a "helping relationship."

4. Utilize local media sources to reach parents and citizens regarding the many resources available at the school.

These attempts to reach parents can be supplemented with more formal procedures after a viable family-school relationship has been established. Informal contacts with families can provide insights regarding their needs. Formal assessment procedures will provide details on the types of needs and concerns families are facing in their lives. The communications process is used in both formal and informal attempts to reach families. As parents sense their concerns are recognized and acted on by school personnel they tend to increase their level of involvement with the school (Swick & Duff, 1978).

Directing the teaching process toward the total family is an essential guideline for organizing a family support program. Involving parents in educational plans, responding to their inquiries in a meaningful way and attending to the individual needs of children are some of the many ways we teach toward the family. A family oriented educational program is developed with input from parents and continually attends to needs that emerge in the family-school situation.

Various needs emerge in family oriented schools. For example, in communities where families are supported by two-parent working teams, extended-day programs may become a valuable source of support. Such extended-day programs might include athletic events, crafts, tutorial work, fine arts options, interest courses and other such activities (Mayesky, 1979). Other needs that may emerge include: (1) adult education, (2) parent education, (3) drug counseling, (4) family management skills, (5) parent-child relations, and (6) the need for infant and toddler care programs. Responding to these types of needs is indicative of an educational perspective that values the "total family" as members of the learning team.

Being accessible to families is yet another guideline for family oriented schools. Accessibility is more than an open door policy. Rather, it is an

236

intentionally designed environment where parents are encouraged to participate in the learning and development of their children. It implies that home and school are mutually supportive environments. Having a "place" in the school where parents can put their belongings, talk with other parents (and school staff) and find materials related to their needs is of utmost importance. Schools where principals, teachers and other school staff "invite" parental participation via conferences, meetings, social events, and a prevailing attitude of "your needed" have an effect on every member of the home-school partnership (Purkey & Novak, 1984).

The involvement of parents in direct modes of school functioning such as serving as classroon aides or in decision making capacities further strengthens a family oriented school program. School policy councils provide a mechanism for parents to speak out on issues affecting families. Additionally, such councils offer educators a chance to share with parents their concerns. Parental involvement in the classroom increases the potential for continued family-school contacts. It provides parents with a chance to assist teachers and children in exploring the curriculum from a broader and hopefully enriched perspective. Further, this type of involvement sensitizes parents to the challenges teachers face in organizing and implementing the instructional program.

Characteristics of Supportive Schools

What are supportive, family oriented schools like? What differentiates these schools from others? Underlying the supportive school is *a philosophy that recognizes the ecological and developmental nature of learning.* That is, children learn not only in school but in many settings and through interactions with many people. Learning requires involvement of the learner in various individual and group arrangements. Indeed, the child who has difficulty in school is usually having problems linking up to various social settings. Supportive schools, recognizing the dynamics of the learning process, *use various human resources* in the educational ecology. Typically, one will find people of all ages working together on common goals and yet doing so in very unique modes (Swick & Miller, 1979).

In supportive schools you will find senior citizens reading stories to young children; high school students "coaching" elementary school children in sports activities; parents serving on policy making boards; teachers sponsoring parent education programs and various other projects that are supportive of family and school development.

A hallmark of family oriented schools is their *emphasis on the uniqueness of each human learner.* Children and parents are treated as individuals with talent and who have human needs and feelings. For example, in supportive schools teachers address children by first names, learn about each child's uniqueness and become sensitive to parental concerns and situations. Children's work and parental involvement products are proudly displayed throughout the school and community. The labeling of children and parents as learners and non-learners is avoided.

Supportive schools have a standard practice of *collaborating with families in the educational planning process.* "Think globally but act locally" is a prevailing viewpoint in these schools. Educators who believe in a supportive school philosophy not only seek parent support of education but actively plan to engage families in planning the school's program. Advisory councils, school study teams, parent-teacher sponsored programs and many other collaborative efforts are found in family oriented schools.

The supportive school is more than anything an inviting place to learn and develop. Purkey and Novak (1984) identify five characteristics of the "inviting school" environment: (1) respect for individual uniqueness, (2) cooperative spirit, (3) sense of belonging, (4) pleasing habitat, and (5) positive expectations. These characteristics, as applied to family involvement in schools, are representative of a highly supportive learning arrangement.

Family uniqueness is respected in the supportive school. Rather than comparing parents with each other, the talents and human depth of all parents are integrated into school practices. Each family contribution is valued and each family problem is recognized and acted upon in the real meaning of the term — supportive.

A school identity is promoted in the supportive school. Children and parents have "a place and a part" in the school's operations. Families have a sense of "ownership" and "pride" in their school as well as a sense of responsibility to support the school in active ways. This sense of belonging is promoted through the engagement of parents and children in many school improvement programs and the involvement of school staff in appropriate family support projects.

An esthetically pleasant environment is typical of supportive schools. For example, schools that value families make room for all members of the family to participate in school functions. A real focus is on helping people feel comfortable in the school environment. Thus you may find plants about the school, children's art work on display and ceramic products made by senior citizens proudly displayed. You may find a "parent room" and other special places for family and community members to use in their learning efforts.

"Expect the best" is an appropriate motto for schools that strive to support total family learning. In many cases teachers of young children can help children achieve their full potential by first helping parents expand their human potential. Children, parents and teachers learn from each other and when they expect each other to succeed and take action to help each other succeed — they are moving toward having a supportive school.

238

REFERENCES

Angle, M. These bosses babysit too. *Parade Magazine* (1980): 10, July 13 issue.

Bell, R., & Harper, L. *Child effects on adults.* Lincoln: University of Nebraska Press, 1977.

Berclay, G.J. *Parent involvement in the schools.* Washington, D.C.: National Education Association, 1977.

Birtchnell, J. The possible consequences of early death. *British Journal of Medical Psychology* 42 (1969): 1–12.

Blanchard, R.W., & Biller, H.B. Father availability and academic perform-ance among third grade boys. *Developmental Psychology* 4 (1979): 944–950.

Bloom, B.S. *All our children learning: a primer for parents, teachers, and other educators.* New York: McGraw-Hill, 1981.

Bradley, R.H. The renaissance of fathering. *Educational Horizons* 59 (1980): 27–33.

Brandt, R.S. *Partners: parents and schools.* Alexandria, VA.: Association for Supervision and Curriculum Development, 1979.

Breedlove, C., & Schweinhart, L. *The cost-effectiveness of high quality early childhood programs.* Ypsilanti, MI: High/Scope Educational Research Foundation, 1982.

Broderick, C.B. Fathers. *The Family Coordinator* 26 (1977): 269–275.

Broderick, C.B. Beyond the five conceptual frameworks: a decade of development in family theory. *A Decade of Family Research and Action.* Minneapolis, MN: National Council on Family Relations, 1971.

Bronfenbrenner, U. *The ecology of human development.* Cambridge, MA: Harvard University Press, 1979.

Bronfenbrenner, U. Contexts of child rearing: problems and prospects. *American Psychologists* 34 (1979): 844–850.

Bronfenbrenner, U. A curriculum for caring. *Instructor* 88 (1979): 34–36.

Brown, C.C. *Infants as risk: assessment and intervention.* Skillman, N.J.: Johnson & Johnson Roundtable Books, 1981.

Brown, M.H. *Neighborhood Support Inventory.* Columbia, South Carolina: University of South Carolina, Unpublished Manuscript, 1978.

Brown, M.H., & Swick, K.J. The neighborhood as a support system for children and families. *The Clearing House* 54 (1979): 350–354.

Bruner, J. *Under five in Britain.* Ypsilanti, MI: High/Scope Press, 1980.

Burgess, E.W., & Locke, H.J. *The family: from institution to companionship.* N.Y.: American Book Co., 1953.

Burkett, C.W. Effects of frequency of home visits on achievement of preschool students in a home-based early childhood education program. *Journal of Educational Research* 76 (1982): 41–44.

Burt, S., & Lessinger, L. *Volunteer industry involvement in public education.* Lexington, MA: D.C. Heath, 1970.

Cammarata, J., & Leighton, F. *The funbook of fatherhood.* Los Angeles, CA: Pinnacle Books, 1978.

Cardenas, B. Enhancing family awareness. *Children Today* 7 (1978): inside cover.

Clarke-Stewart, A. *Daycare.* Cambridge, MA: Harvard University Press, 1982.

Cochran, M.M., & Brossard, J.A. Child development and personal social networks. *Child Development* 50 (1979): 601–616.

Coleman, J. Needed: new means of socialization. *Educational Leadership* 36 (1979): 491–492.

Collins, R.C., & Deloria, D. Head start research: a new chapter. *Children Today* 12 (1983): 15–19.

Colleta, A.J. *Working together: a guide to parent involvement.* Atlanta, Georgia: Humanics Press, 1977.

Cooper, C. Competent infants and their caregivers: the feeling is mutual. in Frost, J. *Understanding and nurturing infant development.* Washington, D.C.: Association for Childhood Education International, 1976.

Davies, D. *Schools where parents make a difference.* Boston, MA: Institute for responsive education, 1976.

Duff, E., Heinz, C., & Husband, C. Toy lending library: linking home and school. *Young Children* 34 (1978): 16–22.

Duff, E., & Stroman, S. The latchkey child: whose responsibility? *Childhood Education* 59 (1982): 76–79.

Duvall, E. *Marriage and family development.* Philadelphia: J.B. Lippincott, 1977.

Education for parenthood: a primary prevention strategy for child abuse and neglect. Denver, CO: Education Commission of the States, 1979.

Elkind, D. *The hurried child: growing up to fast too soon.* Reading, Mass.: Addison-Wesley, 1981.

Elkund, S. Life span development and families. *Dimensions* 9 (1980): 16–19.

Erikson, E. *The life cycle completed: a review.* New York: W.W. Norton, 1982.

Fantini, M., & Cardenas, R. *Parenting in a multicultural society.* New York: Longman, 1980.

Fein, R.A. Men's entrance to parenthood. *The Family Coordinator* 25 (1976): 341–347.

Footsteps: a discussion guide. Baltimore: University Park Press, University of Maryland, 1979.

Fraiberg, S. *The bithrights of children.* New York: Basic Books, 1977.

Frazier, A. *Adventuring, mastering, associating: new strategies for teaching children.* Washington, D.C.: Association for Supervision and Curriculum Development, 1976.

Galinsky, E. *Between generations: the six stages of parenthood.* New York: Times Books, 1981.

Galinsky, E., & Hooks, W. *The new extended family: day care that works.* Boston: Houghton Mifflin, 1977.

Gardner, J. *Self renewal: the individual and the innovative society.* New York: W.W. Norton, 1981 edition.

Gearing, J. Facilitating the birthing process and father-child relationships. *The Counseling Psychologist* 7 (1978): 53–55.

Gilmar, S., & Nelson, J. Centering resources for learning: parents get into the act. *Childhood Education* 51 (1975): 208–210.

Goodlad, J.I. A study of schooling: some findings and hypotheses. *Phi Delta Kappan* 64 (1983): 465–476.

Goodlad, J.I. Can our schools get better? *Phi Delta Kappan* 60 (1979): 342–347.

Goodlad, J.I. *The dynamics of educational change.* New York: McGraw-Hill, 1975.

Gordon, I.J. *Children's views of themselves.* Washington, D.C.: Association for Childhood Education International, 1972.

Gordon, I.J. On the continuity of development. *Childhood Education* 54 (1976): 123–128.

Gordon, I.J. *Research report of parent oriented home-based early childhood education programs.* Gainesville, FL: Institute for Human Development, University of Florida, 1975.

Gordon, I.J. *Parent education: a plethora of approaches.* Gainesville, FL: Institute for Human Development, University of Florida, 1977.

Gordon, I.J., & Breivogel, W. *Building effective home-school relationships.* Boston: Allyn and Bacon, 1977.

Gordon, I.J. Intervention in infant education. in Frost, J. *Understanding and nurturing infant development.* Washington, D.C.: Association for Childhood Education International, 1976.

Gordon, I.J. *The observation of parent-infant interaction in structured educational activities.* Gainesville, FL: Institute for Human Development, University of Florida, 1977.

Gotts, E., ed. *The home visitation kit: training and practitioner materials for paraprofessionals in family settings.* New York: Human Sciences Press, 1977.

Graham, S. On being poor nowdays. *Integrated Education* 12 (1974): 36–38.

Grams, A. Parenting: concept and process. in *Parenting.* Washington, D.C.: Association for Childhood Education International, 1973.

Green, F. Child development: young children in the 80's. in Dickerson, M., & Davis, M., ed.'s. *Young children: issues for the 80's.* Little Rock, AR: Southern Association on Children under Six, 1982.

Greenwood, G.E. Citizen advisory committees. *Theory into Practice* 22 (1977): 7–12.

Hall, E. *The silent language.* Greenwich, CT: Fawcett Publishers, 1959.

Hanes, M. An experience in program evaluation. *Theory into Practice* 22 (1977): 7–10.

Hanes, M. *Parent training: an overview and synthesis.* Paper presented at the 2nd International Symposium on the "At-Risk" Infant, Jerusalem, Israel, 1983.

Hartup, W. The social worlds of childhood. *American Psychologist* 34 (1979): 944–950.

Havighurst, R. Schools and disaffected youth. *Educational Leadership* 34 (1977): 403–405.

Helfer, R., & Kempe, C. *Child abuse and neglect: the family and the community.* Cambridge, MA: Ballinger Publishing, 1976.

Hengstler, H. The impact of flexible working hours on staff productivity. *Association Management* 21 (1974): 61–63.

Hetherington, E.M., Cox, M., & Cox, R. *The development of children in mother-headed families.* Paper presented at the Conference of Families in Contemporary America. Washington, D.C.: George Washington University, 1977.

Hetherington, E.M., Cox, M., & Cox, R. Divorced fathers. *Family Coordinator* 25 (1976): 417–428.

Hetherington, E.M. Divorce: a child's perspective. *American Psychologist* 34 (1979): 851–858.

Hobson, C., Robinson, B., & Skeen, P. Sex-role contributions of male teachers in early childhood education settings. *Childhood Education* 57 (1980): 33–39.

Hoffman, L.W. The father's role in the family and the child's peer-group adjustment. *Merrill-Palmer Quarterly* 7 (1961): 97–105.

Holt, J. How schools can cooperate with home schoolers. *Phi Delta Kappan* 64 (1983): 391–394.

Holloman, J. Discontinuous mothering — expending the alternatives. In Frost, J. *Understanding and nurturing infant development.* Washington, D.C.: Association for Childhood Education International, 1976.

Honig, A. *Parent involvement in early childhood education.* Washington, D.C.: National Association for the education of Young Children, 1975.

Hunt, J. McV. The psychological basis for using pre-school enrichment as an antidote for cultural deprivation. *Merrill-Palmer Quarterly* 19 (1964): 209-245.

Hymes, J. *Teaching the child under six.* Columbus, Ohio: Charles E. Merrill, 1981 edition.

Hymes, J. *Living history of early childhood education.* Washington, D.C.: Childhood Resources, 1972.

Irvine, D.J. *Parent involvement affects children's cognitive growth.* Albany, N.Y.: State Education Department, Division of Research, August, 1979, 12 pages.

Issacs, S., & Keller, M. *The inner parent: raising ourselves, raising our children.* New York: Harcourt Brace Jovanovich, 1979.

Jacobs, L. The meaning of teaching. *Childhood Education* 55 (1978): 222-226.

Jaffe, S., & Viertel, J. *Becoming parents: preparing for the emotional changes of first-time parenthood.* New York: Atheneum Books, 1980.

Kagan, J. Family experience and the child's development. *American Psychologist* 34 (1979): 886–891.

Kamerman, S.B., & Hayes, C.D. *Families that work: children in a changing world.* Washington, D.C.: National Academy Press, 1982.

Kanter, R. Jobs and families: impact of working roles on family life. *Children Today* 7 (1978): 11–15.

Kaplan, L. Parent involvement. *Journal of Teacher Education* 27 (1977): 167–168.

Katz, A.J. Lone fathers: perspective and implications for the family policy. *The Family Coordinator* 28 (1979): 521–528.

Katz, L. *Talks with teachers.* Washington, D.C.: National Association for the Education of Young Children, 1977.

Kempe, C.H., & Kempe, R.S. *Child Abuse.* Cambridge, Mass.: Harvard University Press, 1978.

Keniston, K. *All our children: the American family under pressure.* New York: Harcourt Brace jovanovich, 1978.

Klaus, M., & Robertson, M. *Birth, interaction, and attachment.* Skillman, New Jersey: Johnson and Johnson Roundtable Books, 1982.

Klein, B. Families of handicapped children: a personal account. *Dimensions* 8 (1982): 55–58.

Kirkland, P. Education for parenthood. *Today's Education* 64 (1975): 12–15.

Lamb, M.E. Fathers: forgotten contributors to child development. *Human Development* 18 (1975): 245–266.

Lamb, M.E. Paternal influences and the father's role. *American Psychologist* 34 (1979): 938–943.

Lamb, M.E., & Bronson, S.K. Fathers in the context of family influences: past, present, and future, *School Psychology Review* ((1980): 336–353.

Land, B.L. *Parent-child educational interaction: a longitudinal study of the effects of a kindergarten parent involvement program.* Columbia, South Carolina: Doctoral Dissertation, University of South Carolina, Graduate School, 1983.

Lane, M. *Educating for parenting.* Washington, D.C. National Association for the Education of Young Children, 1975.

Lazar, I., et al. *The persistence of preschool effects: a summary report.* Washington, D.C.: U.S. Government Printing Office, 1976.

Lederer, W., & Jackson, D. *The mirages of marriage.* New York: W.W. Norton, 1969.

Levinger, G. Where is the family going? *The Wilson Quarterly* 1 (1977): 95–102.

Levenstein, P., Roth, H., & Kochman, R. *Manual for replication of the mother-child home program.* Freeport, New York: Verbal Interaction Project, 1971.

Levenstein, P. The mother-child home program. In *The Preschool in action: exploring early childhood programs,* 2nd edition. Ed., M.C. Day & R.K. Parker. Boston: Allyn and Bacon, 1977.

Lewis, K. Single father families: who they are and what they are. *Child Welfare* 57 (1978): 643–651.

Lynn, D.B. *The father: his role in child development.* Monterey, CA: Brooks/Cole Publishing, 1974.

Manning, M.L., & Swick, K.J. Changing father roles: a review of the research. *The Day Care Journal* 1 (1982): 35–38.

Markun, P. *Parenting.* Washington: Association for Childhood Education International, 1973.

Maslow, A. *New knowledge in human values.* New York: Harper Brothers, 1959.

Maxwell, J.W. The keeping fathers in America. *The Family Coordinator* 25 (1976): 387–392.

Mayesky, M. Extended day programs in public schools. *Children Today* 8 (1979): 6–9.

McCarthy, J.L. *Changing parent attitudes and improving language and intellectual ability of culturally disadvantaged four-year-old children through parent involvement.* Bloomington, IN: Indiana University Doctoral Dissertation, 1968.

Mead, M. *Culture and committment: a study of the generation gap.* New York: Doubleday and Company, 1970.

MIDCO. *Perspectives on parent participation in Head Start: an analysis and critique.* Washington: Health, Education, Welfare, 1972.

Miller, M. Des Moine's family learning centers. *Today's Education* 64 (1975): 21–27.

Miller, S., Nunnaly, W., & Wackman, D. *Alive and aware.* Minneapolis, MN: Interpersonal Communication Programs, 1975.

Moore, O.K. Guidelines for choosing hardware to promote synasthetic learning. *Childhood Education* 59 (1983): 237–240.

Morrison, G.S. *Parent involvement in the home, school, and community.* Columbus, Ohio: Charles E. Merrill, 1978.

Nass, G. *Marriage and the family.* New York: W.W. Norton, 1979.

National Parent-Teacher-Association. *Today's family in focus.* Chicago, IL: 500 S. Rush St., 1978.

Nedler, S., & McAfee, O. *Working with parents: guidelines for early childhood and elementary educators.* Belmont, CA: Wadsworth, 1979.

Nieting, P.C. School-age child care: in support of development and learning. *Childhood Education* 60 (1983): 6–11.

Ogg, E. Preparing tomorrow's parents. New York City: Public Affairs Committee, 1975.

Olmsted, P., et. al. *Parent education: the contributions of Ira J. Gordon.* Washington, D.C.: Association for Childhood Education International, 1980.

Osborn, K. *Early childhood education in historical perspective.* Athens, GA: Education Associates, 1980.

Overton, J. *Support system task sheet.* Columbia, S.C.: Family Life Education Center, 1982.

Palme, O. The emancipation of man. *Journal of Social Issues* 28 (1972): 237–246.

Parke, R.D., & Swain, D.B. The father's role in infancy: a reevaluation. *The Family Coordinator* 25 (1976): 365–371.

Paul, M.C. *The effects of formal preschool experience and supportive reading behavior in the home on first grade reading readiness.* Unpublished doctoral dissertation: University of South Carolina, 1975.

Payne, D.C., & Mussen, P.H. Parent-child relations and father identification among adolescent boys. *Journal of Abnormal Social Psychology* 52 (1956): 358–362.

Powell, O.R. Family-environment relations and early childbearing: the role of social networks and neighborhood. *Journal of Research and Development in Education* 13 (1979): 1–11.

Promises: viewers guide. Columbia, South Carolina: South Carolina Educational Television Network, 1982.

Purkey, W.W. *Inviting school success: a self concept approach to teaching and learning.* Belmont, CA: Wadsworth, 1979.

Purkey, W.W., & Novak, J. *Inviting school success: a self concept approach to teaching and learning. Second Edition.* Belmont, CA: Wadsworth, 1984.

Quisenberry, J. *Changing family lifestyles: their effect on children.* Washington, D.C.: Association for Childhood Education International, 1983.

Redina, I., & Dickersheid, J.D. Father-child interaction in a shopping mall: a naturalistic study of father role behavior. *The Journal of Genetic Psychology* 138 (1981): 269–278.

Resnick, J.L., et. al. Fathering classes: a psycho-educational model. *The Counseling Psychologist* 7 (1978): 56–59.

Rich, L. Newark's parent-powered school. *American Education* 4 (1971): 12–15.

Rosenthal, R., & Jacobsen, L. *Pygmalion in the classroom.* New York: Holt, Rinehart, Winston, 1968.

Rotter, J., & Robinson, E. *Parent-teacher conferencing.* Washington: National Education Association, 1982.

Russell, A. Building concepts through verbal interactions: the key to future success in school? *Carnegie Quarterly* 27 (1979): 1–4.

Sasserath, V.J. *Minimizing high risk parenting.* Skillman, N.J.: Johnson and Johnson Roundtable Books, 1983.

Satir, V. *Peoplemaking.* Palo Alto, CA: Science and Behavior Books, 1972.

Schaefer, E.S. Parents as educators: evidence from cross sectional, longitudinal and intervention research. *Young Children* 27 (1972): 227–239.

Schaefer, E.S. *Parent-professional interaction: research, parental, professional, and policy perspectives.* Chapel Hill, North Carolina: University of North Carolina (mimeographed paper available from author), 1983.

Schaefer, E.S., Edgerton, M., & Hunter, W. *Childrearing and child development correlates of maternal focus of control.* Paper presented at the American Psychological Association Annual Meeting, Anaheim, CA, 1983.

Schaefer, E.S., & Edgerton, M. *Modernity-Societal, Regional, Individual, and child academic competence.* Paper presented at Appalachian Conference on Children and Families. Moorhead, KT: June, 1983.

Schaefer, E.S., & Hunter, W. *Mother-infant interaction and maternal psychosocial predictors of kindergarten adaption.* Paper presented at biennal meeting of the Society for Research on Child Development, Detroit, MI: April, 1983.

Schaefer, E.S., & Eegerton, M. *Parental modernity in childrearing and educational attitudes and beliefs.* Paper presented at the biennial meeting of the Society for Research in Child Development, Boston, MA: April, 1981.

Schine, J., & Harrington, D. *Youth participation for early adolescents: learning and serving in the community.* Bloomington, IN: Phi Delta Kappan, 1982.

Schlesinger, B. Single parent. *Children Today* 7 (1978): 12–17.

Shane, H.G. The silicon age II: living and learning in an information age epoch. *Phi Delta Kappan* 65 (1983): 126–129.

Schmitt, B. What teachers need to know about child abuse and neglect. *Childhood Education* 52 (1975): 58–63.

Sinclair, R. *A two way street: home-school cooperation in educational decision making.* Boston, MA: Institute for Responsive Education, 1980.

Sinclair, R., & Ghory, W. Parents and teachers together: directions for developing equality in learning through environments in families and schools. In Sinclair, R. *A two way street: home-school cooperation in educational decision making.* Boston, MA: Institute for Responsive Education, 1980.

Staples, I. Affecting disaffected youth: the Philadelphia story. *Educational Leadership* 34 (1977): 422–428.

Solnit, A. Changing psychological perspectives about children and their families. *Children Today* 5 (1976): 3–8.

Smith, T. *Parents and preschool.* Ypsilanti, MI: High/Scope Press, 1980.

Starr, R.H. Child abuse. *American Psychologist* 34 (1979): 872–878.

Stern, D. *The first relationship: infant and mother.* Cambridge, MA: Harvard University Press, 1977.

Stinnet, N., et. al. *Building family strengths: blueprints for action.* Lincoln, NB: University of Nebraska Press, 1979.

Stinnett, N., et. al. *Family strengths: positive models for family life.* Lincoln, NB: University of Nebraska Press, 1980.

Sunderlin, S. *Parents, children, teachers: communication.* Washington, D.C.: Association for Childhood Education International, 1969.

Swick, K.J. Child abuse: perspectives for helping professionals. *Kappa Delta Pi Record* 17 (1978): 48–50.

Swick, K.J. Parent education. *The University of South Carolina Education Report* 21 (1979): 1–3.

Swick, K.J. Advisory councils: ways to better schools. *The University of South Carolina Education Report* 20 (1978): 1–3.

Swick, K.J. The differentiated parenting team: concept, process, and product. *Dimensions* 6 (1978): 53–60.

Swick, K.J. The need for creating productive attitude climates for learning. *Education* 94 (1973): 305–307.

Swick, K.J. MIxed messages on human usefulness. *Momentum* 10 (1979): 4–9.

Swick, K.J. Parent education: focus on needs and responsibilities. *Dimensions* 11 (1983): 9–12.

Swick, K.J. Home support and language development in young children. *Instructional Psychology* 6 (1979): 19–24.

Swick, K.J. When teachers become real teachers. *Momentum* 14 (1983): 14–18.

Swick, K.J. Business and industry as facilitators of community life. *Childhood Education* 59 (1982): 80–86.

Swick, K.J., Duff, E., & Hobson, C. *Parent involvement: strategies for early childhood educators.* Champaign, IL: Stipes Publishing, 1981.

Swick, K.J., Duff, E., & Hobson, C. *Building successful parent-teacher partnerships.* Atlanta, GA: Humanics Limited, 1979.

Swick, K.J., Duff, E., & Hobson, C. *Working relationships: parents and teachers.* Champaign, IL: Stipes Publishing, 1978.

Swick, K.J., & Duff, E. *Involving children in parenting/caring experiences.* Dubuque, Iowa: Kendall/Hunt, 1982.

Swick, K.J., & Duff, E. *The Parent-Teacher bond: relating, responding, rewarding.* Dubuque, Iowa: Kendall/Hunt, 1978.

Swick, K.J., & Duff, E. *Parenting.* Washington: National Education Association, 1979.

Swick, K.J., & Manning, M. Father involvement in home and school. *Childhood Education* 60 (1983): 128–135.

Swick, K.J., & Miller, H. Community resource use in early childhood settings. *Education* 99 (1979): 330–332.

Swick, K.J., Brown, M., & Watson, T. Perspectives on family assisted learning. *Children Our Concern* 5 (1980): 3–8.

Swick, K.J., & Bollinger, S. Parent education in the 80's. In Dickerson, M., & Davis, M. *Young children: issues for the 80's.* Little Rock, AR: Southern Association for Children Under Six, 1982.

Swick, K.J., & Willis, M. Parents and children in the home environment: implications for the school setting. *Education* 93 (1973): 379–380.

Swick, K.J., & Dennis, L. How to turn homework into homelearning. *Teacher* 91 (1973): 42–43.

Swick, K.J., & Hanley, P. *Teacher renewal: revitalization of classroom teachers.* Washington: National Education Association, 1983.

Swick, K.J., Brown, M., & Robinson, S. *Toward Quality Environments for Young Children.* Champaign, IL: Stipes Publishing, 1983.

Swick, K.J., & Rotter, M. The work place as a family support system. *Day Care and Early Education* 9 (1980): 7–11.

Swick, K.J., & Taylor, S. Parent-child perceptions of their ecological context as related to child performance in school: a conceptual framework. *Instructional Psychology* 9 (1982): 168–175.

Swick, K.J., & Taylor, S. Planning and implementing parent education programs. *Georgia's Children* 3 (1984): in press.

Talbot, N. *Raising children in modern America.* Boston: Little, Brown, and Company, 1976.

Tasch, R. *The role of the father in the family.* Journal of Experimental Education 20 (1952): 319–361.

The portage guide to home teaching. Portage, Wisconsin: Portage Project, 1975.

Vantil, W. Wanted: effective communication. *Phi Delta Kappan* 58 (1977): 78–89.

Wallat, C., & Goldman, R. *Home/School/Community Interaction.* Columbus, Ohio: Charles Merrill, 1979.

Watson, T., Brown, M., & Swick, K.J. The relationship of parents' support to children's school achievement. *Child Welfare* 62 (1983): 175–180.

Weikart, D. *Parent involvement through home teaching.* Ypsilanti, MI: High/Scope Press, 1974.

Williamson, P. Saturday School. *American Education* 9 (1977): 12–16.

Wirth, A. Alternative philosophies of work: some questions for educators. *Phi Delta Kappan* 63 (1982): 677–680.

White, B.L. *The first three years of life.* Englewood Cliffs, N.J.: Prentice-hall, 1975.

White, B.L. *A parent's guide to the first three years.* Englewood Cliffs, N.J.: Prentice-Hall, 1980.

White, B.L., & Kaban, B. *The origins of human competence.* Lexington, MA: Lexington Books, 1979.

Yamamoto, K. *The child and his image: self concept in the early years.* Boston: Houghton Mifflin, 1972.

Zigler, E., & Muenchow, S. Mainstreaming: the proof is in the implementation. *American Psychologist* 34 (1979): 993–996.